The darkest hour

In an isolated cottage on the dunes of Oliver Bay, USA, lives Carla Benson, an attractive middle-aged woman, with only her cat for company. From the wooden porch she watches Atlantic breakers crash on the rocks; at her desk by the window she works on her second novel; and day after day she exults in her escape from the city and her blissful, solitary independence.

But Oliver Bay is no idyllic seaside village – it is old-fashioned, almost feudal, and nearly every inhabitant works in the fish-canning factory, the only industry for miles around. They are hostile to Carla, the feminist, the outsider: women see her as a predator, men as a challenge. 'It's asking for trouble, living alone like you do,' warns the proprietor of the local store.

And trouble certainly comes Carla's way. From wagging tongues and obscene approaches by local youths, to hooligans shrieking round her cottage on summer nights, trouble mounts to an explosion of dreadful violence. And Carla, her own fury uncontrollable, sets out to meet trouble head on . . .

Louna Ford has written a dark and powerful thriller, a story of passion and vengeance in which love and courage, violence and the macabre are compellingly intertwined, and which packs an unforgettable sting into the final pages.

THE DARKEST HOUR

Louna Ford

Constable London

First published in Great Britain 1988
by Constable & Company Ltd
10 Orange Street London WC2H 7EG
Copyright © 1988 by Louna Ford
Photoset in Linotron Palatino 10pt by
Redwood Burn Limited, Trowbridge
Printed in Great Britain by
Redwood Burn Ltd, Trowbridge

British Library CIP data
Ford, Louna
The darkest hour.
I. Title
813'.54[F]   PS3556.O71/

ISBN 0 09 468300 X

Should God punish men for their perverse doings,
He would not leave on earth a moving thing

Holy Koran (16:63)

1

The cottage was perched on a sand dune, slightly askew, but I had the realtor's assurance that its foundations were sound. It was old and had a tired look, in spite of the fresh coat of paint the previous owner had given it before selling. To me. At some stage in the past someone had made an admirable attempt to modernize it, for its windows were large and contrasted oddly with the rest of it. I guess some thirty-odd years ago it had served as a comfortable holiday home for a city family escaping from the stresses of their everyday lives. I could imagine boisterous children riding tricycles on the wide porch, or sitting here, just below the steps, scooping this fine white sand into brightly coloured buckets. There would've been a family dog, of course, playing in the shallow waves, barking excitedly at the restless water and arriving home with a wet belly and sand-covered paws. Yet, today it stood mutely, its architecture sadly outdated, guarding its memories.

On inspection its attributes far outweighed its shortcomings. The rooms were spacious, the ceilings high, lending each a sunny, airy atmosphere. A most delightful feature of the two bedrooms was the window seats with their padded cushions, creating a cosy niche with uninterrupted views over the beach beyond. There was an old-fashioned pantry with genuine oak shelves behind the kitchen, and an adjoining laundry with a large cement wash-basin. The sitting-room had a marble fireplace and a french window leading onto the wide porch. Four steps led one directly onto the beautiful stretch of beach with its oddly-shaped dunes.

The cottage stood forlornly on its dune, well removed from Oliver Bay, the adjacent town. I had bought it for a song during a time when property prices were bordering on the insane. The reason was quite simple – Oliver Bay wasn't geared for the moneyed tourists with their sleek, tanned bodies who invaded other coastal towns during summer, bringing noise and pollution with them. Not only is the water of the Atlantic infamously cold, but the shores of Oliver Bay were fringed with sharp coral reefs rising from the sea like granite boulders, making bathing unsafe. It was a hostile coastline, but produced excellent lobster and mackerel, resulting in another detraction of the town. A large fish factory overshadowed Oliver Bay, its chimneys rising into the sky like elongated fingers, spewing black smoke. During summer a strong north-easterly wind often blew, sweeping the smoke out to sea and dispelling the reek of processed and raw fish. In winter, I was told, it seemed to cling to one's very pores.

Yet none of this had deterred me from buying the cottage. I wasn't a keen swimmer, the cottage was just far enough removed from Oliver Bay not to be in direct line of smell and smoke, and most important – it afforded me complete privacy yet was close enough to town not to be completely isolated. It was the realization of a lifetime's dream and lent me the identity I had sought all my life – that of being a totally independent soul, answerable to no one, and of owning my very own piece of Mother Earth without the invasion of traffic and noise and people. I was a voluntary fugitive from society and the claustrophobic confines of concrete. Here I would at last be able to breathe the air freely, and exist by my own rules.

I compared the cottage and its surroundings to the grim and dark ground floor of the old brownstone I had occupied on east 342nd Street, New York for close on eighteen years. Every morning I had joined the stream of human traffic uptown, spent eight hours in my basement office like a rat in a sewer, then got spewed back onto the congested pavements – a nameless face in a milling crowd, competing for the attentions of flustered cab-drivers. For eighteen years I had merely existed as another traveller on one of life's busy highways, waning to obscurity and being frightened by my nonentity. When I surveyed my newly-acquired property it felt as though I had come home after a very long and arduous journey. It would be fair to say I felt positively smug.

I arrived lock, stock and barrel during the last week of February. The air was still bitterly cold, and the wind blowing in from the Atlantic had a chilly bite to it. I stood in front of the cottage, my hands buried deeply inside the soft lining of my warm jacket, and summarily baptized the cottage Eve's Nook. Why? Because all women have their origin in Eve, and Nook sounded cosy and private. I discarded more important work to spend an entire day painting a signboard that said Eve's Nook in bold, black letters. I fastened it to the front gate, and stood back to admire my handi-work. Doing that was like making an assertive statement about myself and my future, and I had a tremendous sense of achieve-ment. It placed me on the map so to speak.

For an extra fee the removal people put each piece of furniture where I indicated, and there was no particular hurry to get all my crates unpacked. I spent long, lazy days unpacking them, sa-vouring the background melody of the sea lashing against the reefs, the smell of salty spray, the cries of sea-gulls.

Each crate contained a myriad memories – some good, some bad. By the time you reach the half-way point in life, as I had, you've learnt to accept both, the one is as inevitable as the other. I was amazed to discover that things which had caused infinite pain only a few years ago now merely raised a slight twinge of sadness, or a frown, and sometimes even a sentimental smile. There were photographs, some slightly yellowed and faded with age, birthday cards, get-well cards, farewell cards, letters from old friends and long-forgotten lovers. I lingered over each, making a game of recalling names and faces. It became time-consuming, but I enjoyed it thoroughly.

As the last rays of the mild sun shimmered on the ocean I ate my solitary dinners on the porch and talked to myself aloud. It was idyllic, to say the least, and I congratulated myself on my ingenuity in choosing Eve's Nook. I remembered all those cold, inhospitable years in the confines of a city – balancing my em-ployer's books during the days, typing the nights away on my portable typewriter, creating the novel that had sold well enough to pay for this cottage. It finally got into print after two years of collecting rejection slips, but didn't quite make the best-seller list. I had come here with the intention of writing another without the pressures of a full-time career and the distractions that go with the presence of a teenage daughter.

My daughter, Theresa, had left for Israel shortly before Christ-mas, fulfilling a long-standing dream of slogging it out on a kibbutz under a murderous sun. Somehow the concept had appealed to her in a romantic sense, and I had supported her ideal with just a touch of scepticism by buying her a return air ticket. I had received two fun-filled letters since then, both assuring me she was absolutely thrilled with her new life.

I prepared one bedroom for Theresa as though she were likely to arrive back any day. Above her bed I lovingly hung all the framed photographs I had been collecting since she was a ten-day-old baby right up to her nineteenth birthday four months ago. I mused over each, recalling the different stages of her life, which had been different stages of my life too, and marvelled at the metamorphosis that constituted life, each stage a unique learning process. We had enjoyed a good measure of laughter, and many tears too, but it had all contributed to the inner strength I now possessed. Single parenthood had been the toughest challenge of my life, but perhaps the most enriching.

I managed to find a special place for every little memoir, every ornament, every fluffy cushion and rug I had accumulated over the years. I was a sucker for soft, fluffy things, and surrounded myself with them – from cuddly teddy bears with glassy eyes to large Flokati rugs. Potplants too. Every room had a variety of plants, from the simple fern to the exotic tropical blooms, and I tended each with dedication, delighting in each new leaf. After two weeks I finally completed my unpacking and settled down to a form of routine.

My only breathing companion at Eve's Nook was Lulu, my big, fat tabby – a perfect example of feline grace. She was a haphazard mixture of black and white, her glossy fur thick and long. My love for Lulu far exceeded the bounds of most human love for animals and I treasured her companionship. Whenever I talked to her, which was often, she gazed at me with near-human perception in her yellow eyes, uttering the occasional miaow. But unlike humans she never spoke out of turn, or criticized, or made unreasonable demands. I don't think Lulu was as taken with me as I was with her. I liked to carry her round the house like a human baby, but after being touched she spent long periods licking herself fastidiously and with just a trace of disgust, glancing at me accusingly from time to time, as if she associated the human touch with a form of contamination.

Inclined to be a slow riser, I had to discipline myself to rise at 7 a.m. sharp every morning, to do my hour-long exercises to recorded music preferably on the veranda when it wasn't too windy and to eat a well-balanced breakfast. There was a crisp freshness in the early morning air that was positively intoxicating and inspiring, both to body and soul. I stood there, smiling to myself and taking deep breaths of fresh air as though I had just woken from a long slumber. There was comfort in my solitude and I was happier than I had ever been before. Moving here had given me a new lease of life.

Lulu and I settled down to a reclusive and peaceful existence. She claimed one window seat for herself, where she groomed herself and slept while I typed away the hours in front of an open window with the ocean outside to stir my sense of beauty. Words flowed more easily than ever before. Whatever emerged from the typewriter had a poetic ring to it, and I knew beyond a shadow of a doubt that this was going to be a good novel. I was bringing something to life – something of myself that had been incarcerated inside the hard and brittle career-woman I used to be.

I took long breaks from writing to stroll along the deserted stretch of beach, relishing the sense of oneness with nature. I delighted in the abundant marine life on the coral reefs and the untamed fury of the waves breaking against them. Often the wind blew and confined me to the cottage. It shifted sand with startling speed, and at times I feared I'd be buried alive. Yet the cottage stood firmly, as it had for a few decades, and my fears gradually subsided. At night the wind howled round its corners, but the combination of wind and angry sea blended into a sort of rhythm and I slept remarkably well.

The most favourable aspect of my life at Eve's Nook was my total lack of fear at being alone like this. My environment lacked the human debris that spilled onto city pavements after dark – the muggers and murderers and junkies and prostitutes. Or the lonely with their begging eyes, and the mentally-crazed who were ticking away like timebombs. I was now far removed from all the social diseases that made city life unpleasant and unsafe. Living at Eve's Nook was like living in an exclusive and protective cocoon.

Little did I know my new-found peace and happiness were soon to be shattered.

2

A few weeks passed uneventfully. I ate when so inclined and slept when so inclined. I worked when I felt inspired or went for long walks when I didn't. Once a week I took my small Sedan out of the garage, my only hangover from civilization, and drove the short distance into Oliver Bay, where I replenished my simple needs and checked the post box I had rented. Fran Westcott, my literary agent in New York, and Theresa were my only links with the outside world, and occasionally there was another postcard or letter from Theresa, or a small cheque from Fran.

I very soon noticed that the inhabitants of Oliver Bay gave me the cold shoulder but were warm and caring towards their own kind. They were a simple people, whose lives revolved around the fickleness of the sea and the fish factory, and they were suspicious of strangers. The women threw furtive, hostile glances at me, and some stared openly, their eyes saying, Don't approach me, you don't belong here. It became apparent to me that I was an oddity to them – a woman living alone in a macho society where men dominated and made decisions for them. I might even have been considered a danger to the dubious morals of their husbands, fathers and sons, to be side-stepped at all cost. They didn't know it, but this was exactly the kind of relationship I had wanted with them. I had reached the stage in my life where human relationships had little to offer me. They merely distracted me from my more acceptable fantasy world, which was far more interesting than reality. I considered human relationships to be both tedious and emotionally draining. They brought pain and disappointment and anger and resentment, all destructive emotions I had never quite learnt to cope with. Instead I preferred my love-affair with nature and my typewriter and my cat, in that order, all too time consuming to leave room for humans. Other than Theresa, of course. But then, she was no longer with me, and it was impossible for anyone to replace her.

*

Oliver Bay was simultaneously an ugly, smelly town and an historical treasure. It lacked all the characteristics of metropolitan regions, and its easy pace was almost sedating. There was an atmosphere of timelessness, disturbed only by modern features such as McDonald's, Kentucky Fried Chicken and video-game arcades. On the side closest to the ocean was the massive fish factory with its unsightly warehouses, immediately behind it were the central business district, and spreading outwards, the houses of the workers. The narrow, winding streets were lined with an odd mixture of old-world cottages and downright ugly box-like houses. At its farthest reaches were the houses of the more affluent, set well away from the street in spacious gardens.

In a small square in the centre of town I discovered a large marble plaque set on a concrete base, listing all the names of the original settlers – mostly Irish. I couldn't imagine what had attracted them to this region until I learnt of diamond digging that had been popular here at that time. An Indian tribe had related stories of brilliant diamonds the size of a man's hand just waiting beneath the surface of the sand, which caused a flood of fortune-seekers to converge on this coastline. Yet the diamond fever had been short-lived and fruitless. Unlike Fool's Gold there was no such thing as Fool's Diamonds and most had drifted away, bitterly disillusioned.

Oliver Bay's natural harbour had served as a thriving port for slave-traders during the nineteenth century. Just outside the harbour was the clay and cement platform where unscrupulous traders had bargained for human merchandise. The shackles were still embedded in its surface, where manacled slaves had awaited their fate, and surely if I listened closely enough I would hear the anguished cries of fettered men and women piercing the air. There were tragic tales of ships being wrecked on this treacherous shore, spilling their human cargo to the mercy of the Atlantic. The locals claimed that their cries could still be heard in the wail of the wind on dark, moonless nights.

Almost a month after my arrival I joined a guided tour of the factory. What struck me most, in spite of the pervading stench of fish inside, were the very hygienic conditions under which everyone worked. Surfaces were constantly sponged, the floors mopped, the tiled walls kept spotless. The workers wore head-coverings and plastic gloves while handling fish. The tour commenced at the point where the fishing trawlers were offloaded, through the freezing, boiling and canning sections, and finally into the separate pet-food section. The parts of fish unsuitable for human consumption were simply tossed onto a conveyor belt in the main cleaning section. The belt disappeared into a wall and emerged on the other side in the pet-food section, where it conveyed its load to a large mincer. The smell here was almost unbearable, but the final product was an attractively labelled can that said 'Johnson's Pet Food', and in smaller print, 'Pure fish'. I was somewhat appalled by the ingredients that went into the canned fish Lulu enjoyed so much, but since cats eat by smell alone I guessed it was okay.

There was yet another side to Oliver Bay. On the south side, adjacent to the old town, lay the sprawling estate of the Johnsons, sole owners of the fish factory and the impressive fishing fleet. The house was a masterpiece of architecture, protected from prying eyes by an eight-foot-high brick wall and electronically-controlled gates with swivelling television cameras. The property stretched over two miles down the coast, with a ten-foot-high barbed wire fence running its full length. It accommodated the fourth generation Johnsons – Cyril Johnson, his wife, Meryl, and two teenage sons. If you lived in Oliver Bay for any length of time you soon learnt that the Johnsons were demigods to the locals. When one of the Johnsons' limousines drove through town people paused with inbred awe, and kept their eyes discreetly averted.

I also learnt that the Johnsons owned most of Oliver Bay, including its people, and that losing one's job at the factory was the ultimate shame a man could suffer. Cyril Johnson was a progressive employer in that he cared for the well-being of his workers. He had established adequate health and social schemes, but in return he demanded his pound of flesh, and was utterly ruthless when antagonized. A man who had the misfortune to lose his job would subsequently be driven from town in shame and humiliation.

The politics of the town interested me little, but I inadvertently gathered bits of information, mostly from the proprietor of Bay Traders, one of the local stores. Not because I asked, mind, but because Uncle Billy, as he insisted I call him, was a compulsive talker. His full name was William Raymond Reevers, and he was a hangover from a generation now almost extinct. He was a toothless old man with a mane of snow-white hair, a curious accent ranging from a southern drawl to Irish peasant, who still chewed tobacco and spat into a spittoon behind the counter. He was a walking encyclopaedia on Oliver Bay, and knew everything about everyone – young and old alike. I came to the conclusion that he was the type of person who inspired confidence, however misplaced, and people naturally confided their secrets in him. If he noticed the initial reserve in my manner it didn't deter him from befriending me.

'That used to be a grand old cottage you bought out there. Folks by the name of Bennett built it when I was just a youngster. They was from up country, only came for a few weeks each summer. For many years, that was. Same cottage was sold nine times afore you bought it. No one stayed longer'n a year or two.'

'Why is that?' I asked, my curiosity aroused.

'Don't rightly know. It's the wind and sand gets to them 'ventually, I guess. This here ain't no place for a holiday, they soon find out.'

'That's not why I bought it. I need the privacy for my work.'

'Work? I heard say you write books,' he said scoffingly, as though writing had no relation to work.

'You heard right.'

'You got one of them books you write?' he asked again, somewhat contemptuous, yet curious.

'Book,' I corrected him. 'I've only written one. I'm working on the second now.'

' Ain't nobody round here got time to read much. It's a hard life here,' he said, making it sound like an accusation.

'It's a pity. Reading is one of life's rare pleasures,' I replied, inspecting a lampshade made entirely of sea-shells. Judging by the layers of dust I concluded it had been standing in the same spot for many years.

'You ain't exactly a friendly woman, but you know what, Carla Benson? I think I like you,' he conceded, exposing his gums in a broad smile.

Another time he watched me closely from behind the counter, then spoke in a low, confidential tone. 'The folks round here wonder a lot about you, you know. They say it's asking for trouble living alone like you do. Anyone ever bother you up there?'

'Not at all. Why should anyone?'

'Well . . . you're a mighty good-looking woman, if you don't mind my saying so. And there just ain't enough women for all the men here.'

'I'm fortunate that most men my age-group are happily settled into family life, Uncle Billy. Besides, I don't have time for relationships. Tell the women their men are quite safe.'

Uncle Billy frowned. 'It's not the women I'm worried about, lass,' he said before busying himself with my order.

I ignored what I considered the mumbles of a meddling but likeable old man. Compared to the supermarkets I had frequented in the city, the shops here were badly stocked. Any 'special' I required had to be ordered for me, and I soon learnt that most of my requirements were 'special' – my typing paper and ribbons, my favourite shampoo and moisturiser, my particular brand of cigarettes. Fortunately I had stocked up well before leaving New York and wasn't unduly inconvenienced.

During my trips to town the women continued to eye me suspiciously. If Uncle Billy had conveyed my message to them it didn't appear to have had an impact. Since ninety per cent of the men worked either in the factory or on the trawlers, I seldom saw them, but when I did they were everything I had expected them to be – rough, loud-mouthed, hard-drinking, hard-living, intent on preserving the macho image of men who earned a living from the sea, their women created by God for their pleasure and abuse alone. This outdated stance didn't offend me since I had no personal contact with them.

As the days were gradually getting warmer, I often carried a sun umbrella to the beach, and spent lazy hours staring at the constant motion of the sea and putting my thoughts on paper. My new life brought with it a contentment that had been undreamt-of only a few months ago. It was as though my past had been a period of hibernation, as though I had only just woken and every day was unique.

There was only one thing that slightly marred my otherwise perfect existence. It was the unwelcome intruders who came mostly on Sundays, but sometimes on Saturdays too. They converged on the beach with picnic baskets and beach towels, preceded by noisy children and barking dogs, and littered 'my' stretch of beach. They ignored the No Fires signs and grilled their meat on the beach, the offensive smoke infiltrating the cottage. Their transistor radios blared pop music above the melody of the sea, and after a few bottles of wine or a few six-packs of beer they danced in the sand, and laughed uproariously till well after sunset. During these periods I remained in the cottage, sometimes watching them through the lace curtains, wishing them away.

Often people stopped to stare at the cottage, to point fingers and to talk in lowered voices. Sometimes the men exhibited their bravado by making lewd remarks in provocatively loud voices, inviting their womenfolk to squeal with humourless laughter. I greatly resented this uncalled-for interest in my private life and was infinitely grateful when Mondays arrived and I had paradise to myself again.

It was my growing dread of the weekends that first inspired me to go for long, solitary drives along the coast. I would pack a picnic basket and set off with no particular destination in mind. I marvelled at the rugged, unspoilt beauty of the countryside, the flora that thrived in the sandy soil, all the different birds. Oliver Bay was well off the beaten track, the highway running some twelve miles to the west, and it was possible to drive for an hour or more without encountering another living soul. I chose picturesque spots where I ate my solitary lunches and enjoyed the unspoilt scenery.

My favourite spot was Wreckers Strand, thirty-eight miles south from Oliver Bay on the road to Savannah. It was nothing more than a small shingle of beach fringed by angry-looking reefs and large boulders which seemed to have fallen from the hill above. It had earned its name by the number of shipwrecks on its rocky shore, and during low tide one could still see the rusting hulks of trawlers embedded in the reefs. Sometimes I would climb onto a large rock and sit there with the waves breaking against it and sea-gulls crying overhead. At other times I would climb the small hill to enjoy the awesome view from its summit. It made me acutely aware of my insignificance in relation to the vastness of the universe.

It was during one of these Sunday excursions that I encountered him – the young man who was to be the first spoke in the

17

wheel of my misfortune. It was soon after 4 p.m. and I was driving back towards Oliver Bay at a slow pace, humming an old tune under my breath to distract me from the unpleasant driving conditions. I had travelled fifty-six miles south along the coast that day, until I reached a signboard that said 'Savannah – 86 miles'. I had eaten my lunch sitting in the car since a strong, cold wind was blowing, showering everything in its path with fine grains of sand. By 4 p.m. the wind had increased its speed and plucked at the car with frightening strength. Sheets of sand blew against the windscreen, decreasing visibility, and I regretted having come this far. I was rounding a bend in the road when I spotted him, his tall, slender figure hunched against the force of the wind. He was scantily dressed in light blue bermudas, dark blue T-shirt and sneakers, pushing a battered bicycle. At the sound of the car he glanced over his shoulder and raised his hand in what I interpreted as a wave. I waved back and kept going, glancing in my rearview mirror. He presented a pitiful sight indeed, straining against the force of the wind to gain another step, staring after the car with a look of utter defeat.

On impulse I braked and stopped. I had no business taking pity on strangers, I immediately chided myself. All he had to do was stay put until the wind subsided. Besides, he should've known it was foolish cycling on a day like this and so far from the nearest town too. But what if the wind didn't subside? What if it got even stronger and continued to blow throughout the night as it often did? What if his family was waiting for him in Oliver Bay, worrying about his safety? What if . . .?

He reached the car and leaned against the driver's door, his chest heaving. I rolled the window down and yelled against the din of the wind.

'You going into Oliver Bay?'

He nodded, his eyes screwed tight against the wind. I noticed that sand clung to his body in a fine powder and had settled in the grooves of his neck.

'I'll give you a ride but I can't take the bicycle!'

'I'll put it in the trunk!' he cried hoarsely, then coughed violently.

I handed him the key, reluctant to get out of the car and help him. By making the offer of a ride I had committed myself to him, even temporarily, and I didn't like the personal connotations of

18

my gesture. I had come to Oliver Bay to escape people, hadn't I? Taking pity on strangers merely inconvenienced one and complicated one's life. I already regretted my impulse.

There were bumping sounds from the trunk and the small car shook briefly. Then he came running towards the passenger door and got in, along with a few pounds of sand. He wasn't quite as young as I'd thought at first – mid-twenties, perhaps.

'You didn't close the trunk,' I said accusingly.

He looked at me with bloodshot eyes. Sand was clinging to his eyelashes and to the stubble on his face. His blond hair was the colour of ripe corn, if one discarded all the sand in it. As a little girl Theresa had once asked me what Mister Sandman looked like, and I might have described this stranger.

'It won't close . . . not with the bicycle in it,' he explained. There were deep lines of fatigue on his narrow face, his lips were dry and cracked.

'Okay,' I shrugged and pulled away. With the lid of the trunk up I couldn't see in my rearview mirror and my annoyance with myself grew. Damn, he hadn't even thanked me for stopping! That was only one of the things I resented about people – they took everything for granted. The-world-owes-me-something syndrome.

'Have you come far?' I asked, not because I cared one way or the other but because I always felt this irksome obligation to converse when confronted with people.

'Yes,' he croaked.

I glanced at him. He was resting his head against the seat, wiping at his face and eyes with the back of a hand. Sand streamed from him and settled into places where vacuuming was almost impossible. Served me damn right for picking up strangers, I thought.

We drove on in silence. His presence, coupled with the bad weather conditions, increased my state of tension. I had to keep my eyes glued to the road while the wind tossed the small car about, and I was too aware of him to relax. Once, while trying to light a cigarette, I accidentally dropped the lighter between the two front seats and waited for him to retrieve it. When he didn't, I turned to him, a biting remark on my lips. His head had fallen sideways, his mouth was slightly open, and he was snoring lightly. He was sleeping! Well, I'd be damned!

19

I reached Oliver Bay half an hour later. Sand swirled along the deserted streets and accumulated against shop fronts. It was Sunday and there was a ghostly air in town, as though it had been abandoned. I stopped the car beside the concrete circle and turned to him. He was still fast asleep, his face streaked with cloying sand.

'We're here,' I said loudly. He didn't stir. I touched his bare shoulders lightly, felt the abrasive layer of sand on his skin. 'Wake up! We're home!'

He moved his head to the other side, swallowed audibly and started snoring again.

'Time to go!' I persisted, shaking his shoulder more firmly. 'Come on now! Wake up!'

He groaned in protest and turned away from the bothersome touch to his shoulder. Damn! Trust my luck! A car came cruising round the circle and slowed down beside mine. A family of four peered inquisitively at me through their car windows. I shook him again, more roughly.

'Please . . . wake up!' The car continued round the circle and approached me a second time. I put mine into gear and pulled away, deeply annoyed. I would drive home and he could make his own way back to town.

My cottage could only be reached along a two-wheel dirt road that terminated at the garage. I left the car idling while I opened the garage door, then drove it in and switched off the engine. I got out and went round to the passenger side. His head was resting against the closed window. If I opened the door now he would fall out and I might not have the strength to support him. I stared at him, undecided. He looked boyish and vulnerable in sleep, and I wondered why he should be this tired this early in the day. Perhaps I should leave him here. He would wake up in due course and go home.

I returned to the driver's side and opened the window to allow fresh air into the car. The garage was sheltered from the wind, and warm. I left the garage door open too, then ran into the cottage, glad to be home. Lulu met me half-way along the short corridor, and rubbed herself against my legs. I picked her up and carried her into the kitchen, showering her with kisses. The window above the sink had been open all day and a thick layer of sand had settled over everything.

For the first time since my arrival at Eve's Nook my self-created peace had been disturbed, and I felt discontented.

3

When morning dawned the ferocious wind had died down. The air was noticeably warmer, the skies clear and blue, the waters of the ocean rippling playfully on the shore. It was one of those mornings when you feel happy just to be alive, and I decided if there was a heaven it had better be this good.

Cheerfully I put on my tracksuit, fed Lulu in the kitchen, poured myself a glass of orange juice, then went out onto the veranda to do my daily exercises. And then I stopped dead in my tracks. He was sitting on the bottom step, his bare feet buried in the sand, his battered knapsack beside him. At the sound of the door closing he turned round.

'Hi,' he said, smiling uncertainly.

'Hi. I thought you . . .' What had I thought? That he had conveniently disappeared?

'I just wanted to thank you. For the ride,' he said. 'And for letting me sleep in your car.'

Now that the lines of fatigue had been erased by the sleep he looked much younger. Early twenties, maybe less. The sand still clung to his skin and his hair, his lips were still dry. He reminded me a bit of Theresa, perhaps because her hair was the same shade of blond.

I smiled thinly. 'That's okay. I can't imagine it was comfortable, but I couldn't wake you.'

'I'm sorry. I was so hellish tired. Didn't sleep for two days running, and then that wind . . .' He got to his feet.

'Are you going into Oliver Bay?' I asked.

'I guess so. I noticed the chimneys over there. Is that it?' he asked, pointing towards the factory.

'Yes. Haven't you been here before?'

'No.'

'Are you visiting someone?'

'No.'

'Oh. It's less than a mile into town,' I volunteered.

He carelessly flipped the knapsack over one shoulder. I couldn't help but notice how beautifully proportioned he was, how the muscles in his shoulders and arms responded to his every movement. There were blond hairs peeping over the top of his T-shirt, his hands were artistically formed. He wasn't as slender as I'd thought yesterday. His body was strong and sinewy.

'Well . . . thanks a lot,' he repeated, raised a hand in greeting and started walking round the side of the cottage.

'Wait a moment!' I called. He paused and looked back. 'If you don't live here and you're not visiting anyone, where are you going?'

He smiled, shrugging his shoulders. 'Nowhere in particular. I'm just travelling.'

'But . . . you must be hungry. I'll be making breakfast soon. You may join me, if you wish,' I offered, watching him.

A look of surprise crossed his face before it broke into a warm smile. 'That's great. Thanks,' he said simply, and came back.

I watched him in dismay, more at myself than at him. Why was I concerning myself with this boyish-looking drifter in obvious need of a bath and a good meal? I'd become much too emancipated to share even a meal with a stranger. Yet something about him stirred my maternal instincts, besides which it was too late now to retract my invitation. He would bathe, eat and be on his way, I consoled myself.

'Eve's Nook. That's a nice name for a place like this,' he said, pointing to my carefully-painted nameboard.

'That's what I thought too. Do you want to shower while I prepare breakfast?'

He was in close proximity and I could smell stale sweat.

'Do you know something? That's the best offer I've had in months.'

'You couldn't have had very many then,' I said drily.

'You're right, I haven't.'

I preceded him into the cottage. 'The bathroom's on the left. There are clean towels in the cupboard behind the door. Help yourself.'

I went directly to the kitchen, thinking ruefully that I was going

22

to miss my exercises this morning. Lulu was just finishing the last of her pilchards. She licked a paw and started washing her face diligently.

'We have a guest for breakfast, old girl. If you hang around for a while I'll let you have a slice of bacon. Okay?'

With typical feline indifference she ignored me.

I was setting the table when he strolled into the kitchen, wearing the same bermudas but with a clean, white T-shirt. He was clean-shaven, his hair still damp. It struck me that he was a very handsome boy, one of those typical all-blond, all-American boys you saw in ads for Coca-Cola or Beechies, driving fun-coloured convertibles, accompanied by equally ravishing blonde girls with flawless skins and pearly white teeth. They sailed through life with an air of breathless excitement and lots of money to pad the way.

'Can I help with anything?' he asked, standing awkwardly just inside the kitchen.

I shook my head. 'Everything's ready. Please sit down.'

It felt strange having a companion at breakfast again. It wasn't so long ago that Theresa had shared my table, but already it seemed like years ago, in another time and another sphere of existence. Solitude had grown on me at an alarming pace.

I dished up an ample portion of eggs, bacon and mushrooms for him, and invited him to start eating while I toasted more bread. He ate hungrily and with single-minded purpose, while I observed him unobtrusively, strangely pleased. I put the fresh toast on the table and sat down opposite him.

'It's pretty good,' he said, looking up.

For the first time I noticed the unusual green of his eyes. They were almost translucent, like pools of clear water reflecting the sun. There was a clean, untarnished look about him. I smiled my acknowledgement and started eating.

'Has your husband left for work already?' he asked, buttering a slice of toast.

I glanced at him, feeling a now familiar annoyance stir inside me. It didn't matter how young or how old they were, they just couldn't accept the fact that certain women could survive without them. 'Ever heard of women managing on their own?' I asked pointedly.

'Sure. But I thought older women were different,' he said.

23

'This older woman grew up in the sixties when women suddenly got wise to the fact that they had a choice,' I responded, more sharply than I'd intended.

'Was it good? Growing up in the sixties?'

I pondered the question for a moment, aware of his frank gaze. 'The sixties was probably the most revolutionary decade in modern times. Along with the awakening of women as productive and noteworthy members of society we saw the advent of space travel, experienced Beatlemania, suffered the tragic assassination of John Kennedy and confronted the horrors of Vietnam. Yet it was no better than growing up in the seventies or even now in the eighties. Growing up is always painful. There are so many insecurities we don't know how to cope with. It's tragic, in a way, when youth is supposed to be the best time of our lives.'

'I don't think it is . . . the best time, I mean,' he said, buttering a third slice of toast. 'I don't know how it was in the sixties, but today there's too much emphasis on youth and beauty. And pressures to achieve. And when you're young you have an added disadvantage – nobody takes you seriously.'

'And you want to be taken seriously?' I asked with just a trace of amusement.

He looked at me, his eyes examining me. 'I guess you think I'm just another young fool trembling on the threshold of life.'

'I didn't say that,' I fenced. 'Are you?'

'No. I was born old. I can't remember being a child . . . ever,' he said, and bit into the toast.

I sensed that he wanted me to enquire why not, but I refused to take the bait. I didn't desire even a glimpse of his private life. Instead I got up, filled the kettle with water and switched it on. Lulu sauntered into the kitchen from outside, and I handed her the promised slice of bacon. She left the kitchen with it dangling from her mouth.

'That's a lovely cat,' he said. 'I like cats. They don't mess up the garden like dogs do, or stink up the place when they don't get washed regularly.'

'Dogs have their attributes, if you have the love and patience. Some people believe they're more intelligent than cats simply because they're more responsive and dependent. I believe cats have more pride, and they're not stupid enough to trust us implicitly.'

He laughed, displaying a row of perfectly white teeth. Next thing he would take a Gold Leaf from his pocket and light up. And the cameras would roll.

'Do you like living alone?' he asked.

'Very much.'

'I do too. I've been on the road for five months now, and I think it's been the best five months of my life, mainly because I was alone.'

I looked at him, puzzled. 'You mean you travel on that bicycle?'

'Yes. Does it surprise you? It's the best way to enjoy the countryside, you know. Unless it rains or the wind blows, like yesterday,' he grinned.

'But . . . where do you sleep?'

'Wherever,' he shrugged. 'I keep close to the coast. The sand is good enough. When the weather gets real bad I book into a hotel.'

Questions milled about in my head, but I refrained from asking them. I didn't want any further involvement with this young stranger. My hospitality was beginning to wear dangerously thin, and I ached to get back to my typewriter.

He downed two cups of black coffee, then offered to do the dishes. I declined, keen to see the last of him.

'It's some place you have here,' he said admiringly, gazing out the kitchen window towards the sea. 'This is how I want to live one day – alone . . . by the sea.'

'I'm sure it seems pretty romantic to you, but it doesn't suit everyone. The isolation can become a burden,' I said practically.

'But not for you?'

'No.'

'I don't even know your name,' he said again.

'Carla Benson. And yours?'

'Peter Dreifuss-Jones. I have to get going before it gets too late. My target is fifty miles a day, and I must still go into town. Thanks for everything, Carla. You're the nicest person I've come across in five months.'

The compliment was unexpected. I had never considered myself a 'nice' person. I was reclusive, self-opinionated, headstrong, cynical. But how could he know all these things about me?

'I'll be going into town later. I can give you a ride,' I offered half-heartedly.

'Oh no, you've done enough. Thanks, anyway.'

He slung his rucksack over his shoulder. It was decorated with stickers promoting football clubs and signatures from people I presumed were his school or college friends. I accompanied him to the garage where he removed the bicycle from the trunk of my car. He wiped the sand from the saddle, then extended a hand.

'Goodbye, Carla. It was a real pleasure meeting you.'

I took his proffered hand. 'Goodbye, Peter.'

I watched as he pushed the bicycle along the two-wheel track – a lonely figure on the road to nowhere. He looked back and waved. I waved back, relieved to see the last of him.

Two days later, on Wednesday afternoon, I pushed the type-writer back across the desk shortly before 3 p.m. I had woken that morning with a sudden surge of inspiration and had been ham-mering away at the keyboard since 7 a.m., with only two short tea breaks and a hastily consumed sandwich. I had smoked forty cigarettes and now my mouth tasted utterly vile, my throat felt as though it were lined with sandpaper, my head ached dully. In other words, I was badly in need of fresh air and relaxation.

Lulu had disappeared some time during the morning and there was still no sign of her. I guessed she had discovered more interesting and defenceless creatures in the adjacent bush. For the past few days she had been arriving home with partly-chewed field mice, tailless lizards or weakly-struggling locusts. She dumped them wherever she tired of playing with them, leaving me to dispose of the grisly remains. It was very difficult to associate my adorable bundle of fluff with the cruel act of hunting and killing, but the evidence abounded.

I collected my wide-brimmed, straw hat from the hook behind the kitchen door, put it on and left the cottage. The sun was pleasant outside, the warmth enfolded me like a soft blanket. In the absence of a breeze the smell from the fish factory hung strongly in the air. It was low tide and the sea was unusually calm. Dark coral reefs, usually invisible, jutted from its surface like misplaced anthills. I removed my sandals and enjoyed the feel of the warm sand beneath my bare feet. I strolled towards the cluster of rocks directly below my cottage, and came across half a dozen empty beer cans and some greasy fast-food wrappers carelessly strewn about. The weekend visitors seldom cleaned up after partying here but I made a point of cleaning up 'my' stretch of beach every Monday morning. I didn't know how I had missed these.

I climbed onto the rocks and examined their pitted surfaces at leisure, while water lapped gently against them. I still marvelled at the easy pace my life had acquired. My inner clock had still not unwound completely and sometimes I still felt anxious for no apparent reason. A lifetime of habit could not be broken in so short a space of time. I stepped carefully over the sharp edges, pausing at the numerous clear pools of water with their abundant marine life. I inspected a crevice where starfish clung to the jagged surface, and wondered if I would ever tire of the sea. All my life I had loved it with a searing passion and had only ever known true contentment in its vicinity. Its timeless rhythm had a soothing effect on me, its raging waters stirred in me a deep sense of awe.

I sat down in my favourite spot – a flat piece of rock facing the ocean – and allowed my eyes to stray over the vast expanse of water. When I first noticed his head bobbing in and out of the water I mistook it for a piece of seaweed until the seaweed suddenly acquired arms and legs and came swimming towards the rocks where I sat. It surprised me that anyone would brave the cold water, especially at this time of year. I didn't recognize him until he reached the rocks below me and pulled himself from the water. Unaware of my presence he shook the water from his blond hair, shivering noticeably. I admired his lean, hard frame abstractly, as one would admire a timeless and rare work of art. Boys had never looked this good when I was young. Or maybe they had and I just never noticed. Suddenly he looked up, saw me and smiled.

'Hi!' he called, waving.

I didn't know whether to be annoyed or just indifferent. Where had he been since Monday? And why hadn't he moved on? I didn't return his greeting but that didn't deter him from climbing up to where I sat.

'How long have you been sitting here?' he asked.

'A few minutes.'

'Are you going to swim?'

'No. I don't like being cold.'

'It's cold all right, but refreshing too. It clears your head and stimulates your bloodflow. Mind if I sit down?'

'No.' What else could I say?

He sat down beside me and pointed towards the spot where he had just swum. 'You see that sharp point protruding from the water there? It's actually only the tip of a massive underwater reef. It runs all the way up past the factory. They blasted it away at the mouth of the harbour to allow the trawlers a free passage.'

'Where have you been sleeping?' I asked, ignoring the geography lesson.

'Right next to these rocks. There's a sheltered spot the water doesn't reach at high tide.'

'Oh. Does your family know where you are?'

'My family? Any reason why they should?' he asked, his voice suddenly guarded. I looked at him. Drops of water glistened on his three-day-old stubble, his eyes were very clear against the healthy brown of his skin.

'Because they may care. And . . . I'm a mother too. I have a daughter almost your age and I'd hate for her to be alone and unsheltered . . . like you.'

He smiled a slow smile. 'You don't look old enough to have a daughter of twenty-two. That's how old I am. And don't worry, my family doesn't share your sentiments. My father is too engrossed in his business and love affairs and my mother died almost ten years ago.'

'I'm sorry.'

'No need to be. I was only twelve at the time. She was dead for two days before my father came home and realized there was something wrong with her. Those two days were the loneliest of my life. I think I knew all along she was dead but I pretended she wasn't. I was very scared too. She committed suicide and I never forgave her for it. Nor him.'

There was a distinct trace of bitterness in his voice. I turned my face away and stared out across the sea. He had no right to involve me in his tragedy, I told myself, trying to feel indifferent. Yet the vision of a twelve-year-old boy, alone and afraid and sharing a house with his dead mother, tugged at my heart.

'I find the people here downright hostile,' he said again, changing the subject. 'I sense it every time I go into town.'

'Then why do you stay?'

'Because I need a tyre for my bicycle. Mine has a puncture that can't be fixed. The old man at Bay Traders told me he sold the last one over a week ago. He's waiting for stocks to arrive.'

'And when will that be?'

'He doesn't know himself. Places like this have their charm as long as you're not in a hurry to move on.'

'And you are?'

'Not really. I needed a rest and this place is as good as any other. Better, in a lot of ways.'

The sun was burning my unprotected arms and I decided to return to Eve's Nook. I put my sandals back on and got up. He rose too and I noticed that he was a head taller than me – a confusing blend of man and boy.

'Goodbye, Peter,' I said, and made my way down the rocks.

''Bye, Carla,' he called.

I walked hurriedly across the stretch of sand, back to the neutral shelter of Eve's Nook. I knew he was watching me, felt his eyes burn on my back like red-hot pokers. When I closed the door behind me I tried to shut out the lone figure I had left behind on the rocks. For Christ's sake, he was hardly a child, I told myself; he could take care of himself. He had to be tough to have survived five months on the road on a bicycle. Yet time and again I was unwittingly drawn to the window to see if he was still there. The third time I looked he was gone, but the vision of a boy sharing a house with his dead mother for two days remained to haunt me. What had he been eating since Monday? Suddenly I remembered the empty beer cans and food wrappers. So he had money. Then why couldn't I stop fretting and settle down to doing something constructive?

On impulse I decided to air and dust Theresa's room. I removed each framed photograph from the wall and wiped it lovingly before replacing it. Motherhood had been one of my rare successes in life, and I liked to view myself as a liberated, supportive mother, who had shared every triumph and every disaster with her offspring. It had been an uphill road all the way, but together we had survived her drug-experimenting stage, her adolescent crises about identity and self-worth, her sexual awakening. She had left my comfortable nest not as a woman of inferior physique and intellect but as a dignified human being, firmly established. The rest was up to her.

I had never consciously intended to be a bra-burning women's libber. I had grown up during an era when girls were expressly reared for matrimony and motherhood. My needs had been very basic and conventional for my time and place. Like all 'good girls' I had desired little from life other than a kind, considerate husband and a stable family life. My divorce at the tender age of twenty-two had left me sadly disillusioned with the stereotype romances portrayed in Mills & Boon books. With a baby to support I had been cast into the reluctant role of career woman and it hadn't been until my late twenties that I actually started enjoying the independence that accompanied my single status. I don't think Theresa and I would have had such a close, successful relationship if we'd had to share our lives with a third person. But perhaps that was a selfish conclusion on my part.

When the sun hung low in the west I carried a cane chair and portable gas cooker onto the veranda. I poured a Miller into a tall glass and drank it while I grilled a lamb chop and piece of beef sausage. When the delicous aroma of grilling meat wafted from the cooker, Lulu arrived home and curled herself up at my feet. The meat done, I helped myself to the fresh tossed salad I had made earlier and settled down to eat. Only to find that I couldn't. I remembered the greasy food wrappers, the empty beer cans half-buried in the sand, the aloneness of his slender figure. Was he hungry? Could he smell the aroma of the meat right now, and worse still, was he watching me this very moment?

You may ask why I was so concerned about a perfect stranger when I had escaped from New York for the express purpose of divorcing myself from people and the demands they made. I was the type of person who couldn't pass a stray animal on the street without comforting it or giving it something to eat, and Peter Dreifuss-Jones very much reminded me of a stray animal. In New York we would've passed each other on a busy pavement without as much as a second glance, but here, in the confines of our surroundings we each had an identity. I picked at the food. It was tasteless and greasy. I finished the salad and left the meat for Lulu who rubbed herself against me in a gesture of gratitude. I suddenly wished I had never laid eyes on Peter Dreifuss-Jones.

Later that night, while peering through the curtains, I thought I saw his lone figure sitting on the rocks. The moon was full, throwing pale shadows across the landscape, and I might've imagined it. My thoughts strayed to Theresa, but just before I dozed off her face was replaced by his. And he was only a young boy, friendless and directionless, deprived of his mother's love at the age of twelve.

4

Bay Traders was an old store, a remnant from another civilization. There were five steps leading to its weather-beaten and rickety front door. The railing along its porch was badly rusted and broken in places, the wooden floorboards inside creaked when one walked across them, and the stale stench of tobacco blended with the pungent smell of onions. There was a slightly more modern superette closer to the factory, but somehow Uncle Billy appealed to me and I preferred shopping here.

In the semi-dark interior Uncle Billy was resting his elbows on the counter, reading a week-old, oil-stained newspaper. He folded it the moment he saw me and beamed a toothless grin.

'Good morning, Uncle Billy,' I greeted.

'And a good morning to you. Ain't you up early this morning?'

'Am I?' I looked at my watch. 'It's after eight. I've been up since six.'

'Lord A'mighty, I didn't know writers get up early too. If you're here 'bout that typing paper it's too early in the day. They don't deliver till after noon, gotta come off the highway, you know.'

'No, that's not why I'm here. I've come to enquire about a bicycle tyre. I believe you have some on order.'

'A bicycle tyre? You have a bicycle?'

'No, but I need a tyre for a friend. When do you expect the stocks to arrive?'

'If it's only a tyre you want I got plenty in the back here. Lots a folks here ride bicycles. Place ain't big enough for a car,' he laughed toothlessly. 'What type a bicycle is it?'

'I don't know offhand, but you do have them in stock?'

'Sure. All sorts. You wanna see them?'

31

'Er . . . not right now. I'll be back for one as soon as I know the make of bicycle,' I lied smoothly.

'You just let me know and I'll fix you up,' Uncle Billy said, and spat behind the counter.

'Yes, I'll do that. And . . . thank you, Uncle Billy. While I'm here I'll take a few tins of cat food. Make it ten,' I said.

'Sure thing. How many cats you got out there?'

'Only the one, but she eats enough for two.'

'Me, I like cats too. Used to keep a whole bunch a the things till the wife died back in '68. Those were the days afore the factory made that pet food and we had to go up there every day to collect scraps. But at least we didn't have to pay for it.'

'So what happened to them when your wife died?' I asked.

'There was no one to feed 'em. Gave 'em all away. She was a good woman, was my wife. Would've wanted it that way. Only son I had never was interested in this here store, so I carried on alone. But folks aren't what they used to be, prefer the self-service places these days. Walk in and walk out without as much as a good day to you. Ain't much point in carrying on here 'cept it gets damn lonely at home.'

'Your son . . . what does he do?'

'My son? What do you think the boy did? Fathered a child, he did, then volunteered for 'Nam and got killed in a jungle he had no business being in. They brought him home in pieces, I tell you. Goddamn war was no American war but my boy got killed in it.'

I didn't want to be drawn into the moral of a stale war that still littered American society with traumatized victims and provided a whip for people's pet hates. While he packed the tins in a small carton with painstaking precision, my eyes strayed over the store. It was April already, but the remains of last Christmas's decorations still adorned the store. Or maybe it went back a few Christmasses. Faded strips of crinkle paper hung limply from thumb tacks attached to the ceiling. A pitiful pine tree stood in a dark corner, decorated with glitter balls now covered in dust.

Uncle Billy noticed my inspection. 'Don't much care for Christmas like I used to,' he said, and put a fresh piece of tobacco in his mouth. 'Was a time I joined every party and ate 'n drank with the fittest of 'em folk. Now . . . I'm just an old man, plagued by rheumatism, even in summer.'

'I don't much care for Christmas myself.'

Uncle Billy nodded his head in approval, his toothless jaws working mechanically on the tobacco. 'Good sense you have too. Come Christmas you just stay up there at that cottage a yours, you hear? Some folks here forget it's the birth of Christ. The hooligans sure take over at Christmas and New Year. Now don't you go saying I said so, you hear? But the good, clean fun sure's gone outa Christmas here, I tell you.'

'It's happened everywhere, I'm afraid,' I agreed, and paid for the pet food.

'The youngsters have changed so much it makes my old head spin. No respect for nothing good these days. It's the devil they worship here, if you ask me. And the worst is when the factory shuts for the summer vacation. The Johnsons go to Europe then, and you know how it is . . . cat's gone, mice play. Only every year it gets rougher. You wanna know what happened last year?'

I didn't, but there was no stopping him now.

'The two Bester brothers got burnt to cinders out at Jutters Point. They was good boys, ran the lumber business just out a town. Whole bunch a them went out to the Point partying, made a big bonfire on the beach, they did. Then some fighting broke out and someone pushed them into the fire. I heard say they yelled blue murder, but no one helped 'em. Just stood there watching and laughing. Them boys burnt so bad their own mothers didn't recognize them. Afterwards them youngsters all swore they saw nothing, heard nothing. They was all somewhere else at the time. So no one's been brought to justice. Makes one wonder – what happens this year?'

The story left me somewhat uneasy. It wasn't hard to imagine a bunch of rowdy and drunken fishermen partying on the beach and killing each other in the process. Suddenly Oliver Bay wasn't just a sleepy small town anymore, it too nursed the rot that had crept into the human race. I picked up the carton, ready to leave.

'Where's Jutters Point?' I asked.

'The north side a the factory, right aside the pet-food section. It's a good stretch of beach if you don't mind the stink. This year . . .'

'I'll be back for my paper this afternoon,' I cut him short, and left. My car was parked directly in front of the store. A short and stockily built man was leaning against the driver's door, his arms folded across his chest. He wore faded jeans, a stained check shirt

33

and a dark blue jockey cap. He watched me approach, his jaws working on a piece of gum, a slight smile playing on his fleshy lips. His age was difficult to determine. These men of the sea led a tough life and it showed on their faces at an early age, so that when a man was twenty he could look anything up to forty.

Ignoring him, I went round to the passenger side, opened the door and put the carton on the seat. When I came round to the driver's side he didn't budge.

'Please stand aside,' I said coldly. 'This is my car.'

'I already know that. Only one of its kind here. I'm Ax Reevers. It's short for Alexander,' he said, smiling. His teeth were uneven and stained.

'That's very nice, Ax,' I said sarcastically. 'Now please . . .'

'Uncle Billy's my grandpa. He told me your name's Carla. It's a nice name, classy like,' he continued, unperturbed. His accent was flat, his small eyes moved constantly in his fleshy face. I noticed the thick layer of black hair on his arms and the back of his hands.

'Thank you. Now please stand aside. I'm in a hurry,' I said, making no attempt to conceal my irritation. I felt threatened by him and didn't like the sensation at all.

'The monthly dance is next Saturday night. They clear the main warehouse for it, plenty of dancing space. And the local band is good, plays anything from Latin American to country and pop. You wanna go with me?'

I fixed him with a cold stare. 'No, thank you. I don't dance and I don't like crowds. Neither do I like men who impose themselves on women.'

The expression on his face didn't change. On the opposite side of the road I noticed two men sitting on the bonnet of a beat-up truck, watching us and grinning. I presumed they were his friends.

'Aw, come on, Carla. Don't be so damn uppity. You're one of us now,' he persisted, chewing and smiling. 'What's a pretty woman like you wanna do locking herself away in that God-forsaken cottage?'

'Hey, you! Ax! Get away from that car!'

Uncle Billy had emerged from the store and was pointing a gnarled finger at Ax. His mane of white hair blew outwards in the breeze, his eyes were ablaze, giving him a fearsome appearance.

To my surprise Ax obeyed immediately. 'Only being sociable, grandpa,' he said, standing aside.

'You come right on up here! Right this minute!' Uncle Billy barked.

I quickly got into the car and drove away. When I passed the truck I noticed the two men laughing. The encounter had unnerved me. I had never quite grown accustomed to the way some men use the advantage of their physical superiority over women. It is intimidating and puts women at a distinct disadvantage, with no means of retaliating. In the cave-age I guessed it had served a useful purpose, in the twentieth century it seemed downright offensive.

Another surprise awaited me at Eve's Nook. Peter Dreifuss-Jones was in my garden, lifting weeds from the flower-beds with a spade. He had removed his T-shirt and stood bare-chested beside a pile of weeds. When he saw me he leaned on the upright spade, wiped sweat from his forehead and smiled boyishly. The sight infuriated me. The sanctity of my privacy had been violated. I started trembling.

'What do you think you're doing?' I asked angrily.

His smile disappeared rapidly, his face fell. 'I wanted to do something for you . . .'

'You owe me nothing! You hear? Nothing whatsoever. Get off my property. At once!'

The vehemence of my attack startled even myself, but I had no control over my unreasonable anger. He wiped his hands on his shorts and walked backwards, hurt surprise on his face.

'I'm sorry . . . I thought . . .'

'You thought wrong!' I snapped.

He turned, left through the gate and walked away across the sand. His posture seemed to sag with each step, and just as suddenly as the anger had gripped me it let go. I stood there, watching him leave, feeling as though I had just ripped a toy from a child's hand and crushed it underfoot.

I went into the cottage, unpacked the cat food and made myself a cup of tea. His face swam before me. I saw the confusion and hurt in his clear, green eyes, the sensitive lines along his mouth, the slumped shoulders as he walked away, and I felt like a total creep. But goddamn it, he shouldn't have done that without my permission! I hadn't intended being quite so harsh, but it was that

35

episode in town that triggered my reaction to his presence. And the fact that he had lied to me about the bicycle tyre.

I paced the kitchen restlessly, wringing my hands together. The vision that assailed me was that of a twelve-year-old boy living in the same house with his dead mother for two days and being too afraid to confront the truth. How had a twelve-year-old boy processed such pain? On impulse I left the cottage and ran across the stretch of beach towards the rocks. There was no sign of him. I examined the spot where he had said he slept. The bicycle was under an overhanging rock, both tyres intact. His rucksack was there too, so were the greasy food wrappers and empty beer cans. It resembled the lair of a lost animal. I noticed something else too. He had washed his clothes – in the ocean, I presumed – and left them on the rocks to dry. Anyone who lived the way he did and still kept himself so clean had to be admired.

'Peter!' I called, then climbed the rocks. I examined the stretch of sea in front of me, but nothing unusual stirred in it. The seaweed was genuine seaweed and the sea-gulls bobbing on the water didn't have arms. From here I could see all the way down the beach to the point where the trawlers docked at the factory's harbour. It was deserted.

I returned to the cottage, feeling awful, and went directly to my desk. The blank sheet in my typewriter stared back at me, accusing me of slacking. I needed a clear mind and total dedication to complete this novel and shouldn't have allowed people like Ax Reevers and Peter Dreifuss-Jones to ruffle my calm and distract me from the more important business of establishing myself as an author. Fran had enquired about my progress in her last letter and I owed her a reply. The minutes ticked by while the blank sheet seemed to challenge me, knowing I would retreat. Had she hugged him before ending her life? Had she tried at all to imagine his shock and grief? Had she left anything of herself behind? And why had he returned here with a lie?

I walked over to the window seat where Lulu lay curled up. I buried my hand in her thick, soft fur, felt the warmth of her body underneath. She yawned and eyed me sleepily.

'Your life is so wonderfully uncomplicated, Lulu,' I murmured, stroking her absently. 'No hidden motives, no uncontrolled desires, no guilt, no sorrow. I thought I'd left all that behind, that I'd never look back on emotions again. But it isn't that simple, you see. Not for us humans.'

She stretched lazily and yawned again. I gazed out of the open window. The lace curtains stirred in the warm breeze. Every time I saw the scenery outside it was like seeing it for the first time. Its tranquil beauty never faltered. I wanted to grow old and die here – peacefully and contentedly. And preferably with the sun shining, like now, and the smell of the sea in my nostrils. And alone, of course. Dying was a lonely business, not to be shared with anyone.

He entered my line of vision, walking towards the clump of rocks, clutching a brown paper bag. He carried his T-shirt too, the muscles on his bare chest rippled as he walked, his shorts fitted snugly over his narrow hips. For a few moments I remained still, admiring the careless grace of his lean body and the confidence in his stride, then rushed outside.

'Peter!' I called, but my voice was drowned by the roar of the ocean. He continued his brisk pace until he disappeared behind the rocks. I hesitated only briefly, then ran across the sand. I found him sitting under the overhanging rock, eating a piece of fried fish with his hands. The brown paper bag lay at his feet.

'Peter?'

He looked up and stopped chewing, his eyes suddenly wary.

'I'm sorry . . . about this morning. I didn't mean to be quite so nasty,' I apologized.

'It's okay,' he said and continued eating. I didn't think it was okay.

'Something unpleasant happened in town and . . . and I arrived home and found you there. It sort of frightened me, I guess,' I explained. I wanted him to forgive me but at the same time I wanted him to go away from here and never come back.

He picked at the fish with his fingers. 'I said it's okay. Really it is. Forget it.'

Good, I had apologized. Now why didn't I just walk away and forget it?

'If you still want to work in the garden it's perfectly all right. I intended doing it myself but never got round to it. I . . . I'll pay you.'

He looked up. 'I don't need money.'

There were traces of cooking oil on his lips and blond stubble. While I watched he carefully removed a long fish bone from his mouth and stabbed it into the sand beside him. I didn't know what else to say. Suddenly I felt foolish standing here, almost begging a young drifter to come and work in my garden.

'I'll be up later,' he said casually.

'Fine. See you then,' I said, turned and walked back to Eve's Nook.

From the garage I fetched a few garden implements left behind by the previous owner, and a refuse bag from the kitchen. The patch where he had worked looked much better and I started putting the pile of weeds into the bag. To say the garden was neglected was a vast understatement. It had been neglected when I arrived here and my lack of attention to it was evident. Weeds were having a field-day suffocating everything in their path and the spiky grass made a brave but futile attempt to grow. I didn't hear him approach and was startled when he spoke directly behind me.

'Leave that to me. I like gardening.'

I turned to him and smiled. 'So do I. I'll help you once I've made tea. Or would you prefer something cold?'

'Tea's fine,' he said. He seemed to have recovered from my earlier snub.

For the remainder of the morning we worked side by side without feeling the need to talk. I thoroughly enjoyed this outdoor diversion and the team spirit between us. Against a wall we discovered two wild pomegranate bushes, the buds of their red blossoms sprouting in the mild spring air, but other than this promise of colour there was no order in the garden and we soon realized it was a bigger task than we had anticipated.

At lunchtime we retired to the porch to enjoy a cold meal and even colder beer. The day was quite warm and the cool of the veranda was refreshing. Yet a nagging voice in my head kept telling me I was wasting time, that I should be working on my novel. I had broken my routine for two days running and broken routines were difficult to re-establish.

'What happened in town this morning?' he asked between mouthfuls.

'Oh . . . nothing much. Maybe I just don't understand the people here,' I shrugged.

'They're a queer bunch all right. Every time I go into town they want to know what I'm doing in Oliver Bay and when I intend moving on. I've seen it before, in other small towns. Once people know you're on the road you're treated little better than scum.'

'Why are you on the road?' I asked, trying to keep my eyes from the perfect shape of his sculptured body.

'It's something to do. For now,' he responded.

'Is that all? Something to do?'

'Yes. What's the alternative? Cutting throats in the business world until I reach the top and grow ulcers and a fat belly? And be washed out before I'm forty? I just don't fit into that sort of framework,' he said soberly.

'Surely that isn't the only alternative. Why typecast the entire social structure?'

'You ask a lot of questions, Carla, but since I like you I'll tell you. My mother conformed to society's norms and it killed her. She supported my father through law school, she was a model wife and a model mother. She lived in a model house in a model suburb, she had model friends, a late model car, a model pool. But when you add it all up it just isn't enough. She was a naïve and compassionate woman, qualities the world mistakes for weakness. Everyone abused her, including my father. I'm very much like her and I don't want to be a punching bag for punch-drunk people.'

'What is it you want then?' I prodded.

He shrugged his shoulders carelessly. 'I don't know. I need more time to chew it over. But whatever it is, it'll be as far removed from people as possible. I discovered something very early in life: everyone lies – politicians, professors, lovers, friends . . . even family. It all starts with Father Christmas and ends on your deathbed, when everyone assures you you're going to be just fine. Lies depress me even more than ruthless ambition. I went to university, more to please my father than through personal ambition. I observed my fellow students there, saw the burning ambition and greed in their eyes, the killer instinct that propels them. I just didn't belong there. I'm not sure where I belong.'

'Did you drop out?'

'Yeah. I didn't want to ride the same wave of self-destruction most people seem to ride. There has to be more to life than that, only I need more time to figure it out.'

'And you think you'll figure it out by cycling around the country?' I asked sceptically.

'Maybe. Maybe not,' he answered simply.

I offered him a cigarette but he lit one of his own Camels. I drained the last of my orange juice and stared out to sea, enjoying its calming effect.

'You're compassionate too, Carla,' he said again. 'You try to hide it behind a hard façade, but not well enough. It's in your eyes when you drop your guard. Is that why you're hiding yourself away here?'

'I'm not hiding. I just happen to enjoy my own company more.'

'I don't believe you, Carla. You have a real need for something more than your own company,' he said softly. I looked at him, met his gaze. His eyes challenged me to deny it, but I didn't. God, he was only a boy, hardly out of adolescence! He had no right to probe my soul.

'You're wrong,' I said abruptly, and looked away.

'My mother was a proud woman too,' he said softly.

'Is that why I remind you of her?' I asked quietly.

He threw his head back and laughed spontaneously. His teeth were very white against the healthy brown of his skin. 'God, no. You're nothing like my mother. She was very blonde and very frail-looking. You're dark and strong.'

I gathered the lunch plates and empty glasses. Immediately he jumped to his feet and helped me. Together we carried them into the kitchen and stacked them in the sink.

'I have to go back to town, Peter, and afterwards I have work to do. I don't think it's a good idea to continue in the garden today. The sun is too hot.'

'I like working in the sun,' he said, a silent plea in his clear eyes. I shook my head firmly.

'No, you're sunburnt. You should go now,' I said. Go? Where to? I ignored the question in his eyes and ran hot water onto the dishes.

'Let me do that for you,' he offered.

'No. It'll only take a minute.'

He remained standing there, as though waiting, and I blamed

myself. I shouldn't have encouraged him. I should've remained immune to the hunger in his eyes.

'Will you come for a swim later?' he asked. 'The water's not so cold once you're in.'

I looked at him, ready to decline. But then I wondered why the hell not. It might even be fun. 'All right. I'll be down later this afternoon.'

Fool! Up to that point I had still had time to turn my back on him, to walk away from his need. And my own.

'Don't mind Ax, you hear?' Uncle Billy said. 'He's a cheeky boy but he don't mean no harm.'

I ignored the reference to his grandson and wrote out a cheque for my purchases. I had waited five weeks for them and most were now urgently required.

'It's them friends of his, I tell you. That Sam Shroder and Doughie Steyl . . . now there're two real mean boys. Never out a trouble since they was this high,' he continued, indicating with his hand. 'Never did listen to me when I told him to lay off those scoundrels. One day they're gonna get him into real trouble, you mark my words.'

I handed him the cheque. 'Will you place the same order again?'

'Sure thing. He was only four years old when his pa ran off to 'Nam. His mother never was no good, ran off with a passing salesman two years later. Last I heard she was washing dishes in a two-bit spot in L.A. Ax give you any more trouble you come right on over here and tell me, you hear? I ain't too old to give the boy a damn good strapping.'

'I can look after myself, Uncle Billy,' I assured him, but not myself. How did one handle men like Ax Reevers?

Curious glances followed me when I called on the adjacent butcher, where I bought a week's supply of meat for myself and Lulu. People stared openly when I emerged and got into my car. Oliver Bay's inhabitants could no more adapt to me than I could to them, but I didn't want it any other way. I would only intrude in their small world and they in mine.

Back home I absorbed myself for two hours doing revision on completed chapters, then changed into my bathing suit. I examined my body critically in the full-length mirror, and cursed the deterioration of my once firm and slim figure. This was one of the hardest things I'd had to cope with in life – the gradual and irreversible collapse of the body after thirty-five. It is something so totally beyond our control we can only look on in helpless frustration. No amount of exercise can restore the elasticity of an ageing skin, the firm hips and thighs. My breasts were still firm, like those of a young girl, but everything else said I was pushing forty.

I slipped into my sandals, reprimanding myself for fretting over something as inescapable as ageing. I put on my straw hat and left the cottage. He must've been watching the cottage for he came towards me from the rocks, smiling broadly.

The cold water was a shock to my system, and I screamed in genuine anguish. Peter laughed out loud and I joined in. Together we swam away from the cluster of rocks towards the open sea. He had been right. After a while you didn't feel the cold for the simple reason that it numbed you. The tide had a strong pull too and I opted to return to the beach and blessed sunlight. Shivering and spluttering I emerged from the water, Peter close behind me.

Upon reflection, it was a fun afternoon. We lay stretched out on our beach towels, soaking up the warm sun. We smoked, drank Coke and chatted idly about places we had seen and things we had experienced. I discovered another side to his serious nature. He was witty and intelligent, and an interesting source of information. For one so young he had travelled extensively and described places to me I hadn't known existed. At times he had me laughing out loud, something I hadn't done for some time. Sea-gulls gathered on the rocks above us and their shrill cries rang out like laughter, blending with ours.

He lay close beside me – a bronzed and beautiful young man whose every movement hinted at sensuality. Once I had the crazy impulse to run my fingers through the blond hairs on his chest, to touch his sensitive mouth with my fingertips. Disgusted with myself I turned away and concentrated on the soothing tone of his voice instead. When the sun hung low in the west I gathered my things, while Peter watched, suddenly silent. I sensed he was waiting for an invitation, reluctant to be left alone. What did I have to lose? I asked myself. He was only a boy in need of a friend. And I? I owed him something for the pleasure he had given me today, however fleeting.

'Will you join me for supper?' I asked. 'I'm a pretty lousy cook but we can grill hamburgers on the porch.'

His face lit up noticeably. 'I'd love to.'

'You may use the bathroom while you're there,' I offered, feeling generous. 'I think you can do with a shave too.'

He ran a hand over the stubble on his face. 'Do you think so? I was beginning to like it. A beard is more practical for someone like me.'

'Probably,' I conceded. 'It wasn't meant as a criticism.'

Side by side we strolled back to Eve's Nook, a companionable silence between us. While he showered I prepared the meat and rolls. Afterwards I relaxed in my cushioned cane chair and observed him while he grilled the meat. His clean, blond hair was almost aglow in the fading light, his long, lean legs a healthy brown. Whenever he looked at me I was struck by the unusual colour of his eyes. They were almost luminous in this half-light. I wondered if he had a girlfriend back home and decided he probably had more than one.

Lulu strolled onto the veranda, attracted by the aroma of roasting meat. Peter picked her up and stroked her, murmuring silly words of endearment, and to my surprise she leaned against him, totally at ease. Typical feline – their loyalty was always questionable.

The night was suddenly chilled when a slight breeze started blowing in from the sea. As darkness settled a full moon illuminated the landscape, throwing an eerie, pale light over the ocean. In the distance the din of factory machinery mingled with the roar of the sea, reminding me that this wasn't paradise, even if it was the closest I'd ever get to it.

We washed down the hamburgers with Millers. Talking to him was quite easy and I found myself telling him about Theresa and her new life on the kibbutz.

'Where's her father?' he wanted to know.

'I don't know,' I replied honestly. 'And yours?'

'Back in Los Angeles . . . with a new wife half his age. It's his fourth in so many years. The older he gets the younger they get. There's no fool like an old fool. Whoever said that knew what he was talking about.'

'Do you hate him?' I asked bluntly.

He considered the question briefly, then shook his head. 'Hate is too strong a word. Hate is exhaustive and destructive and time-consuming. I'd like to believe I'm indifferent to him, but sometimes I remember how he treated my mother and . . . and I imagine I hate him. It's funny, but when I was little I used to think he was strong and invincible and well-informed. Almost God-like, you know. Now . . . I know he's weak and vain and self-indulgent. Sometimes I even feel sorry for him.'

'Does he support you?'

That closed look crossed his face. 'I have money of my own.'

We finished the meal but remained sitting in comfortable silence. Various sounds blended in the night – the sea, cricket-song, the wind, stronger now, stirring the bushes next to my property. For the first time since Theresa had left I felt totally at ease with another person. If I had borne a son instead of a daughter I would've wanted him to be like Peter. I was still not ready to admit to myself that Peter was more than a body to me. All I admitted was that most people offended me in some way or another, but not he. I wondered again why he had found it necessary to lie about the bicycle tyre, but there was only one way to find out.

'Peter, about the bicycle tyre . . . I saw the bike this morning and both tyres seemed okay.'

There was no embarrassment on his part when he met my gaze. 'They are okay. I thought you needed an excuse for me to be here, so I invented one.'

'Why are you here?'

'I told you . . . you're the nicest person I've come across in five months. I wanted to see you again.'

'And you have. When are you leaving?' I asked shortly.

'Soon. I want to reach New York before it gets too hot.'

'Why New York?'

'Why not? It's a goal, so to speak.'

'And you think you're going to reach it on that bicycle?' I asked incredulously.

'I don't know but I'm sure going to give it a try,' he grinned.

By the time we had carried everything back inside the wind was scooping sand onto the veranda and the chill had deepened. A bank of dark clouds was moving in from the sea, darkening the night. I washed the dishes while he dried. Neither of us said anything, there was no need to. I thought of sending him back into the night soon, imagined how he would huddle against the rocks, unable to protect his body from the cold wind and flying sand. Yet, if I offered him the shelter of Eve's Nook, would he move on within a day or two, or would he take advantage and stay? It was a difficult decision to make. I had moved to Oliver Bay to be alone, to work in solitude, to savour my independent lifestyle. I didn't want complications at this stage, or any other stage, for that matter.

'Thank you for letting me share your meal, Carla. I guess I'd better go, you must be tired,' he said, turning to leave.

'Peter . . .' I started, then stopped. He looked at me expectantly. 'Thank you . . . for a very pleasant day,' I said, avoiding his eyes.

'I'm glad you enjoyed it. I did too,' he said, moving towards the door. There was still time to change my mind, to offer him the shelter of my home. But what if he moved in and didn't leave soon? Would I have the heart to tell him to go? Would I want him to go again?

'Good-night, Carla.' He had reached the door and I let him go.

'Good-night, Peter,' I replied without looking up.

It started raining soon after I went to bed, and the wind howled wetly round the cottage. I lay stiffly in bed, haunted by the vision of a young man huddling against the rocks, exposed to every drop of rain, every cold gust of wind. Cursing myself, I got up, put a raincoat over my nightgown and went outside. Barefoot I ran across the stretch of beach, my head down against the driving rain. The night was pitch-dark, and I almost ran straight into the rocks before realizing I was there.

'Peter!' I called above the howl of the wind.

'Carla? Is that you?'

I couldn't see him in the dark. 'Yes! Come on up to the cottage! I have a spare room!' He didn't reply and I thought he hadn't heard me. 'Peter?'

'You don't have to do this, Carla! I've been caught in the rain before! Go back!'

'No! I want you to come with me!'

45

The next moment he was beside me, reaching for my hand in the dark. Our cold, wet fingers closed round each other's, and together we ran back to the cottage. I closed the front door behind us and turned to him. His wet hair was plastered to his forehead, water ran down his face and dripped onto his soaked T-shirt. His face was blue with cold, his teeth clattered. I resisted a strong urge to fold him into my arms.

'God . . . I'm so sorry,' I muttered, genuinely remorseful.

'For what?' he asked, surprised.

'For not inviting you earlier tonight. Have a hot shower immediately. It'll warm you up. Theresa's room is the last door on the left.'

Without waiting for a response I returned to my bedroom, removing my raincoat. For a while I lay there in the dark, listening to the unfamiliar sounds of another human body at Eve's Nook. It was both disturbing and comforting. Once he became still and I knew he was safely in bed, I dozed off.

5

My inner clock woke me a few minutes before seven. I stirred lazily in bed and disturbed Lulu sleeping at the foot of my bed.

'Morning, old girl,' I greeted. She miaowed and curled up again. 'Gosh, you must be the laziest cat this side of the equator. What happened to all your natural instincts?'

Suddenly I remembered last night and started listening for unusual sounds in the cottage. When they came it was from the kitchen. My guest was hungry, no doubt. I lay there, propped up against the pillow, and remembered another blond young man I had picked up years ago on a crowded Manhattan pavement. Theresa had been away at summer camp, and I had felt lonely and depressed enough to go to a café frequented by artists and writers. All I had wanted was a quick snack and a bit of Bohemian chatter.

He had followed me afterwards, a young, healthy-looking boy with freckles across his nose and a warm, friendly smile. Like

Peter he was young and virile, an attraction in itself, but it hadn't been desire that had motivated me to invite him in for a drink. I had simply been in need of that warm smile and the companionship. Once inside, the blond Adonis had stripped himself in my sitting-room and snorted coke sitting cross-legged on the settee, his flaccid penis dangling between his thighs. He had merely scoffed at my indignation and laughed when I asked him to leave immediately.

'Pep up, sister. You picked me up for a reason, so why the act?'

The bright city lights hadn't revealed the cold, calculating expression in his green eyes, the madness lurking just beneath the surface of his friendly veneer. I was just another brainless broad in need of a 'service', so why pretend otherwise, his eyes said. When I tried to reach the telephone he had ripped the cord from it and broke a Grecian vase I had discovered at one of those messy jumble sales that sometimes produced priceless treasures. He had threatened to shred my face with one of the shards unless I submitted to his demands, and of course I had done so, the horrors of venereal disease far less potent than the fear of getting my face slashed. The only consolation was that Adonis had preferred a docile subject, and I hadn't been required to take an active part in our emotionless coupling, which lasted until the watery rays of the sun broke through the gloom of the brownstone. Too ashamed to report the encounter and confess my naïvety to an uncaring world I had soaked myself for hours in a very hot bath, grateful only that he hadn't hurt me physically.

I wondered why this episode was plaguing me now, especially since there was no connection between that young man and Peter. I was stronger now, didn't need companionship any more, and there was no madness lurking in his green eyes. And this was Oliver Bay, not New York.

I reached out and switched on the Sony clock radio. I had neither a telephone nor a television and this portable radio was my only link with the world outside Oliver Bay. For a few minutes I listened to a news broadcast. President Reagan and Colonel Gaddafi were snarling at each other across two continents, a hurricane had lashed the city of Miami last night, causing extensive damage, a farmer on the Mexican border had shot and killed two trespassers on his land.

I got out of bed and tiptoed to the bathroom, careful not to

47

attract Peter's attention. I went through the paces of my morning toilet, all the time aware of the sounds coming from the kitchen. Perhaps he would leave today, restoring my private peace and tranquillity. I believed I had grown too selfish to share them with anyone. Back in my room I dressed in shorts and a cool top, then brushed my shoulder-length hair with quick, hard strokes before twisting it into a French braid. My dark hair was streaked with a few strands of grey, but I had resolved years ago not to dye it. I wanted to grow old with dignity. For a few moments I stared at my reflection in the mirror. It was an ordinary face, the nose perhaps too long, the cheekbones too high, the mouth too wide. The only good feature was my eyes. They were hazel, very large, the gaze direct. I could emphasize them by using mascara, but when I left New York I had also left my cosmetics and nail varnish behind. I hadn't wanted to be reminded of all those years I had sat patiently in front of the mirror every morning, painting on a face for a world where being pretty still had more merit than a good brain. There was nothing artificial about my life here and I wanted it to remain that way.

When I entered the kitchen he was standing in front of the stove, looking young and healthy. The table was attractively laid, the kitchen smelled of bacon and mushrooms.

'Hi,' he said over his shoulder, smiling.

'Hi.'

'You're just in time for breakfast. Sit down and I'll dish up.'

'Oh, Peter . . . this isn't necessary,' I objected lamely, secretly pleased. 'Besides, I should've done my exercises first.'

'Yes, I know. I watched you from the rocks earlier this week, going through your paces. You have a good body, Carla. One morning won't make a difference.'

A good body? I didn't think he had noticed, and the casual compliment left me feeling somewhat shy.

His healthy appetite was indeed amazing. He seemed to enjoy eating as thoroughly as he enjoyed everything else I had seen him do. I also noticed that he had shaved and wore the clean clothes I had seen drying on the rocks yesterday. In spite of his lifestyle he always managed to look clean, which was a feat in itself. I had to admit a growing admiration for him.

'Did you sleep well?' I asked.

'Like a rock. I almost forgot how good a mattress feels. It beats

48

the sand any day.' We laughed. 'Theresa is a lovely girl. She has warm eyes, like yours,' he said casually. 'You must love her very much.'

'I do,' I replied, wondering why I couldn't ever get bacon this crisp.

'She's lucky to have you,' he said quietly. I looked up, noticed a trace of sadness in his eyes. 'It feels as though I know her. All those photographs . . .'

'They're all I have now. Setting your children free graciously is the ultimate sacrifice a parent has to make, and when they go they take a part of you with them. One day you'll understand what I mean. That is, if you care enough.'

'I'll care enough.'

'Somehow I feel men don't love their children as much as women. They release them too easily.'

'Not all women have the capacity to be good mothers,' he said, and I knew he was referring to the woman who had left him uncared for at the age of twelve.

'Do you ever get lonely?' he asked again after a while.

I shook my head. 'Not any more. Do you?'

'Sometimes. It's mostly when I wonder where I fit in. When I travel like this I see a lot of people . . . mostly family people. It always awakens this yearning to belong inside me.'

'Why don't you go home, Peter?'

'Home? I don't have a place I can call home. The last time I visited my father his new wife made a pass at me, and when I turned her down she got real nasty. And why don't you stop treating me like a disobedient child?'

'If I was it was unintentional. Don't be so sensitive about it.'

After breakfast he stacked the dirty dishes in the sink, ignoring my protestations that I'd wash them.

'I'll clean the kitchen, then get stuck into the gardening. There's a lot to do still.'

'Peter, stop acting as though you owe me something. I haven't done anything to deserve it.'

He paused and looked at me. 'Why? Because I made breakfast or because I want to work in the garden?'

'Both.'

'I want to, Carla. There's no other reason,' he said sincerely and I wanted to believe him.

I returned to my bedroom and started working on my novel. He brought me a cup of tea mid-morning, reminding me he was still around with no immediate plans for leaving. He left as unobtrusively as he had entered. At lunchtime I heard him in the kitchen and pushed my typewriter aside, meaning to join him there, but he entered with sandwiches and a pot of coffee. I thanked him and invited him to join me but he declined, saying he didn't want to disturb me. I admitted to myself then that I liked Peter Dreifuss-Jones.

Later that afternoon, when I emerged from the cottage, he was still busy in the garden. The transformation was astonishing, and he smiled proudly when he noticed my pleasant surprise.

'Doesn't this look more like home?' he asked. I looked at him. Yours or mine? I wanted to ask, but didn't.

'It certainly does. You did a marvellous job. And you know what else? You've fired my imagination. I think if we put more shrubs against the wall there, it'll give the cottage a more "lived-in" appearance. And the lawn . . . I could buy a lawn-mower, trim the edges.'

'Leave all that to me. You don't have to worry about a thing,' he said, leaning on the spade.

How could I? He would be gone in another day or two. Unless, unless . . . no, I didn't want to consider the possibility. There was no place in my life or my cottage for him. He had to leave soon.

'Think you're brave enough to join me for another swim?' he challenged.

'Why not?' I accepted the challenge.

Later, while walking across the sand, something disturbing happened. Peter reached for my hand. His long fingers closed round mine before I realized the significance of the casual gesture. It seemed so natural at first I didn't react. When I did I withdrew my hand hastily without looking at him. Confusion raged inside me. Was he crazy? I was seventeen years his senior, besides which I had no desire to enter into a brief affair with anyone, let alone a boy young enough to have been my son. I had absorbed all the pain and disappointment it was possible to absorb in any one lifetime. I had progressed beyond that, I was an untouchable. The mating games that men and women play no longer had any appeal for me. There were always winners and losers and somehow I always ended up being the loser.

50

This time I was prepared for the cold water, but even so I yelled when the waves splashed against me. When Peter laughed I tried to join in, but suddenly the natural ease between us was gone. A new awareness had crept in and I couldn't quite look directly at him. I decided to return to the cottage, but as I turned to go a freak wave broke directly behind me, knocking me off my feet. I plunged head first into the raging water and almost immediately Peter was there, reaching for me. His grip was surprisingly strong when he pulled me to my feet. I clung to him unsteadily, wiping water from my burning eyes, while the strong backwash tugged at our legs. His arms were round me, holding me close, and when I tried to pull away his grip tightened. I looked up at him. His face was very close to mine, his wet, nude chest rising and falling against mine. There was a hunger in his eyes that had nothing to do with food, and suddenly I realized that I had been mistaken about Peter, that he wasn't a boy any more. And the closeness of our wet bodies seemed suddenly obscene.

'Let . . . me . . . go,' I panted, pushing against his chest with both hands.

He released me abruptly. 'Are you okay?' he asked anxiously.

'Of course,' I snapped, and backed away from him. I reached the water's edge while he watched me, a strange expression on his face. I turned and ran back to Eve's Nook.

I closed the front door behind me and leaned against it, panting. He had to go! Tonight. Or tomorrow, at the latest. For his own sake and mine. For the desire he had stirred in me back there in the water left me aghast. I was no longer a physical person, I was a spiritual person. Desire just didn't form part of my scenario anymore. Hell, I never even masturbated. It was so . . . so self-indulgent. I was a woman of the world, in full control of myself, and surrendering to desire wasn't being in control.

I tried to see the situation in perspective. Peter was alone and homeless, I probably resembled the type of woman he had wanted his mother to be. And I, I was attracted by his lean, hard body that promised sensual pleasure. My response back there had no connection with all the empty years behind me, or the lack of physical contact in my life.

I put a chicken in the oven and prepared an assortment of vegetables. He didn't fit into my scheme of things any more than I fitted into his life. He would have to leave tomorrow morning,

51

and early too. It was Saturday tomorrow and the picnickers would come again. I didn't want anyone to see him here and start any malicious gossip about us.

He came in through the front door soon after dusk fell and went directly to the bathroom. I listened to his movements with rising apprehension. I feared confronting him again. I was sure that the hunger in my eyes had been equally transparent, and what could we say to each other, now that our needs had been laid bare? He had to go, but would he go willingly or would I have to be quite firm about it? After a while I heard him go to Theresa's room.

I left everything on low heat and decided to have a shower before supper. He had left the bathroom immaculately clean. I showered and changed, then brushed my hair and left it hanging loose on my shoulders. I inspected myself in the mirror, wondering why I was tormenting myself like this. Wasn't I ready yet to admit to myself that I felt attracted to him, that my earlier maternal feelings had made way for the hidden woman in me?

He was in the kitchen when I returned, inspecting the carefully laid table. He looked up when I entered and became still. Our eyes met and held. It was there in his eyes, the thing I was resisting myself.

'Will you cut the chicken?' I asked. My voice sounded unnaturally loud.

'Of course,' he said, and removed the chicken from the oven. It was brown and crispy, one of my better efforts.

Without speaking we sat down to eat, but the silence between us tonight was different. We were aware of each other. Dear Lord, how many times had I pitied older women prancing around on the arms of younger men! It had seemed so pitiful, so . . . hungry. Peter . . . Peter was alone and disillusioned with life. Please God, don't let me misconstrue his need for me, I prayed silently. He was drawn to me for all the wrong reasons. I had extended a flicker of warmth to him in a world gone cold, and he didn't know how to cope with his gratitude.

'Carla . . .'

'Peter . . .'

We spoke at the same time and fell silent at the same time.

'Yes, Peter?'

'Carla . . . for some time now I've been wanting to spend some time in Jerusalem. Will you go with me?'

I stared at him. 'Jerusalem? You mean the Jerusalem in Israel?'

'Yes. We could fly there within a day or two, hire a camper and tour the country.'

'But . . .'

'I'll pay for everything,' he added quickly.

'You have that much money?'

'I told you I have money of my own. We could see Theresa while we're there,' he continued. 'I'm sure you'd like that and so would she.'

'But . . why me? I'm sure you have a number of young friends who'd be delighted to go with you,' I said, the food on my plate forgotten.

'I prefer being with you,' he said simply, his voice soft. 'Can you understand that?'

'You don't know me, don't know anything about me,' I objected, my voice rising in pitch.

'I know enough,' he said, holding my gaze.

I thought of Theresa in Israel. What would she say if I arrived there with this young man? Would she laugh openly or behind my back? Or pity me? Or would she think I had deliberately followed her there, unable to release her?

'It's totally out of the question,' I said abruptly. 'I have work to do.'

'The novel can wait, Carla. It's . . .'

'Novel? How did you know about the novel?'

'The old man at the store told me. He likes to talk . . .'

'You mean you discussed me with Uncle Billy?'

'No. He discussed you with me. He said I was the second stranger in town during the past few weeks, and when I asked him who the first was he told me about you,' he explained.

'When was that?'

'On Monday.'

'Was that why you came back here? Because you thought there was something appealing about a woman living alone in an isolated cottage by the sea, writing for a living?'

The hurt look crept back into his eyes. 'No. I . . . I needed to see you again.'

'Why?' I cried. 'Are you looking for someone to replace your dead mother?'

He paled visibly; his green eyes hardened. I regretted the words almost as soon as I'd spoken them. They hung heavily between us while we stared at each other across the table.

'Nobody can take her place,' he said coldly, put down his knife and fork and pushed back his chair. 'God, you're so bogged down with complexes it would've been funny if it wasn't quite so pathetic. Your whole attitude says – don't touch me, I'm tough, I can make it on my own. Well, let me tell you something – you can't. You need me as much as I need you, Carla. It's in your eyes when you forget your guard. We're two of a kind. We're outcasts, living on the fringe of society, looking in. We don't know how to forgive and forget.'

'How dare you . . . ?'

'Shut up and listen! I don't know who the hell hurt you so much, but you have no right to punish me for it. You no longer have your daughter to use as a shield against the world. You're exposed, Carla. And if you don't take care you're going to start bleeding soon.'

He stormed past me out of the kitchen. I remained sitting, speechless. With a few words this . . . this young boy had lifted the lid off my smug existence and laid bare all the hidden hurt and mistrust, all the old pain that made up my core. How could he have known, someone so young and inexperienced?

I heard him in Theresa's room, then a door slammed and he came back along the corridor behind me. I tensed. But instead of returning to the kitchen, he left by the front door. Stunned, I got up and went to the bedroom he had occupied. His belongings were gone. Good, I should be grateful, I told myself. He was gone, never to return. He had briefly disturbed the tranquillity of my existence, stirred feelings of desire in my dormant body, but now he was gone. Never to return. *Never to return.* Then why wasn't I feeling happy? Why was I feeling so hellishly empty?

I returned to the kitchen and stared at the untouched food. Where had he gone? Lulu sat beside her empty food bowl and miaowed, bringing me back to reality. I put a large portion of chicken in her bowl and cut it into smaller pieces. She purred while she waited. Dear God, why couldn't humans be this easy to please? Give them a bowl of chicken and they're happy. Pat their

54

heads occasionally, give them fresh water every day. I leaned against the cupboard and laughed. The empty refrain echoed through Eve's Nook.

The silence in the cottage was different tonight. It had a lonely quality. The roof creaked frequently, occasionally a window frame rattled slightly in the breeze. As though sensing my confused state of mind, Lulu crept onto my chest and buried her head in my neck. I stroked her absently, staring into empty space, smoking one cigarette after another.

I had never wanted to belong to anyone in the way that lovers belonged to each other, bonded by their need for each other. When you belonged you became a slave to your emotions, entrapped in a pitiful need to please your partner, for your own happiness depended on his. My stormy and short-lived marriage to Arthur Benson had permanently cured me of that need. Yet the feelings Peter had stirred in me vividly evoked the past.

Arthur had been a boyishly handsome man, ten years older than me in age but twenty in experience. He had been well-dressed and well-spoken, a good prospect for any aspiring young wife. I wasn't sure now if I had loved him. At least, not with the starry-eyed, all-consuming love some people seemed to experience. I hadn't been much of a prize myself – still afflicted with teenage acne, unsure of myself, hung up about my recent childhood. And he . . . he had seemed so worldly and self-assured I considered myself lucky to become his wife.

Three days before the wedding I had learnt for the first time that he had been married before. It had seemed so immaterial then. His ex-wife had been a flighty girl who had run off with one of his best friends. Or that was what he told me. By the time I discovered that she too had been a victim of his Jekyll and Hyde personality it was already too late. I was pregnant and financially dependent on him. And soon learnt to be terrified of him too. His handsome face could twist into a mask of hatred for no apparent reason, directed at me. The obscenities and curses that burst from his lips still left me cringing after all these years, however undeserved they had been. His hands had hurt me and left permanent scars, but not nearly as much as his cruel accusations had hurt.

55

The world had seemed a very confusing and dangerous place to me then, or at least, the world occupied by men. I had escaped the trials of an abused childhood to walk smack bang into the clutches of an even more horrifying situation. But unlike my father, Arthur had obtained a licence to abuse me physically and mentally. After the divorce I had decided that an existence linked to the male species had to be avoided at all cost. A world without men was bound to be a safer world, the art was to learn to live without them, to smother the desire to love and be loved in return. A feat I had accomplished. Or so I had thought.

Shortly after midnight the bed became a prison. Suddenly the mattress was too hard, the bedding too heavy and hot, the pillow too soft. I got up, went to the kitchen and switched the kettle on. I made myself a cup of tea and drank it sitting at the kitchen table. We were two of a kind, he had said, living on the fringe of society. We didn't know how to forgive and forget. We needed each other.

There was a light tap on the front door. I froze. Had he come back? And if so, did I want him? Could I throw myself wide-open to his need and surrender to my own without getting bruised in the process? No. All I had to do was ignore his summons. He would go away and I would forget the sensual structure of his body and the brief desire it had stirred in me. But . . . would I ever forgive myself for turning my back on even a brief glimpse of happiness? Wasn't it better to have isolated spasms of exhilaration than to exist on an even keel that touched the borders of boredom sometimes?

I walked to the front door. My hand hesitated on the doorknob. There was still time to change my mind. I could turn my back now and walk away, and I would never see him again. Never. The finality of the word terrified me. I unlocked the door and opened it.

There was a naked plea in his luminous eyes. It said, Don't die on me and leave me alone. I need shelter for a while, it's pretty grim out there. 'I saw the light,' he said quietly. For a while we stared at each other, then I stood aside, allowing him in. I locked the door behind him, and without speaking I went to my bedroom. He followed me, bringing the salty odour of the sea with him. Just inside the room I turned to him, but he spoke first.

'Carla . . . all my life I've been searching for a place where I belong. Ever since my mother died I've merely been drifting through life. Until I met you. Now I know I belong here . . . with you. Don't send me away . . . please.'

He approached me, slowly but deliberately. I backed away, trying to still the crazy beat of my heart. This was madness. God-awful madness.

'Carla . . .'

'No.'

I reached the wall beside my bed. There was nowhere else to go. He reached me and laid his hands on my shoulders.

'Carla . . .'

'No,' I groaned.

He drew me closer and I didn't resist. His lips came down on mine, hot and searching. They weren't the lips of a boy but the lips of a man – hungry and passionate, demanding response. And dear God, I responded with all the pent-up fire inside me. We clung to each other, two desperate people drowning in a flood of emotions. His hands moved over my body and mine over his – searching and grasping. We were on the bed, undressing each other with an obsessive hunger, our mouths open against each other's, our tongues touching. Naked, our bodies met and melted into one. His lips and hands were hot, moving over my naked flesh, lingering in deliciously moist places where no man had been for a lifetime, and the ecstasy was almost unbearable. I couldn't wait and strained myself against him, my every fibre crying out for fulfilment. I spread my legs wide to receive him, and when he entered me I cried out like an animal in pain. Nothing had ever felt this good and this right before. Surely I had lived all my life for this moment, and maybe, just maybe it would never end.

Passion was a wave, sweeping us along on its crest. We were saying things to each other, things that made sense, like I love you, I love you, I love you. Then all too soon our passion exploded like a burning flame, and we clung to each other, one flesh, one breath, one beating heart.

Afterwards we lay spent, like rag dolls, our sweating bodies intertwined. No words were necessary. The merging of our bodies and souls was complete.

And nothing else mattered.

6

I woke on Saturday morning with an instant awareness of him. Outside there was the soft whoosh as waves broke on the shore, inside – Peter's regular breathing. I shifted to my side, propped my head on my palm and gazed down at his sleeping face. His sensitive mouth was slack in sleep, his skin deeply tanned, his blond eyelashes thick and long. He didn't have to open his eyes for me to know how clear and green they were. I ached to reach out and touch his cheek, to run a hand over his bare shoulder and through the soft, corn-coloured hair. A confusing blend of tenderness and desire coursed through me, with the desire more prominent, causing a tight feeling in my groin.

The musky scent of our sex still hung in the room. I relived our raw passion of last night when, for a few hours, we had possessed each other body and soul. Just for a few hours I had felt young and desirable again, not middle-aged and sexless. If he left today there would be no recriminations. He had given me more pleasure last night than I had known for too many years to remember and I would treasure the memory for years to come.

Unable to resist the temptation I reached out and touched the strands of blond hair on the pillow. It felt like silk. Suddenly he opened his eyes and looked directly into mine. They were even more striking than I remembered. Feeling somewhat embarrassed, I moved away across the bed, but he reached for me and pulled me closer.

'Where're you going?' he asked sleepily.

'Peter . . .'

'No, don't go,' he said, and buried his face in my neck. His hand ran the full length of my naked body, setting my skin on fire. The tightness in my groin became a pulsing ache that left me breathless and trembling against him. No, this couldn't be! Last night had merely been the uncontrolled madness people sometimes experienced in the thin hours of the night, not in broad daylight, like this. Surely he knew that.

His erection throbbed against the smooth skin of my thigh, while his hands moved gently over the swelling of my breasts. He teased my nipples until they hardened, then moved down until his lips closed over one, so hot I wanted to cry out from the pleasure it gave. I groaned when his hands moved down to my Venus mound and touched the outer lips of my vulva. 'Peter, Peter,' I mumbled, delirious with my need.

Our lovemaking was different this time, now that the urgency was gone. It was deliciously unhurried and protracted and gentle. It was the total absorption of two people in each other, the total giving and total taking of unselfish pleasure. For one so young he was an experienced lover, both considerate and demanding. Uninhibitedly we explored each other's bodies with our hands and our tongues, savouring each ecstatic moment. When he finally lowered himself onto me I took his rigid phallus into my hands and guided him into me. He slid in slowly and smoothly, his lips on my face, seeking mine.

We rose and fell in a slow rhythm, and when our passion reached a peak it was almost as though it happened in slow motion. The intensity of my orgasm left me shuddering uncontrollably. Finally we lay against each other, satiated and happy. He lit one of his Camels and I lit a Cameo. I lay against his chest while we smoked, heard his heart beating, smelled the male odour exuding from him. He stroked my hair gently.

'You're beautiful, Carla. More beautiful than anyone I've ever known,' he said lazily.

'Please don't say anything. It isn't necessary,' I objected softly. I had surpassed the need for banal utterances by passing lovers.

'Why not? I've never given myself as totally to anyone as I've given myself to you . . . last night and this morning. It feels as though I've come home after wandering in the desert for a long time. You know how to give and how to love, and I'll never disappoint you.'

Never? What was he saying? One night of love did not bind him to me emotionally or physically, yet he sounded so sincere I wanted to believe him. Being this close to him suddenly made me realize just how uneventful my life had been and how conveniently I had steered clear of pitfalls and temptations. The please-don't-bruise-my-fragile-soul complex. Now I was a big girl and not nearly as vulnerable as I had been when younger, and the allure of his closeness had such a strong pull I couldn't resist it.

Much later we showered together. My newly acquired devil-may-care attitude was exhilarating and I was intent only on savouring each moment to the full. While the lukewarm water cascaded over our bodies, we soaped each other, our lips touching, our tongues playing with each other's. And again passion was aroused, only this time our bodies wouldn't co-operate. After a while we started laughing, holding and rocking each other.

It was late morning before we breakfasted on the veranda. By then the Saturday picnickers had arrived and the peace was rudely disturbed by loud voices, screaming children and barking dogs. Today it didn't irk me though. Nothing could disturb my inner state of bliss. We packed our own picnic basket and drove along the coast to Wreckers Strand. I wanted to share its beauty with Peter, enjoy a quiet afternoon with him. We spread a blanket in the shade of an overhanging rock and lay side by side, our bodies touching in a natural way. Twice during the afternoon we splashed about in the shallow waves like children, the sound of our laughter carrying on the breeze. We strolled along the un-spoilt stretch of coast, my hand comfortably buried in his. I didn't want to question his motives for being with me any more than I wanted to question mine for being with him. I had just spent a lifetime shying away from love and kindness, and if the only way to experience it was with this young drifter, then so be it. I would value whatever time he gave, for however long or short. I would not weep when he left, for he had given me something more precious than money could buy. Tomorrow would take care of itself.

'Carla, how long have you lived alone?' he asked during our stroll.

'Not for long. Theresa left five months ago.'

'That isn't what I meant,' he said, but I already knew that.

'Oh . . . for a number of years. No, for most of my life.'

'But why? Why didn't you get married again?'

'Most marriages are traps, Peter, emotionally destructive traps. Some people flourish better on their own. I'm one of them,' I replied.

'Was it very bad? Your marriage?'

'Bad enough.'

'Do you still love him?'

I stopped and turned to him. 'What is this? Twenty questions? Can't you just leave the past where it belongs?'

He tried to kiss me but I turned my face away.

'Carla . . . I'm only trying to understand how someone as loving and sexually alive as you could've survived on your own. If it offends you I'm sorry I mentioned it,' he said, and drew me closer. I leaned with my cheek against his chest, and we stood like that for a long time before his hands crept up and cupped my face. I raised my lips to his and allowed myself to drown in the tenderness of the kiss.

We returned to Eve's Nook in the late afternoon. A group of picnickers was still on the beach, sitting around the glowing remains of a fire – men and women in bathing suits, their oiled bodies suntanned. Their loud voices carried into the cottage and there was no escape from them. Someone played a guitar while the group swayed with the rhythm and sang bawdy songs accompanied by raucous laughter.

Once, when I peered through the window I recognized Ax Reevers among them. His eyes often strayed to the cottage, but he couldn't see me behind the lace curtains and in the fading light. Something about him bothered me, something I hadn't been able to pinpoint at our first meeting. It was the brute sensuality about him, coupled with the mean streak on his fleshy face. Once he slapped a young girl viciously on her buttocks and roared with laughter at her scream of pain. I decided Ax's was a distinctly unpleasant personality, like a volcano simmering just beneath the surface.

The monthly dance was being held tonight and they left soon after sunset. I watched them go and noticed that Ax looked back at the cottage twice before disappearing from sight. I felt vaguely uneasy until Peter came up from behind, put his arms round me and kissed my neck. His hands closed round my breasts and immediately Ax Reevers was forgotten.

As each day dawned I expected him to leave but he didn't. To say I was happy sounds far too mild. It was a happiness so total it saturated my every living fibre and oozed from my every pore. It was a now happiness; a happiness that asked no questions, demanded no tomorrows, that lived only for the present. Peter was a lively, considerate, loving companion and I flourished in the glow of his spontaneous love. Whenever I looked at my reflection in the mirror there was a new radiance about me, a smouldering light in my hazel eyes. I was no longer plain.

Ours was a physical love, at first. The hunger inside me didn't subside, it continued to respond eagerly to his. It was his youth that appealed to me and my maturity that appealed to him, I tried to tell myself, but each day seemed to close the gap in our ages and bring us closer together. I lost all my inhibitions and sometimes demanded that he just lie there while I explored the delights of his young body. Yet when we weren't making love there was a close camaraderie between us, a friendship that grew by the day.

Peter had no difficulty in persuading me to buy a bicycle for myself, and I soon discovered the simple pleasure of cycling with the wind in my hair, a fresh sea breeze on my skin. Together we cycled up the coast on wind-free days, and into town to do our shopping and to explore. Together we visited the old slave quarters and invented stories for each feature. We cycled along Oliver Bay's narrow avenues and discussed the architecture. We bought dripping ice-creams at the ice-cream parlour and licked them leaning against the bicycles. We laughed a lot and generally acted like teenagers on a summer vacation.

We maintained our private periods too, during which I worked on my novel and Peter pottered about the cottage. He seemed to take delight in the domesticity of our existence. He cooked exotic meals or vacuumed the carpets or dusted the cottage, totally comfortable with the domestic chores. The garden completed the transformation and gave the cottage a new air of neatness. We removed shrubs from their natural environment and transplanted them to the garden, and soon it was our own little Garden of Eden. That done, he set about painting Eve's Nook a pale yellow, the gutters and window frames a dark brown. And as the weeks progressed towards summer the garden came alive with colour and Eve's Nook resembled something from a picture postcard. The sounds of his constant presence were reassuring and neither of us ever mentioned his leaving again. Suddenly it was difficult to imagine a time when he hadn't been there.

Gossip was inevitable, of course. We couldn't go anywhere without attracting attention, but we made it a point not to touch each other in public. Instead we caressed with our eyes and shared secret smiles that spoke much louder than words.

'That young boy . . . is he visiting you?' Uncle Billy asked one morning.

'Peter? Yes, he's my nephew,' I lied smoothly.

He slapped an open palm on the counter. 'Now that's exactly what I told 'em. Folks been saying things 'bout the two of you, not that I'll repeat any of it, mind. They say that young boy's a drifter, just passing through, and you picked him up. I told 'em it's stupid,' he snorted.

'Very stupid indeed, Uncle Billy,' I agreed.

I preferred to turn a blind eye and deaf ear to the people of Oliver Bay. They weren't aware of my emotionally starved past, didn't know the quality of happiness I now shared with Peter, irrespective of our age difference, and I didn't see any reason why they should.

There were lazy days in the sun under the umbrella, our hands buried in each other's, our lips touching from time to time, stirring the passion that was ever present between us. Our love-making became an intrinsic part of our relationship and our desire for each other seemed to increase. Something as innocent as the accidental brushing of our hands while passing a cup or glass would have us flinging ourselves at each other, our lips meeting hungrily, our bodies straining against each other's. There were endless nights of passion when time seemed to stand still for us, when he tried to get deeper and deeper inside me, and I took all of him until I cried out with the ecstasy of his giving.

During this period there was one incident that marred our otherwise perfect existence. One afternoon we extended our lazy stroll down the beach right up to the factory. It had closed two days earlier for the summer vacation, and now it towered from the sand like a giant brick monster, temporarily asleep. The trawlers were anchored in the harbour, swaying and creaking with the motion of the wind and sea. Sea-gulls were sitting on the deserted decks, pecking at invisible morsels and preening themselves. We climbed onto the pier and strolled right up to the massive doors of the factory, now tightly shut and barred.

'What a monstrosity,' Peter mused. 'But then . . . I suppose it's the heartbeat of this town.'

'Oh, yes. Without it a town like Oliver Bay would simply disappear off the map. The first Johnson knew what he was about when he built this factory. With the food source right on his doorstep, how could he go wrong?'

'Whatever made you decide on Oliver Bay?' he asked curiously.

I shrugged. 'Nothing in particular. The price of the cottage was right, for starters. Its isolation clinched the deal.'

'I'm not sure this is the right place for us, Carla,' he said pensively.

'Why ever not?'

'The people . . . there's something about them I don't like. It's resentment in their eyes when they look at us. And a hint of violence lurking just beneath the surface. I get the impression they hate us for being so happy.'

'Oh, you're imaginative,' I laughed, and laid a hand on his arm. I felt the tension in his body.

'I hope that is all it is . . . imagination,' he said and turned to go. I followed him, but bumped into him from behind when he suddenly stopped in his tracks. I opened my mouth to say something, then closed it. On a cement boulder directly above our heads were the figures of three men, watching us silently. One was sitting with his legs dangling from the boulder, the other two were standing behind him. There was something vaguely sinister in their stillness.

'Let's go,' I said, and brushed past Peter. At the same time one of the men jumped from the boulder and confronted me boldly. It was Ax, bare-chested and barefoot. His faded jeans clung to his heavy figure, the bulge of his stomach hung over his beltline.

'Hello, Carla,' he drawled, his snake-like eyes sweeping over my face and neck, making me feel naked and dirty. He was chewing gum again, his jaws working mechanically. A rusty length of chain dangled from his left hand and he tapped it playfully against his leg.

I felt intimidated by his stance and the sheer evil that exuded

64

from him, and felt compelled to respond. 'Hello, Ax,' I said, and tried to brush past him. He moved with cat-like speed and blocked my path. A provocative smile played round his fleshy lips.

'What's the hurry? You haven't introduced me to your nephew here,' he said, looking over at Peter. The emphasis on the word 'nephew' didn't escape my notice.

I turned to Peter, who looked from me to Ax, puzzled. 'Peter, this is Ax Reevers. He's Uncle Billy's grandson,' I introduced them, forcing myself to appear calm. There was no sense in letting Peter know how alarmed I was.

'Peter, is it?' Ax almost sneered, and extended a bulky hand with dirty fingernails. Peter hesitated only briefly before taking it. A fatal mistake. It was a few moments before I realized what was happening. Ax was deliberately squeezing Peter's hand, grinning broadly and chewing gum. Peter retaliated until the muscles in his upper arm trembled visibly, but he was no match for the older, more heavily built man, who had battled with the sea for most of his life. His face twisted in pain.

'Stop that immediately!' I snapped angrily.

Ax released Peter's hand abruptly and slapped him unnecessarily hard on the shoulder.

'Aw, he can take a joke, can't you, Peter? Yeah, he's a real sport,' he chuckled, much to the delight of his two friends. 'Now, I want you to meet my mates over there. That one sitting is Sam Shroder, behind him is Doughie Steyl. Greet the folks, guys.'

The two men giggled, raising their hands in greeting. Like Ax they too were heavily built, but taller. Sam's face was almost square, resting on a massive neck. Doughie's eyes were bulbous, his complexion ruddy. These were the 'bad boys' Uncle Billy had referred to. A cold shiver ran down my spine in spite of the heat. Before Ax turned back to me I noticed the large warts on his bare and hairy back. He was easily the most repulsive man I had ever met.

'We missed you at the dance, Carla. Everybody comes to the dance, it's custom, you know,' he drawled, tapping the chain rhythmically. His restless eyes made my flesh crawl.

Suddenly my fear turned to anger. 'I told you I don't dance. Now please stand aside.'

His eyes acquired a dangerous glint, the sneer left his fleshy lips. He raised the chain and brought it down against the cement boulder with a loud crack, startling me.

'It's a shame you're in such a hurry, Carla. A *rreeaall* shame. Me and the boys here wanted to show you where we work, thought you'd like to know about the pet-food section, seeing you got a pet eating the junk. There's a conveyor belt, you see, which makes a helluva whining racket when it moves. Me, Sam and Doughie work in shifts, keeping it going. We throw all the mangled fish on the belt, all the heads and tails and entrails. Sometimes shark and octopus too. It kicks up a helluva stink and there's plenty of blood everywhere, but it all goes into the big mincer and comes out the other side in cans of Johnson's Pet Food.'

'Tell her what else we do, Ax!' Doughie shouted from above.

'Oh yeah, we piss in there too. And once Sam had a cat he didn't like any more and we threw it in there. Wanna go on up to peek a closer look?'

Above us the other two men giggled again, and I realized this was some kind of a game for them. I'd had enough. 'Stand aside,' I hissed.

Peter came closer and put a protective arm round my waist. Together we walked away along the pier while the derisive laughter of the three men followed us. The encounter left me strangely weak, and Peter's earlier words echoed in my mind, a prophetic ring to them.

'Where did you meet Ax?' Peter asked, visibly shaken too.

'You don't meet men like Ax Reevers. You accidentally stumble across them and wish you never had. Just forget it.'

Later that night he raised the subject again. 'Let's go somewhere else, Carla. There's some land further south. I noticed "For sale" signs when I was cycling along there. We could buy a plot and build another cottage.'

'Oh, Peter . . . stop fretting. The people here are a simple people, they have different values but they don't mean any harm.'

'Those men . . .'

'They're the proverbial bad boys. Every town has them. People tolerate them as long as they don't hurt anyone,' I argued.

'And what makes you think they won't hurt anyone? They're more than just bad boys. They're downright evil,' he persisted.

I sighed exasperatedly and rose from the settee, but Peter grabbed my hand and pulled me back. I fell heavily against him and immediately sensed the tension in his body that gripped mine too. We sought refuge in each other's comforting touch, and soon the unpleasant episode was forgotten. We made love right there on the settee and again in the shower before finally falling asleep in each other's arms.

A second incident occurred which left a sour taste behind and added a new aspect to our relationship. One morning we took the car into town. I needed gas for the car and a few things from the drugstore, while Peter wanted more paint for the interior of the cottage. I dropped him at the hardware store, then proceeded to the filling station. We had arranged to meet at the post office at a certain time, but I arrived there fifteen minutes early and found him inside the only public telephone booth in town, in earnest conversation with someone. He didn't see me approach, not even when I went right up to the door, which was slightly ajar.

'. . . tell Dad not to worry,' he said, then listened. 'So? What's another month or two? I said I'd make it, didn't I?'

I hurried away from the booth, went into the post office and emptied my box. There was a letter from Theresa and two mail shots which I threw away. When I emerged he was leaning against the car, holding two cans of paint. He smiled when he saw me, but I sensed a guilty reserve in his manner.

'When did you get here?' he asked, making an admirable attempt to sound casual.

'A few minutes ago. I saw you in the phone booth so I emptied the box in the meantime.'

'Oh, that,' he said, licking his lips. 'I phoned the realtor about that land down south. He said he may be able to come up with something suitable soon.'

Without replying I got into the car. Why did he have to lie? If he had wanted to leave a message for his father why couldn't he just say so? The lie hurt me more than I wanted it to. It also reminded me that he had a life apart from the one he had been sharing with me, and that soon he would have to get on with it. One didn't go places by lying in the sun and making love to an older woman.

It was this realization that caused me to withdraw from him to a certain extent. I had to start preparing myself for the day he would leave. In spite of my initial resolve, he had grown on me and settled somewhere in my heart, and I would miss him deeply once he left. There was a bothersome pain in my chest whenever I looked at him now so I avoided looking at him. Sometimes at night, when he reached for me, I lay limply against him, unable to respond even though my body ached to. It was just my way of trying to cushion the hurt when it finally came.

Peter sensed my withdrawal and became increasingly anxious. Like a child he strove to please me in every way, and during the week following the telephone call and lie, I came to realize that his need for love and affection went much deeper than my own. It was a need that had little connection with sex, but sex was a vessel of expression and he used it often. One night, when I failed to respond to his foreplay, he forced my legs apart and tried to enter me. When I struggled against him he suddenly slumped and buried his face in my neck, his shoulders heaving with sobs.

'Carla . . . I . . . love you,' he sobbed. 'Love me too!'

The result was that we both wept and made desperate love, as though this was our last hour together. During the days he hovered near me, usually within sight and sound. I often caught him watching me, his expressive eyes anxious. He was painting the interior of the cottage, but often abandoned the work to sit with me, his eyes resting on me while I worked.

One morning I climbed up the ladder to the attic to look for something in a trunk. I heard Peter run from room to room, calling my name. When I answered he didn't seem to hear, and the tone of his voice grew more panic-stricken until it verged on hysteria. Alarmed, I climbed down the ladder, calling to him. When he rushed up to me there was blind panic on his face, tears clinging wetly to his eyelashes.

'Carla! Thank God!' he sobbed, embracing me with a frightening intensity. His body trembled against mine, while he stroked my hair and mumbled my name over and over. His reaction disturbed me deeply, and I wondered if the trauma of his mother's death had been responsible for his insecurities. I asked him about it one night.

'I worshipped her,' he said. 'I never imagined I'd have to live without her. She was a goddess to me – blonde and beautiful and fragile. I was so terribly proud of her. I remember how quiet the house was during those two days. She was such a lively person, always surrounded by people. The bedroom door remained shut and I told her callers she was sick. My father had forbidden me to enter their bedroom when the door was closed, but on that first afternoon I couldn't stand her absence any more. My father hadn't been home for almost a week, and I thought she wouldn't mind if I went in and kept her company. She hated being alone, you see. She was lying with her back to me when I entered. I couldn't understand why she was so tired, sleeping all the time. I . . . I got into bed with her and talked to her, but she didn't answer me. I remember she was naked and very cold, and . . . and there was a peculiar, sweetish smell in the room. I took another blanket from the linen cupboard and covered her, but her skin stayed cold. I slept with her that night and stayed with her the next day, hoping she'd wake up and say it was all a game. My father came home the next night and called the doctor, but she'd been dead for two days. An overdose of the sleeping pills she couldn't live without. The worst thing was – she didn't even leave a note. Most suicides leave notes, but not her. I just couldn't believe she didn't have a message for me, not when she'd loved me so much. I preferred to believe my father had killed her and made it look like suicide. Until her will was read. She asked us both to forgive her, and left all her money to me. Maybe she thought it would compensate for what she'd done. But how could it?'

My heart bled for him. I held him against my chest like a child, stroking his straight, blond hair and kissing his forehead. 'Did you continue to live with your father then?'

'For a while. Until he sent me away to boarding school. I interfered with his lifestyle. There were always young girls in the house when I came home for holidays. Some of them he married, others were just decorating the place between marriages. He was always away somewhere, on business or whatever. At first the girls tried to mother me, but when I got older they took me into their beds while my father was away. I didn't think he'd mind, but even if he did, it was a way to getting back at him for not loving my mother.'

'Now I know where you got your training,' I teased, trying to dispel the gloom.

He laughed and rubbed his nose against mine. 'Is it good or bad?'

'Excellent,' I assured him, glad to see him smile again. Yet I couldn't respond to his advances just then. To have done so would've been akin to committing incest. It was like holding a child in need of love and reassurance. He raised himself, pushing me back against the pillows. His face was above mine, a hurt expression in his eyes.

'Carla, is something wrong?' he asked, fear clouding his green eyes.

'Oh, no. Nothing. Can we just hold each other tonight? Just be close, like this?'

'You've changed,' he said again. 'Did I do something wrong?'

I thought of the telephone call, but dismissed it as insignificant. I shook my head, stroking his cheek. His lips touched mine briefly.

'I love you, Carla. I can't bear the thought of losing you. Ever,' he whispered, his breath sweet on my fact.

'You won't. I love you too,' I whispered, not sure if it was indeed love that bonded us. We held each other, two battered souls who had found solace in each other's touch. When the time came, perhaps God would lend me the strength to release him unconditionally. And to continue with my life.

7

With the summer vacation in progress, the locals spent a lot of time on the beach below Eve's Nook and the privacy we had treasured before became a rare commodity. We came to dread the nights when they partied on the beach till late. I often noticed Ax among them, and concluded that he was some kind of leader among his group. He always sang the loudest, talked the loudest and laughed the most uproariously. He wore skimpy, white bathing trunks which, when wet, became transparent and clung obscenely to his bulging sexual organs. He reminded me of other men I had seen loitering in the subways of Manhattan, the knowledge of all evil in their eyes. Like vultures they preyed on human misery, selling dope and sex and destruction, and while their victims succumbed to their weaknesses they lived on by the power of their evil.

One afternoon, while working on my book, I looked up and watched with dismay as Ax strolled towards the cottage, a swagger in his stride. He rapped loudly on the french window. Peter was in the garage, washing the car, and I went to the window with an anger born from fear and revulsion.

'Yes?' I asked coldly. Unruffled by my manner he leant against the doorframe, his hairy arms folded across his chest.

'Can you spare a glass of water?' he asked, his eyes sweeping the length of my body, undressing me.

'Wait here,' I said shortly and shut the door in his face. I doubted that he needed the water, suspected instead that he wanted to rile me. Yet how could I refuse such a basic request?

When I returned he took it and drained it in one gulp. I noticed his skin was tanned a dark brown by the hot, summer sun, and it accentuated his ape-like appearance. He held the glass towards me, but when I took it his fingers closed round mine and held fast. I recoiled as though struck by a snake.

'Your nephew still here?' he asked, trying to look past me into the cottage.

'Please excuse me, I have work to do. Leave the glass outside the door,' I said, and started closing the door. His bare foot shot out and kept it ajar, his small eyes glittering with a hard light.

'Why don't you like me, Carla?' he asked through the narrow gap between us.

'I neither like nor dislike you, Ax. I told you I have work to do.'

'Then prove you don't dislike me. Come down to the beach tonight. We're having a party. You can even bring your nephew along, how about that? I promise you'll have a real good time.'

'I'm having all the good times I need right here. Go now, Ax,' I replied.

'Oh, I'm sure you have. That nephew of yours is a mighty good-looking boy. Must be damn hard keeping him happy here,' he said sarcastically, and chuckled.

Behind me Peter was coming down the passage, calling my

name. Ax suddenly removed his foot and the door slammed shut. I locked it with trembling fingers and thudding heart. What could I do about the disturbing effect Ax Reevers had on me? Could I go to the local police station and say I wanted to make a complaint? Ax Reevers offends me, Sheriff. No, he hasn't done anything to warrant this complaint, he offends me just being himself. Won't you arrest him and ship him off to a penitentiary in another state? You will? Thanks, Sheriff. That's mighty good of you. Knew you'd understand.

Shortly after midnight that night we were awoken by loud, cracking sounds outside on the beach. The deep laughter and shrill cries of women rang out. Peter got out of bed and peered through the window.

'What is it?' I asked, sitting up in bed.

'People down on the beach, shooting fireworks,' he answered. 'With all that beach out there why do they keep coming here?'

I thought of Ax and the warts on his hairy back. 'I don't know,' I said, unable to control the cold shiver that ran down my spine.

He returned to bed and put his arms around me. I lay against his chest, listening to the noise outside which continued unabated for another hour. Once someone threw a fire cracker against our bedroom window. There was a sharp crack and the room was briefly lit up. Laughter followed quite close to Eve's Nook, and the cottage which had seemed such a private haven a short while before now seemed to be exposed to every unfavourable element. Suddenly I understood why it had been sold so frequently in the past. The beach was public property and I had no right to ask them to clear out, but their inconsideration infuriated me.

Once silence was restored to Eve's Nook, it was after 1 a.m. and we were both wide-awake and subdued. Peter fetched a bottle of cold wine from the refrigerator, we lit two candles and sipped the wine by candle-light, making a brave attempt at cheerful conversation. At 2 a.m. we decided we were peckish and went to the kitchen to raid the fridge, both naked. Peter playfully pinched my bare buttocks, but when I tried to do the same to him he caught my hands expertly, laughing at my ineffectual struggles.

'It's not fair,' I cried. Suddenly we both heard a dull thud just outside the kitchen window, like someone falling. We fell silent abruptly. The curtains were slightly apart, something neither of us had noticed before. We looked at each other.

'Bastards,' Peter hissed, then ran to the front door.

'No, Peter! Come back!' I cried, but he had already thrown the front door wide open. 'Get the hell away from here!' he yelled. I joined him and together we listened to the soft whoosh as someone ran away across the sand.

I took his hand, pulled him back inside and locked the door. 'Let's go back to bed,' I said sombrely.

'Someone was actually watching us. Christ, it's sick,' he fumed.

'I know, I know, but they're drunk. It's over now. Forget it.'

Yet I couldn't forget it. I lay awake for what remained of the night, while Peter snored softly beside me. I kept seeing Ax's fleshy face at the kitchen window, peeping at our naked bodies. I tried to convince myself I was mistaken, that it could've been a number of other people, but the vision wouldn't go away. It had been Ax all right.

Peter woke me shortly after 9 a.m. by nuzzling his face in my neck. I groaned in protest and tried to turn away from him.

'Carla, wake up! I've just had a brilliant idea. Want to hear about it?'

'Not really,' I replied sleepily.

'I'm going to tell you anyway. We both haven't been happy here these last few days. I thought we could just pack our bags, get into the car and drive along the coast until we reach a town that appeals to us.'

'And then?'

'And then we become tourists too and behave as outrageously as everyone else. No one will know us. We can swim and lie in the sun and dance all night and do just about everything we can't do here. How about that?'

I turned and looked at him. He was serious.

'I'm at a crucial stage in my novel,' I objected mildly.

'It'll keep. You need a break too. You work much too hard. Come on, say yes. We can be on the road within an hour.'

'Can't. What about Lulu?'

'Damn! I knew there'd be a snag. Can't we ask someone to feed her?'

'Who?'

'Hmm . . . let me think. How about Uncle Billy? Didn't he tell you he used to keep cats?'

'He's old, Peter. He wouldn't want to be bothered.'

'If I ask him and he says yes, will you agree?'

How could I refuse without being a stick in the mud? 'Yes.'

His arms circled me and drew me closer. 'I knew you'd agree. I want to love you in public as much as in private. It's going to be the best time of our lives.'

He kissed my neck, at the same time cupping my breasts, and I surrendered to the ever-present desire between us, last night forgotten.

Mackerel Bay was symbolic of hundreds of other seaside resorts along the east coast. It offered golden beaches and nightclubs and casinos and funfairs. The neon lights beckoned tourists in garish fashion to spend their hard-earned – as well as their not-so-hard-earned – dollars. The hotels and motels were cramped to the seams. Sleek, expensive cars thronged the wide streets, bikini-clad girls exhibited their bronzed bodies while potbellied men tried their best not to leer. There were professional gamblers and gypsies and prostitutes and pimps, all working the summer crowds, who had no qualms about extracting cash from their easy prey. After all, everyone was on their summer vacation.

In spite of all this I enjoyed the festive air in Mackerel Bay. We stayed at a third-rate motel called Jakes Seaside Motel, which reminded me somewhat of the Bates Motel from the *Psycho* movies, only the paint here was fresher. We hadn't booked and were fortunate to arrive soon after a cancellation. Or perhaps we hadn't been so fortunate. The level of noise never diminished throughout the night. There were radios and televisions blaring, rowdy parties outside in the garden, yelling couples and cursing drunks. A baby cried incessantly nearby, sounding like a she-cat on heat.

If I'd been worried about going public with my young lover, my mind was soon put at ease. No one in Mackerel Bay cared. There were old men, smoking expensive cigars and reeking of money, with young, voluptuous girls hanging onto their every word. There were older women, whose wrinkled necks were in sharp contrast to their faces stretched tight by too many face-lifts, wearing dime-sized diamonds, with muscled young men hovering near them and attending to their every need. There were young lovers and not-so-young lovers, all too busy having a good time to take any notice of us. .

Our anonymity was a blessing, and for the first time we didn't have to disguise our relationship in public. Now that we were together like this, Peter regained his confidence in our relationship and laughed more often. We gambled, lost and retreated, we frolicked in the waves and tanned and enjoyed lazy meals in the best restaurants, we visited the funfair and went on a roller-coaster ride which left us helpless with laughter, we bought each other small gifts at the various stalls, we danced at night-spots until the early hours of the morning. There were hot, lazy nights when we remained in the room, making love, our sweating bodies sticking together. Here in Mackerel Bay I was finally enjoying the youth I had lost with my early marriage and subsequent motherhood.

The third day after our arrival I noticed a man on the beach watching us. I guessed he was about thirty, even though he was balding and running to fat. He sat with his legs drawn up, his arms folded across his knees. A towel was draped over his freckled back and shoulders, a limp sunhat shaded his face. Occasionally he brushed the sand off his legs with disgust, or rubbed oil onto his burnt nose. He seemed misplaced in the holiday crowd and didn't look as though he was enjoying the sun at all. When I first noticed him staring, I thought he was mistaking me for a rich society broad holidaying with her gigolo. Determined not to be ruffled by a perfect stranger, I ignored him, yet that same night we were dancing at a club when I noticed him on the edge of the dance floor, watching us. When he caught my eye he moved back a bit, but time and again I saw his face elsewhere, searching for us.

The next afternoon, when we got back to the motel, exhausted but happy, the desk clerk handed Peter a folded note. While he read it, he deliberately held it away from me, then crumpled it up and dropped it into a clay pot beside the reception desk.

'What was that?' I asked.

'A message from an old acquaintance. He spotted me on the beach and asked if we could have a drink together,' he explained casually, putting an arm around my shoulders.

'A man's been watching us since yesterday, Peter. Early thirties, overweight, freckles on his arms and shoulders, sandy hair. Is that him?'

'Could be. I haven't seen him for at least four years. People change. Let's forget it and get ready for a night on the town.'

Later, while showering together, something else came to mind. 'But if he knows you, why didn't he approach you on the beach, or at that club last night? I get the impression he's following us.'

'He's always been a queer sort of guy. Will you forget it? Please?' he answered, and slid his soaped hands over my naked flesh. I shuddered when his hands slid through the cleft of my buttocks and between my thighs, the stranger discarded as unimportant.

Later that night, while dining at Sasha's, a popular seafront restaurant, I excused myself to visit the toilet, and when I returned a few minutes later, I noticed the same man talking to Peter at our table. There was an annoyed expression on Peter's handsome face, and he gestured with his hands to emphasize a point. Just before I reached the table the man abruptly walked away, leaving Peter to stare after him.

'Was that your friend?' I asked, sitting down.

'Who? Oh . . . you mean Allen? We've never really been friends. He worked for my father a few years back, lost his job when my father caught him drinking at work. He wanted to know if I could lend him a few bucks.'

'Why didn't you invite him to join us?'

His eyes met mine. 'Because firstly . . . I don't like him, and secondly, I want you all to myself. Have I told you lately how very happy I am with you?'

'No.'

I didn't see Allen again, and by the time we were preparing to leave, seven days after arriving, I had forgotten all about him.

Back at Eve's Nook the last four days of the summer vacation passed in relative quiet as people started preparing for the re-opening of the factory on Monday. Except for the occasional stroller wandering onto our stretch of beach, the days passed in lazy harmony. We cycled every day, spent lazy hours on the beach sunbathing or collecting oddly-shaped shells, listened to old records, mostly from the nostalgic sixties, and continued to take delight in each other's bodies and minds. Sometimes we sat on the rocks for hours and fed the sea-gulls, or watched the day fade away to a crimson dusk. There was a close accord between us now as we settled into the relationship. When I worked on my book Peter would sit cross-legged on the floor beside me, making ornaments from the shells we had collected. Our emotional accord had reached near-perfection, and we often found we were thinking exactly the same thoughts at exactly the same time. Sometimes at night we woke simultaneously, as though governed by the same internal clock, and responded to each other's hunger. Peter was a constant source of wonder, and sometimes I couldn't believe he was real and a part of my life now. It all seemed like a beautiful dream.

One night I was lying in the crook of his arm, running my hand through the blond hairs on his chest. A hot breeze was blowing into the room from outside, but we suffered no discomfort this close together. Idly I ran a hand over the flat, hard muscles of his stomach, marvelling yet again at the perfection of his young frame.

'Tell me about your childhood,' he said suddenly, stroking my hair.

'My childhood? What do you want to know?'

'Everything. Where you grew up, what your parents were like, things like that. You've told me all about your life in New York and with Theresa, but what comes before that?'

And for the first time ever I could relate to another person the childhood that lurked in my past like a dark presence, occasionally popping up its ugly head.

'I was born in Sacramento. My father was a truck-driver for a canned-food wholesaler. He was a very cruel man – tough, loud-mouthed, hard-drinking. He scared the hell out of me and my mother. She was a weak, timid woman, the classical martyr. He beat her regularly for the sheer hell of it. According to him women and dogs had to be beaten regularly, just to keep them in their place, you know. Her only reaction was to cry and plead. I hated him for what he did to her, but I hated her even more for allowing him to.

'He didn't come home often, I guess he had other women in other towns who were more interesting than the little mouse he had married. When I was about eight, my mother got a job in a sleazy uptown diner, and supported the two of us the best she could. When we were alone we had a good relationship . . . at first. Later I despised her too much to care one way or the other. Every time he came home she allowed him to take her money and didn't even defend herself when he accused her of whoring for it.'

'That sounds like a pretty raw deal . . . for you,' he said sympathetically.

'No, the raw deal was the sexual abuse he subjected me to. He used to come into my bedroom at night and . . . and make me do things. I was so terrified of him I didn't know how to resist. I once told my mother, begged her to take me away, somewhere far where he couldn't find us, but she slapped me and told me never to repeat such lies about my father, to honour him like the Bible says. When he came home that time she told him what I'd said, and he . . . he took me into the bedroom and told me to undress. I was crying and begging but he made me do it. Then he removed his belt. It was a black leather one with studs on, I still remember that some of the studs were rusted. He belted me while I screamed and screamed for my mother, but she never came to my rescue. And then . . . then he suddenly folded double, panting like a dog. His trousers had fallen to his knees and he was ejaculating on my bedspread.'

'Carla, Carla,' he murmured, holding me against his chest.

There was much more, but I couldn't continue just then. I trembled against him, experiencing again the fear and horror of the past. I was a child again, in need of protection, and Peter gave it unselfishly.

Long afterwards he said: 'Where are they now?'

'Last I heard they were still living in Sacramento. He had a stroke a few years back which left him paralysed down the left side of his body. She cares for him on welfare money. I've disassociated myself from them.'

'And your marriage was bad too?'

'Bad enough. I was nineteen when I married him. I'd just finished high school and was in the process of running away from home. I stole my mother's pay-packet and took the first train to New York. I met Arthur Benson on the train. He was repping for a pharmaceutical company, on his way home from a sales seminar. I was so damned naïve at the time I thought New York would welcome me with open arms, that jobs were just there for the picking, that I'd never be short of money. He destroyed my illusions on the train and by the time we pulled into New York station I'd agreed to live with him.'

'And to marry him?'

'Not then. He married me seven months later when I fell pregnant with Theresa. I divorced him three years later, to salvage my own sanity and my child's physical well-being.'

'Hasn't there been anyone since Arthur?' he asked, stroking my neck and shoulders. It had a therapeutic effect, and eased the tension that accompanied memory.

'No one special. The odd lover, the odd friend. Nothing lasted long. I withdrew emotionally from people after Arthur, and focused all my love and attention on Theresa. Giving her a stable home life and good education were the most important tasks I set for myself, and they were time-consuming enough. There wasn't much room for anything else.'

'But what about yourself? You're important too.'

'I am. Now. I have the life I've always wanted. Theresa is happy in Israel and now there's you. What more could I want?'

'You're the best thing that's ever happened to me, Carla. For the first time in my life I'm happy. Really happy.'

One night I snuggled up to him and said: 'If I ever had doubts about God, I believe in Him now. This is the closest thing to rapture I'd ever imagined – us.'

'I'm not so keen on the concept of God. Just when you think He's smiling on you, something really bad happens,' Peter said soberly.

'Do you believe in evolution then?' I wanted to know.

'No. I don't know which concept is more bizarre – the one that we originate from pre-historic fish or the one that we were created from dust. It's safer to believe a little of both.'

'That's too easy. It doesn't call for a commitment,' I objected.

'Why be committed to either? Will it make a difference to your way of life?'

'I guess not,' I conceded, then 'Peter . . . what can happen that is really bad?'

'Hush,' he said softly, and leaned over to kiss me. 'Don't even think about that.'

Just before we fell asleep, he spoke again. 'Carla?'

'Hmm?'

'I love you.'

'I love you too.'

We had just had our last day of happiness, but neither knew it yet.

8

The sharing of precious commodities such as love and happiness put me in the vulnerable bracket. Life had taught me that just when one feels most complacent, tragedy strikes in some form or another. I should've known that happiness is but a fragile bubble, ready to burst at the slightest touch, that every moment of every day we were just one teetering step away from it.

The last Saturday of the summer vacation dawned exceptionally hot. The weather bureau warned that temperatures were expected to soar to a hundred degrees or more. A misty haze was hanging over the coast and the humidity was unusually high. We swam early that day, enjoying the icy cold of the Atlantic before the picnickers and sunbathers arrived. Yet as soon as we emerged from the water the heat engulfed us and drained us of energy.

Soon after lunch I left for town alone, having persuaded Peter to give me a private interlude. I desperately needed to speak to Theresa on the telephone, since I'd been feeling increasingly guilty about my own happiness and not knowing about hers.

It was too hot to cycle so I took the car. At the post office I went into the public telephone booth and waited for the operator to connect me to the number in Israel. While I waited my eyes strayed over the town. A few cars were parked at the Oyster Inn, Oliver Bay's only hotel, but otherwise the streets were deserted. Uncle Billy had told me the annual summer ball was being held at the hotel tonight, and I imagined everyone would be there.

'You're connected to your number. Insert your coins now,' the operator said.

'Kibbutz Aliyni,' a male voice responded. I asked for Theresa Benson but had to repeat myself twice before the heavily accented voice understood. When she came onto the line a few minutes later I was ecstatic.

'Honey, it's me . . . Mom.'

'Mom? Is that really you?' she yelled excitedly.

'Yes, really.'

'Oh, this is great! How are you?'

'Grand. Just grand. And you?'

'Wonderful. Except that I miss you so much. Did you get my last letter?'

'Day before yesterday, yes.'

'What do you think of Gavin?'

'He sounds really nice. Are you very much in love?' I wanted to know.

'Oh, yes! We're going to Tel Aviv tomorrow. His parents are coming from Canada and he wants me to meet them,' she said breathlessly.

'Is it that serious?' I teased.

'I think so,' she giggled. 'When my year is up here he wants me to go to Canada with him for a month or two. But here I am . . . prattling away about myself. What about you? Are you very lonely?'

'Lonely? Heavens, no. I'm much too busy to be lonely,' I said lightly, thinking of Peter back at the cottage.

'Are you sure? Have you made friends there?'

'You know how I feel about friends. I simply don't have the time or the energy they demand.' I didn't want her to know about Peter. Yet.

'Oh, Mom, I really do worry about you. Are you ever going to crawl out of that shell of yours and discover there are in fact people you can trust?'

'There are lots of people I can trust, but not with my time and emotions. Stop worrying about me,' I assured her, then asked the question that had driven me here. 'Are you happy, darling? Really happy?'

'Oh yes! Very. And you? Do you like living in Oliver Bay?'

'Very much. I think it's the second best thing I've ever done, moving here. The first was having you.'

'Oh, Mom . . . I love you.'

'I love you too, honey.'

The line was deteriorating fast. 'When are you coming to Israel? I want you to meet Gavin. I just know you'll like him.'

'Soon. I need another three to four months to complete the book.'

Suddenly she was gone and I stood there with the receiver in my hand, listening to the crackling on the line. I replaced it and stared at it for a few moments. My little girl had finally grown up and no longer needed me for survival. She was at the other end of the earth, in love with a Canadian boy, perfectly capable of running her own life. I had spent many years preparing myself for the severing of the cord that bound us together, but even so her absence left a void that was only partly filled by Peter. I would go to Israel towards the end of the year and meet the young man who would finally take her away from me. If not him then someone like him.

When I left the telephone booth Uncle Billy was just locking up his store. His old figure was thin as a rake, but he walked with the precise gait of a much younger man. I waved to him and he waved back before disappearing round a corner. During our absence he had gone to Eve's Nook every day on his little Vespa scooter to feed Lulu, whom he referred to as a 'real lady'. The drinkers at the Oyster Inn were rowdy, and it was with a sense of apprehension that I recalled the burning of the Bester brothers last year. Would they party at Jutters Point again tonight?

When night settled the coast was enveloped in a thick blanket of fog. It was still very hot and the fog was like steam, swirling about the cottage. It was the first time since my arrival at Oliver Bay that dense fog had blanketed the coastline. Uncle Billy had often told me about the fog and the havoc it created when the fishing fleet was out at sea, but this was the first time I had first-hand experience of it. Sleep was impossible in the stifling heat. It drove us out of Eve's Nook and to the clump of rocks in search of some cool air.

It was an eerie sensation, sitting on the rocks late at night, surrounded by the misty white that constantly changed shape like thin, restless fingers. The night was hardly cooler outside, but occasionally a large wave broke against the rocks and released a spray of damp sea air over us, bringing a small measure of relief. We sat side by side, listening to the roar of the ocean and the intermittent mournful blow of the fog-horn. We might have been the only people left on earth.

'I want to do something for you, Carla,' Peter said, absently stroking my bare arm. 'Something permanent.'

'Permanent? Like what?'

'I want to take you away from this stinking town . . . somewhere where the air is fresh and clean. While you were away this afternoon I went to see the realtor. He gave me a list of plots to see further down the coast. I want to build you a castle you can't imagine in your wildest dreams, something that'll stand for generations, a monument to our love. I want to surround you with beautiful, priceless things, spoil you, see that loving light in your eyes every day of my life.'

'You spoil me enough,' I objected smilingly. 'And I am surrounded by beautiful, priceless things. I have you and Eve's Nook and the sea. What more is there?'

'Leave it to me. Soon I'm going to build us a paradise where no one can penetrate,' he said, then leaned across and kissed my neck.

'A paradise costs money, Peter. I doubt we have enough between the two of us,' I said realistically.

'Carla, I think it's about time I told you I have more money than I can possibly spend in one lifetime. It's old money – the Dreifuss money. It originates from breakfast cereals and dried fruit. My father married my mother for it and she never knew a day's happiness. It ruined so many people's lives I think there's a curse on it. All the Dreifusses have died violent deaths. And she left it all to me.'

For a while I sat silently, trying to absorb this new facet to his life. It was difficult to imagine him a wealthy heir to an old fortune when he was so unspoilt and giving. The corrupting power of money hadn't taken its toll on him, not yet anyway.

'Where does the Jones come into it?'

'My father is Jones. Mother insisted that I carry the Dreifuss name too. She was the last of the Dreifuss clan, and she inherited it all. She played the final joke on my father when she left it all to me.'

I stared at his familiar profile in the dark. 'But, Peter, with that kind of money, why were you travelling on a bicycle?'

He laughed and kissed my cheek. 'If I hadn't I wouldn't have met you. Besides, bicycles are much healthier than planes or cars. Safer too.'

'But certainly not comfortable.'

'Agreed, but I wanted to travel incognito, be a penniless drifter for a while. The moment I became the legal heir, at twenty-one, people swamped me with faked friendships. For almost a year they tried to turn me into something I just couldn't be, and I wanted to get away from it all, wanted to establish an identity for myself without the money. Now I have.'

At about the same time we heard people partying further up the beach. It was fourteen minutes past midnight and the dance must've come to an end. Again there were the loud cracks of fireworks, girlish screams and raucous male laughter.

'Let's go back,' I said, suddenly uneasy.

'Not yet,' Peter said. 'No one will see us here.'

There were muffled voices coming closer now, and men laughing drunkenly. It increased my unease, especially since we couldn't see further than the rocks we were sitting on.

'Peter . . . please let's go back,' I urged. He sensed my concern and agreed reluctantly. Together we climbed down the rocks, holding hands tightly.

They were waiting for us – Ax and Sam and Doughie. They circled us as soon as we touched sand. All three wore jeans and nothing else, their semi-nude bodies glistening with sweat and the damp of the fog.

'Bah!' Ax yelled, spraying saliva into my face. He reeked of stale sweat and nicotine and alcohol. The other two giggled girlishly.

'If it ain't the two love-birds, sneaking off to their nest! Going

84

fucking, darlings?' Ax sneered. The other two whistled suggestively through their teeth and laughed.

'You're disgusting,' I said contemptuously.

Ax turned to his friends. 'Are we disgusting, guys, or are we simply disgusting?'

'We're disgusting!' they cried in unison, laughing. Ax raised a half-empty bottle of champagne and shoved it against my lips, bruising them.

'Have a swig, sweetheart! Go on! Have a swig! Fucking improves with champagne.'

I backed away, shocked and disgusted by their behaviour, and bumped into one of the others. Immediately two strong arms circled me from behind like clamps of steel. I struggled angrily to free myself, while Ax threw his head back and roared with laughter. Peter shot forward, his handsome face twisted in fury.

'Hey! Let her go!' he yelled, but Doughie grabbed him from behind and threw him to the ground with amazing ease. Immediately Ax's foot shot out and kicked him on the side of his face. The senseless brutality of the act appalled me, and I struggled more fiercely in the iron grip.

'Bastards! Let her go!' Peter yelled, getting to his feet shakily. Ax and Doughie circled him playfully, like opponents in a boxing ring, laughing drunkenly and uttering wet, sucking sounds.

'Come on, lover boy. Come on, kiss my arse. It ain't no different from a pussy,' Ax taunted drunkenly.

Peter released a low, animal cry and threw himself at Ax. The men reacted with amazing swiftness. Ax hit Peter a crushing blow in the ribs, from behind the heavier built Doughie kicked him in the small of his back. Peter fell heavily on his knees, his face twisted in pain. I gasped with shock, unable to comprehend this unfolding nightmare. While I watched, the two men continued to circle him excitedly. Doughie giggled drunkenly, his protruding eyes aglow with malicious glee.

'No! Leave him alone!' I cried, struggling desperately against Sam's superior strength. I kicked backward against his legs but it caused me more pain than it did him.

'Come on, get up, lover boy!' Ax taunted, but when Peter raised himself Doughie's foot shot out again and kicked at his face. Peter fell backwards, then rolled onto his stomach and curled into a foetal position, groaning with pain. Blood flowed from his nose and mouth and dripped onto the white sand.

'Oh God, no! No, no! Stop!' I screamed hysterically.

My mind reeled at the horror of the scene. This couldn't be happening. Surely to God they were going to back off any moment now and say it had all been a joke. We would shake hands and go our separate ways, none the worse for wear.

'Ain't you gonna get up, lover boy?' Ax sneered, prodding Peter with his foot. Peter shuddered and blood bubbled at his mouth and nose.

'Ax! Why are you doing this?' I cried. 'Why, in God's name, why?'

Ax strolled over to me, his fleshy lips drawn back in a drunken sneer. While Sam held me, he slowly unbuttoned my blouse. With both hands he ripped the front of my bra apart, and my breasts fell free from their restraint. Both his hairy, dirty hands closed round them, squeezing. The other two uttered short, girlish giggles, while a few feet away Peter spat blood and sand from his mouth.

'Why? Why?' Ax mimicked shrilly, his repulsive face an inch from mine, his sour breath on my face. 'I'll tell you why, bitch. 'Cause you think you're better than us. You parade your haughty manners in town and pull your nose up at our customs, while back here you're fucking this young shit like any two-bit whore. Well, me and my mates here wanna share in the fun. Fun's for sharing, ain't it?'

'Give it to her, man. She's begging for it,' Doughie said excitedly, his bulbous eyes focused on my naked breasts.

'You're committing a serious crime, all three of you. Don't you realize that? Let us go now, Ax. We'll forget this ever happened,' I appealed to him.

'Since when is fucking a crime, sister?' Ax asked, pinching my nipples viciously between his thumbs and forefingers. His tongue flicked out and licked at my face. I squirmed in disgust and twisted my face away, while the other two howled with laughter. Ax lowered his head and sucked wetly at my nipples.

'Bastard!' I sobbed, sickened, and kicked out at him. He raised the champagne bottle and slowly emptied its contents over my head. I coughed and spluttered while the cold liquid ran into my nose and mouth, and their laughter rang in my ears.

Peter was on his feet again, staggering towards the men. His face was a mask of blood and sand, his breathing laboured.

'No, Peter! Run! Get help!' I screamed, but he kept coming. His fist shot out with lightning speed and caught Ax on the side of his head. Ax fell sideways onto the sand and Peter threw himself at him with a grunt. For a few moments the two men rolled in the sand while Doughie waited for an opportunity to join in.

'No! In the name of God, stop this madness!' I begged, shaking my head from side to side in an effort to dispel this awful vision. It had to be a vision.

He fought bravely. Dear God, how bravely he fought! But he was no match for these tough, rugged men of the sea, who had age and experience on their side. Unable to witness their callous cruelty I closed my eyes and prayed for the first time since I was a child. While they hit and kicked him brutally, I heard bone crunching and the soggy connection of fist on broken flesh. He coughed and choked on his own blood, but they kept going for him. When God rejected my wordless pleas I screamed and cursed and pleaded, all to no avail. These men were mindless animals, governed by their evil souls, their hearts eaten away by rot.

Finally he lay still, bloodied and broken, and I sobbed hysterically in Sam's iron grip, unable to grasp the monstrous quality of this unexpected nightmare. But it had only just begun. For me.

Ax, his eyes glinting with sick excitement, ripped the remaining clothes from my body, while Sam held me. He smeared his bloody hands on my naked flesh in a macabre ritual, leaving streaks of Peter's blood on me. I was a sacrificial lamb, being prepared for the slaughter. I kicked wildly and ineffectually at them, succeeding only in amusing them more. Then, unceremoniously, they spread-eagled me on the sand, impervious to my screams of rage and fear. Ax struggled out of his faded jeans while the other two egged him on excitedly.

'She wants it *rreeaall* bad, man. She's so hot for it she's sizzling,' and 'Yeah, man, give it to her.'

Naked, he positioned himself between my parted legs. He towered above me like a man-sized ape, the black, curly hair reaching from just below his neck down to his crotch. His erection sprouted from the thick pubic hair like an obscene dagger.

'It's a man you need, whore, not a shit-eating little arsehole. I'll show you what *rreeaall* fucking is all about,' Ax said, licking his thick lips.

'Let her have it, man!' Sam yelled impatiently.

'No, please . . . please, don't!' I cried, hoping against all odds to reach them at this last minute.

Ax hit me a vicious blow with the back of his hand. Immediately I tasted blood in my mouth.

'Shut the fuck up, bitch!' he snarled, threw himself on me and penetrated me roughly, while the other two held my arms and legs.

Each thrust pierced me with the pain of outrage. I was merely a thing to them, stripped of identity, stupefied by my inability to defend myself. My body no longer belonged to me, but I was imprisoned in it and unable to escape. Suddenly I was a child again and my father was hurting me, hurting me very badly while my mother ignored my screams.

Rape is the ultimate outrage perpetrated on women, the worst form of humiliation a human being can suffer. Fear and hatred and rage merged inside me and twisted my gut like a knife. I tried to shut off my mind from this brutal act of violence, just as I had done all those years back, but I experienced each thrust to the full, smelled the repulsive reek of stale sweat and alcohol, felt each splash of cold spit that dripped from his open mouth onto my face. A few feet away lay Peter's form, bloodied and lifeless. When Ax finally shuddered and fell heavily onto my defenceless body, it knocked my breath away. I gasped for air. Please God, no more. Let this be the end.

'You see? You're no better than any of us, bitch,' Ax heaved, raised himself from me. 'You're just like any other two-bit whore, loving every minute of it.'

But it wasn't over yet. Doughie was next. He was even more vicious, his lust aroused to a frenzy by having watched Ax. His teeth sank into the tender flesh of my breasts, while the others laughed and egged him on. My screams of pain pierced the night and blended with their howls of laughter. No one came to my rescue. There were only the fog and the night to witness my agony and destruction as a human being. With him it was over soon. He ejaculated in spasms and with small, shrill cries which had the other two in fits of hysterical laughter.

Sam was the worst. He was the untamed monster of horror

movies, the one whose face was never revealed until the last minute. At first he couldn't get an erection, and when the others mocked him, he spent his frustration on me.

'Take it in your mouth, whore! Go on! Take it in your mouth!' he shouted, shoving his limp phallus in my face. I groaned through swollen lips and twisted my head away from it. Unexpectedly his fists rained down on my unprotected face, while he called me every vile name in the book. There was blood in my nose and my mouth and my eyes. Once he hit me viciously in the pit of my stomach, causing me to gasp in agony. I gagged; vomit rose in my throat and threatened to choke me.

While he tried to enter me, Ax took his belt and brought it down on Sam's bare buttocks. The reaction was instantaneous. I continued to scream until my voice was hoarse, praying that someone would hear me and rescue me from this insane horror. Then, as though I hadn't suffered enough, he turned me over onto my stomach, parted my buttocks and entered me from behind. The pain was excruciating. With each thrust Ax brought the belt down on him, and his animalistic cries were louder than my screams of agony.

Suddenly and exquisitely I ceased to feel any pain. I was trapped in the clutches of a nightmare so terrifying my mind rejected it. I knew it had to end. Nothing this vile could last forever, and as long as I believed that I could hold onto my sanity. When he finally ejaculated he pressed my face into the sand and twisted it. There was sand in my eyes and nose and mouth. And just when I thought I would surely die, it was over. He rolled away from me, while Ax pushed me onto my back again. I lay like a broken doll, my breath wheezing through my broken nose and swollen lips. Tears ran from my eyes and cleansed the sand from them. Warm blood ran from my face and congealed in my ears and hair. The salty taste of blood and the putrid taste of vomit burnt in my throat.

They sat down on the sand beside me and opened another bottle of champagne, congratulating themselves on the 'lesson' they had taught me. Their coarse voices came to me from afar, as I lay paralysed by the horror of this night.

'So what do we do with them now?' Sam asked, wiping champagne from his chin.

'Kill them,' Ax said callously.

'Yeah? How?'

Ax picked his jeans up, his hand disappeared into a pocket and reappeared with a flick knife. The razor-sharp blade sprang from its sheath.

'Hey! Knock that shit off,' Doughie said uneasily.

'Why? You chicken shit?' Ax snarled.

'No, man, but I ain't gonna be party to another killing.'

'So what do you say we do with them? Leave them here so they can tell the whole fucking world what we did to them? You wanna go to jail?'

'No, man, but . . .'

'Then shut the fuck up! You're in this with us.'

'You were quite happy to burn those Bester arseholes last year,' Sam said. 'Didn't hear you complain then.'

'Yeah, but burning don't show no murder . . . like with a knife.'

'So what you want? You want us to burn them too? Is that it?' Ax asked.

There was a short silence, then 'I don't see how we can do that without a fire.'

'Yeah, now you're beginning to see the light.'

'You think champagne burns?' Sam asked.

Another silence. 'Could do. Why not give it a try?'

The next moment cold champagne was being poured over my lifeless body, then they threw burning matches on me, but I didn't feel the pain.

'It ain't working,' Ax concluded ruefully.

A few feet away Peter groaned and stirred. He coughed weakly. It penetrated my stupid daze, brought me back to reality. 'Peter, Peter!' I cried, but no sound emerged from my stricken throat. I tried to move but my ravaged body wouldn't obey.

'Go on! Shut him up!' Ax yelled. Sam and Doughie moved away. 'No!' I cried wordlessly. A few dull thuds followed and Peter was silent again.

'Now take him away! You know what to do with him. Go on! Get!'

There was the sound of a body being dragged across the sand, then I was alone with Ax. And the knife. He leaned over me, holding it aloft, a vicious expression on his fleshy face. His eyes glinted with an uncontrolled madness while he stared down at me, smiling. He was going to kill me. All my life I had prided myself on my pragmatic approach to death. It was our ultimate destiny, hovering in everyone's future, to be confronted at some stage. I had always found it ironic that while everyone knows death to be an integral part of life, whenever someone dies it is inevitably referred to as a 'tragedy'. Loved ones wail and mourn the dead, as though they themselves were exempt from it. I had made Theresa promise many times that she would not grieve when I died, that she would merely see it for what it was – the final chapter of my life. But never, dear God, had I anticipated the death that awaited me now. While that sharp blade glistened wetly in the fog, I suddenly thought – I don't want to die! At least, not like this! Not naked and bleeding and spread-eagled on the sand, stripped of all my dignity and in pain. Suddenly death seemed like a dark, bottomless pit from which there was no return.

Ax brought the knife closer and laid its blade against my cheek. It was cold, so very, very cold. I shivered involuntarily.

'I like you, Carla,' he whispered, his stale breath on my face. 'I've always been a sucker for classy ladies. I've decided to let you live, but you know what'll happen if you tell, don't you? I'll be back for you, only next time it'll be worse. It'll be so bad you'll beg me to cut your throat like a wild dog's. Do you get my drift?'

'Yes,' I croaked through swollen lips. He smiled his cruel smile, closed the knife and walked away. The fog swallowed him. I listened to the footsteps fading away in the night. All that were left were me and the fog and the roar of the ocean. But then who was weeping so bitterly? Whose heart-rending sobs were tearing through the night, creating a sound so utterly forlorn and abandoned?

Then above the sobs there were other sounds. Those of people approaching, laughing their carefree laughter. There were sensations of light too, penetrating the fog. And then someone screamed. The light was in my eyes, hurting me. Someone covered me with something warm. There were hushed voices and cool hands on my burning flesh. I was being lifted and carried across the sand.

'Peter, Peter,' my aching heart cried.

9

I was adrift on a different sphere of existence, where pain was an abstract companion with a life of its own. It came in pulsing waves, some mild, some agonizing, but ever present. My injuries were multiple. I had a ruptured spleen, a broken left arm, my jawbone was broken in two places, four teeth simply crumbled at a touch and had to be surgically removed, my nose was broken, my anus was torn and had to be stitched, blood vessels had burst in both my eyes. Yet the body is an amazing vessel. In spite of the severity of my injuries, it immediately set about restoring itself, aided by modern medicine. But even though it seemed to overcome its own pain, pain lingered on in my mind and left ripples of shock behind which could perhaps be dispelled by time, and perhaps not.

Like most other things in Oliver Bay, the hospital was owned and financed by the Johnsons. It was well-equipped and adequately staffed. Nasty accidents often happened on fishing trawlers and the hospital was prepared for every eventuality. They wheeled me into an operating theatre, cut me open and patched me up and sewed me up again. They fed me intravenously and injected me with pain-relieving drugs, but while they set about repairing my body they couldn't touch my shattered mind. They couldn't cut it open and patch it up and sew it up again. The nightmare was for ever locked into its casing, to be relived over and over again. I repeatedly called for Peter through the fog of pain and terror, only it didn't sound like my voice at all and the word not like Peter at all. They sedated me and ignored the awful moans emerging from my throat.

One morning I woke to find a strange and beautiful woman standing beside my bed. She was wearing a pale yellow outfit that seemed to glow in the soft light of the morning sunshine streaming through the window above my head. Her face was very pale, her ash-blonde hair swept away from its bony structure, but what struck me most were her smouldering blue eyes, focused on me.

She remained so still I wondered if I were hallucinating, but then her lips moved and she said something I couldn't quite grasp.

'They'll pay for this.'

'Peter,' I mumbled, but the sound that burst from my throat was a horrible, disjointed grunt.

'Oh yes, they'll pay for this,' she repeated, her lips drawn into a thin line.

I turned my battered face away from her and closed my eyes, surrendering to the magnetic pull of oblivion. Much later, when I opened them again, she was gone and I was certain it had merely been an hallucination.

Dr Richard Mallen was a soft-spoken man with a receding hairline and a preoccupied manner, but behind the heavy spectacles his eyes were compassionate, his hands cool, bringing blessed relief to my hot and aching flesh. When all I wanted to do was die, he was there to pull me back from the clutches of the dark, gaping void that hovered all round me. I learnt to hate him for it, for I wanted no part of a world in which one human being could destroy another in the space of a few hours. I had been reduced to a grunting animal in pain, whose mind was locked in a recurring nightmare from which there was no escape.

I woke one morning with the strong smell of medical alcohol in my nose and saw Dr Mallen standing at the foot of my bed, writing something in a flat folder.

'Peter?' I asked, but since my jaw was still wired it emerged as a grunt.

'Don't try to speak, Ms Benson. There'll be plenty of time for that later. You must rest now,' he said, coming closer.

'Peter!' I cried, panic-stricken, my eyes stretched wide in plea.

'Yes, I know,' he said soothingly, laying a hand on my arm. 'You had a dreadful experience but you're safe now. Try to rest.'

Dear God in heaven, what about Peter? Where was Peter? Why couldn't this man understand me, tell me what I wanted to know? That Peter was alive and well and waiting for me at Eve's Nook?

'Peter, Peter, Peter,' I mumbled, trying to raise myself. Sensations of pain assaulted me from every direction, causing me to break out in a cold sweat.

He filled a syringe from an ampoule. 'This is a sedative. It'll help you to relax.'

'No, no, no!'

The needle plunged into my arm and paralysis rapidly spread throughout my body. Of course this was only an extension of the nightmare. I would wake later and Peter would be standing beside the bed, his clear, green eyes smiling reassuringly. He would take me away from here, build me a paradise further down the coast and nothing bad would ever happen again.

The nurses were efficient and humane. They were always there, adjusting my IV, taking my blood pressure, smoothing the bedding. They spoke in cheerful voices while they sponged my burning body and brushed my hair. When I tried to ask them about Peter they placated me with the assurance that everything was going to be just fine, and I desperately needed to believe them. If only Peter hadn't been dragged away across the sand – lifeless and bleeding, the fog the only witness to his fate.

One morning a man in a sheriff's uniform entered the room, pulled a chair up to the bed and sat down. He removed his wide brimmed hat and ran a hand through his thinning hair. His forehead was high, his nose bulbous, his mouth small and puckered. He reminded me of a clown I had seen in a circus many years ago, pulling faces and making me laugh. Yet this man wasn't a clown, this wasn't a circus, and he wasn't here to amuse me. I watched him wearily. By now I had learnt not to reveal my anxiety for fear of that sedating needle, and I kept very still while I stared at him.

'Good day, Miss Benson. I'm Sheriff Witmore,' he introduced himself. I nodded my head in acknowledgement. At last here was someone who would tell me about Peter, who would allay my worst fears. All I had to do was wait.

'Dr Mallen tells me you're not quite ready to talk, but I'd like to get working on the case. All I have at the moment is a name.'

A name? Then he knew who my attackers were?

'He's a young layabout, name of Peter. What I don't know is his last name, where he came from, where he was going to,' he continued.

I stared at him. What was he saying?

'Damn boy should be strung up by the balls for what he done to you. It ain't human. But don't you worry now, I have a full and accurate description of him. He may have left the state already, but I've circulated his description to all the surrounding states.

We're gonna pick him up in no time. With your help, of course. I want you to write his full names in this notebook here. And everything else you know about him. Think you can do that?'

I shook my head, slowly at first, then faster and faster. 'No. You've got it all wrong. It was Ax and his friends,' I cried, but the words were all garbled.

He raised a hand. 'It's quite all right. Don't you go get excited now. If you don't feel up to it I'll come back tomorrow.'

I reached out and grabbed the notebook from his hand. He handed me the pen.

It was Ax Reevers and Sam Shroder and Doughie Steyl, I wrote in big, bold letters. I handed it to him and watched while he read it.

'Well, I'll be damned. You sure about this?' he asked, frowning.

I nodded frantically, then reached for the notebook again. 'Where is Peter?' I wrote.

'You mean you don't know? I thought he . . . someone said he ran away from the spot where they found you.'

'No,' I groaned. I scribbled hastily: They dragged him away. I think they killed him.

He read the words, his eyes suddenly hard. 'Sons of bitches,' he muttered. 'If this is the truth, miss, they're sure as hell gonna answer for it. I'll be back tomorrow, but I'm gonna leave this notebook with you. I want you to write it all down, everything, just as you remember it. Okay?'

I nodded, grateful that at last here was someone who was going to help me. 'Find Peter!' I wrote.

'I'll try my best,' he assured me and got to his feet.

Wait, I scribbled again. My cat is at the cottage. Will you feed her?

'Someone's already taking care of that. Don't you worry 'bout a thing now,' he said and was gone.

Reliving every moment of the attack on paper was like revisiting the deepest recesses of hell, but I forced myself to do it. That night was for ever engraved on my mind, every little detail crystal-clear. I felt strangely weak and had to rest often, but I omitted nothing.

He returned the next day and sat on the same chair beside the bed. I watched him anxiously while he read the pages I had filled.

From time to time he paused to look at me, a frown on his face. I waited impatiently. I had to know about Peter.

Finally he closed the notebook and looked at me. 'This here story sounds real enough, Miss Benson. It must've taken some time concocting it. Only trouble is, the three boys you accuse were somewhere else at the time of your . . . er . . . assault. Fourteen witnesses swear they were partying with them at Jutters Point, almost a mile away.'

His words were like hammer-blows, thundering through the room, stunning me. Holy mother of Jesus, this couldn't be happening! Peter! All he had to do was find Peter! Peter would tell him everything, substantiate my story.

'And the young man you say was assaulted and dragged away has disappeared without a trace. We searched your cottage and couldn't even find a piece of clothing belonging to him. The way I see it . . . he assaulted you and bolted. Why are you protecting him?'

I turned my face to the wall, hot tears stinging my eyes. I shut them, hoping to shut out the unreality of this turn of events. It was really very simple – he didn't understand. Once my jaw had healed I would tell him, explain it in more detail. He would understand everything once I explained it properly.

'What hold does that boy have over you, Miss Benson?' he asked again. The question cut into my soul like a knife. He loves me, Sheriff, that's the hold. He is the only man who had ever treated me with kindness. He had even tried to protect me in the face of all odds, and they had killed him for it. My heart wept, but my body didn't open up its sluices of grief.

Ten days later they put me on a trolley and wheeled me back into the operating theatre. When they returned me to my bed an hour later my jaw was mobile again, the stitches removed from my healing scars. The pain that had been my constant companion for ten days started abating and I could communicate again.

'Peter . . . please tell them to find Peter,' I pleaded with Dr Mallen.

'Ms Benson . . . Carla . . . may I call you Carla?'

I nodded.

'Sheriff Witmore told me a bit about your case. If it's of any consolation I'm inclined to believe you were attacked by more than one man. I'd like to help you if I can.'

'Then please find Peter,' I pleaded.

He seated himself on the edge of the bed and laid a cool hand on mine. 'Do you feel ready to talk about it? Once I know exactly what happened I'll see that the wheels of justice start rolling.'

His manner was sympathetic, his eyes caring. I looked into them and believed that he meant it. And I talked. My voice was toneless and quivered only when I reached the part where Sam Shroder had sodomised me. There was nothing I could hide from him, not after he had tended my every injury for ten days. Unlike Sheriff Witmore he believed me. I could see it in his eyes, feel it in his touch. His expression was almost sad when he spoke.

'Carla, I want to tell you a story,' he said. 'Many years ago, when I was still at high school, something similar happened here. The girl was also from out of town, never quite accepted here. She was young and pretty and vivacious, her eyes filled with a thousand dreams. One night, after visiting the local cinema, she was abducted, driven to the cemetery just outside town and brutally raped and beaten. She accused two of the local fishermen, but they were never brought to trial. There were at least twenty people who swore they'd been drinking at the Oyster Inn that night and never left. She recovered but the dreams in her eyes died, were replaced by a vacant look that was much worse than the damage to her body.'

'How can they protect such monsters?' I asked bitterly.

'You have to understand a little about Oliver Bay. Many years ago, when the fishing fleet wasn't so modern, many men perished in the sea or in accidents on the trawlers. Their widows raised their children to live one day at a time and to share the tragedies of their townsfolk. It bonded them in a way that is still accepted today. They not only protect their own, they also punish their own and resent strangers. The men you accuse are rotten apples, everyone knows that, but the people will protect them because you're an outsider. They belong here and you don't.'

'I belong here too! I bought Eve's Nook. It's mine.'

'Eve's Nook?'

'My cottage. I had a right to live my life there the way I wanted to, but they destroyed it. And they . . . they killed Peter, that's why he can't be found. They cold-bloodedly killed a young man in the prime of his life. Oh Jesus, tell me he's alive,' I moaned, clinging to his sleeve.

97

'Don't distress yourself so,' he placated me, patting my hand as though I was a child. I cringed at the touch. He had lied! He was one of them! He was no more going to help me than the Sheriff with his mean and suspicious eyes. They both belonged to Oliver Bay and its sinister customs.

'Go away,' I said tonelessly.

'If they killed him, what do you think they did with the body?'

'I don't know. Just go away.'

'We'll discuss this again when you're feeling better. Try to rest now.'

I was left alone with the white walls and the silence and the memories. Once I tried to leave the hospital, determined to find Peter myself, but I collapsed in the corridor just outside the room. Dr Mallen threatened me with restraints should I attempt it again, and I had to wait for my body to heal itself.

Sheriff Witmore returned a number of times, and I slowly learnt to hate him and everything he stood for. He wore the badge of justice, yet there was no justice in his treatment of me and his indifference to Peter's fate. He accused me of lying and insisted that I was protecting Peter.

'There's a nation-wide manhunt on for your attacker, but we need more information,' he said. 'What was his last name? Where was he headed? What did he wear the last time you saw him?'

'I told you who attacked me,' I said, staring out the window.

'Miss Benson, the men you accuse were nowhere near your place that night. I have sworn statements from fourteen people. Why are you still persisting with that accusation?'

'They're all lying.'

'It's common knowledge that this Peter was staying at your cottage. You were seen together many times, the last on the afternoon of June 11, swimming together. Why are you protecting him?'

'They killed him.'

'From what I gather he's a nice-looking boy. No one blames you for picking him up. A woman your age . . . well, I suppose it was very flattering for you. But he's proved to be dangerous and he must be stopped before he attacks someone else. Don't you agree with that?'

'Leave me alone.'

'Don't you want me to continue with this investigation? Is that what you're trying to say?'

'Yes. Now leave me alone. I have nothing more to say.'

'It's up to you, of course, but I think you're making a mistake. How do you know he won't come back?' he persisted.

Dear God, if only he could come back. 'Because he's dead.'

I begged Dr Mallen to keep him away from me and he agreed reluctantly.

'He wants to help you but he can't unless you want him to. If he arrests those men my medical evidence will be of vital importance to the case, but I can't help you either if you don't want to be helped.'

I wanted to be helped, all right. Not by being made to stand up in a biased court in Oliver Bay and publicly humiliated, but by having the past few weeks of my life erased. But since nobody could do that for me I wasn't prepared to become a public spectacle for a sensation-starved town.

'I don't want to see him again. And I don't want your help,' I said dully.

I was starting to accept the fact that Peter had died in the fog, his body buried somewhere along the desolate coastline. They would stand up in court with their phony witnesses, make a farce of justice and laugh at my defeat. I would not give them that pleasure.

I was getting up every day now, sitting in the sun by the window, chain-smoking. The window looked out over a small, square piece of serene garden, with the sea in the background. It should've been a peaceful scene, instead the horror lurking in my mind blinded me to its beauty. Most of the swelling on my face had subsided, but the bruising had turned a sickly yellow. I still avoided looking at myself in the mirror since I resembled a reconstruction of a Frankenstein monster. My battered face reminded me of each blow that had rained down on it and the men who had violated my body and killed my lover. Breathing didn't hurt so much any more. I could sit again comfortably on an area where a short while ago there had only been pain, my jaw ached less and the teeth in my mouth had been replaced with dentures.

I was almost ready to go home – to an empty house filled with memories and nothing else.

10

Dr Richard Mallen discharged me four weeks after the horrendous ordeal that still occupied my every waking thought and my dreams too. When he offered to drive me home I had no choice but to accept, since Oliver Bay had no cabs and it was more than a mile to Eve's Nook. I sat stiffly and stared silently out the window while we drove through Oliver Bay, wondering why I hadn't noticed before just how old and ugly this town really was, how offensive the stench of fish, how morbidly the wind howled through its narrow, winding streets with their weather-beaten houses. People stopped to stare at the passing car, but when they recognized me they looked away hurriedly. This was to be the precedent for my future relationship with them. They all knew those men were guilty, but as long as they didn't have to look me in the eye it was acceptable. To them, but not to me.

We left the outskirts of town and soon drove along the familiar two-wheel track that led to Eve's Nook. A dull ache started in my chest and grew steadily worse until each heartbeat was hammering in my chest, leaving me dizzy and short of breath. He parked the car in front of the cottage and turned to me.

'Is there anything I can do for you?' he asked.

Sure, Doctor. You healed my body, now prescribe medication to restore my peace of mind and give me another chance at sanity. 'Yes. Please arrange a telephone for me. Today.'

'No problem. Anything else?'

Oh yes. While you're at it please give Peter another chance at the life that had hardly begun for him. 'No.'

Eve's Nook stood on its sand dune, an abandoned air about it, a place that held bitter-sweet memories of a young man and the love he had given so freely. I stood in front of the door with aching heart, listening to the sound of the car engine fading away. With trembling fingers I unlocked the front door and entered. A layer of dust and sand had settled over everything, the air was stale. As soon as I closed the front door behind me I heard a distinct sound coming from the kitchen. I froze in my tracks. Peter! Peter was here! Oh, thank God!

'Peter?' I called breathlessly, then rushed down the short corridor. There was no one in the kitchen but Lulu, who miaowed and rubbed herself against my legs. I stood just inside the room, breathing heavily as though I had just run a long distance. The table was still laid, the plates of our last supper still neatly stacked in the sink. We had intended washing them the next morning. I had been too hot that night and we wanted to get outside. To disaster and tragedy. Neither of us had suspected we wouldn't be coming back to Eve's Nook that night, and that one of us would never return.

For a while I stood rooted to one spot, while the blackest despair washed over me, then Lulu miaowed and drew me from its clutches. I picked her up and pressed my face into her long fur. There was a great dam of grief inside me, but the floodgates were securely locked. Lulu purred contentedly, unaware of the pain that stabbed my heart with every beat. I carried her from room to room, drawing a certain measure of warmth from the familiarity of her body.

There was no remnant of his presence in the cottage. Theresa's room was stripped of his things, the bed neatly made, the cupboard empty. A faint trace of his aftershave lotion still hung in the room, but that was all. I proceeded to the bathroom. His razor and shaving brush were gone, his toothbrush too. I caught my reflection in the mirror above the basin and stared at it in disbelief. The flesh on my face appeared to have shrunk, leaving hollows where my cheeks and eye-sockets used to be, my pallor was sickly, my lips bloodless. It was like staring at a familiar stranger from another and now-distant world. That ravaged face with the haunted eyes couldn't possibly belong to me – Carla Benson, the author who had worked so hard to carve a little niche for herself in life, and who had found love for the first time at the age of thirty-nine.

Lulu got restless so I put her down. Immediately she jumped onto the window sill and disappeared through the open window. She hadn't missed me. The only value I had was in the plate of food I handed her every day, but she could get that anywhere. So why did I have the misconception that she was as dedicated to me as I was to her? But then, why should it even matter? Why should anything at all matter?

I walked listlessly to my bedroom. The typewriter stood on the desk by the window, reminding me that once upon a time I had experienced enough emotion to be creative. That was before I had died inside. It was like inspecting a stranger's room. There were soft, fluffy rugs and teddy bears, padded cushions on the window seats and potplants which someone had watered regularly. The person who had lived here had been a happy person, the two people who had made love on this large bed had left a trace of themselves behind – the musky scent of two sweating bodies melted into one, of a passion that had consumed them both.

There was nothing of him in this room either. Except the memories, of course. And the woman . . . she had died with him on a stretch of sand beside the rocks on a hot, fog-filled night. I knew the killers had been here, had removed every shred of evidence of his stay.

I walked aimlessly from room to room, searching for something that no longer existed. The food in the refrigerator had gone stale. Mould, like green and spiky fingers, was growing on the cheese, the left-over chicken, the sponge cake we had baked together that last afternoon. I looked at it indifferently. Food was intended for the living, not for the dead, and since I had died with Peter I no longer needed it. I drank a glass of water, then leaned against the sink, suddenly weak and nauseated.

It's a lovely place you have here. One day I'd like to live like this . . . alone, by the sea.

His voice echoed through the silent cottage. He had wanted to live, now he was dead. What had they done with the body? Why, in God's name, had they deprived him of a decent burial? Even a dog deserved a decent burial.

He brought the telephone in the afternoon – a thickset man with a grey overcoat and a leering expression. His eyes were bold and seemed to be laughing at me and lingering on my breasts unashamedly. I brusquely told him to hurry up and get out, then locked myself in my bedroom until his van disappeared down the track. Next I telephoned the only locksmith in town and requested that the locks on my doors be changed and additional

102

security installed. I offered double rates for immediate service, and he worked until after dark to complete the task. When I handed him the cheque he deliberately brushed my fingers with his and I felt like screaming.

Once Lulu was inside I locked and bolted every door and closed all the windows. From a secret compartment in an old travel bag I removed my .32 snub-nose Colt revolver with its crude, home-made silencer. I had bought it from a pawnbroker in Greenwich Village two years ago simply because he had offered it at a bargain price, never intending to use it. Ax had warned me that night he would be back if I told, and since I had, I expected him to come. While I sat there on the edge of the bed, the cold steel of the gun lying heavily in my hand, I realized that I wanted him to come back, wanted to see the surprise on his face when I shot him in cold blood. I counted the bullets – fifteen in all. For an hour or more I cleaned and lubricated the gun carefully, then loaded it and hid it under the pillow next to me.

Sleep escaped me this night and the next and the next. I didn't have sedatives to help me through the long, painful hours of the nights, when demons taunted me from every corner of the cottage. Often I thought I heard Peter whistling in the adjacent room, or snoring lightly beside me on the bed, and each time I saw with startling clarity his bloody face twisted in helpless fury while he tried in vain to protect me. For most of the night I sat in front of the window, staring out over the moon-drenched landscape. Often I imagined I saw him sitting on the rocks, his blond hair shining in the pale light of the moon. I would fling the window wide-open and call to him across the stretch of sand, but the vision would clear and leave only black shadows in the night. And a great emptiness inside me.

The ghosts were present day and night. Peter's ghost was there, in every room, crying out for revenge. The perpetrators of the evil deeds were laughing ghosts, mocking me from every corner of every room. They were scot-free, protected by their own kind. No law in the world could touch them. They could kill and destroy a life again with the same callous disregard, and no one could touch them as long as their own kind protected them. My father's ghost was there too, offering me candy bars to forget the pain, like he used to when I was a child, only now the left side of his face was contorted by his disease.

Richard Mallen called on the fourth day after discharging me from hospital. I heard the car coming and looked through the window. My first impulse was to ignore him, to allow him to go away again and leave me to my fate, but I desperately needed something to help me sleep. The voices in my head were becoming more persistent and sometimes I wanted to scream and scream with fear and terror until they went away.

I was so weak I trembled when I walked to the front door and opened it. I knew I was a pathetic sight. My hair hung in oily strands, my sunken eyes were bloodshot from lack of sleep, my complexion was wax-like. There were deep lines along my mouth that hadn't been there before. And I was cold, so very, very cold.

'Carla!' he exclaimed, and I recognized the shock and pity in his dark eyes. 'What happened to you?'

His concern annoyed me, but I kept my voice level when I replied. 'I died. Can't you see that?'

He looked at me, puzzled. 'You know you don't mean that. You're upset because I didn't come sooner. There was a nasty accident at sea day before yesterday, and I battled for two days to save the lives of two men. I'm sorry.'

I nodded mutely. He followed me inside, noticed the state of the cottage and looked at me searchingly. The walk to the front door had exhausted me and I leaned against a wall, fighting the waves of dizziness that assailed me.

'I shouldn't have discharged you so soon. You're not well enough to be on your own. I want you to come back to the hospital with me. Now.'

'No. I'm not ill,' I said, my chest heaving from exertion.

'I don't want you to be alone like this. If you won't come back to the hospital I'll bring a private nurse to stay with you.'

'I don't need a nurse,' I said dully. 'I need sedatives to help me sleep.'

'Has it been that bad?' he asked softly.

I stared at him silently. How in God's name did he think it had been? Good? He read the answer in my eyes.

'Have you been eating? Have you done anything since I left you here?' he wanted to know.

The room behind him seemed to sway. Mildly at first, then sharply to the left. I clutched at the air with both hands before tumbling into the dark pit that opened all round me. And he was there to catch me.

Her name was Ella Murdock, but she insisted that I call her Dock. She came every day, immaculate in her white uniform, the epitome of efficiency. She asked no personal questions and treated me like an invalid. The cottage had a spring-clean at her capable hands, she cooked healthy meals which she bullied me into eating, she forced me to sit outside on the veranda, to go for short walks on the beach. I hated and mistrusted her. She belonged to this town, was party to the evil deeds perpetrated by three of its men. She was the candy offered by the town to alleviate my pain and shut me up.

Every morning she telephoned the factory superette and had the day's requirements delivered, insisting that everything be fresh. I watched her suspiciously and eavesdropped on her conversations. Whenever she laughed it cut into my soul like a knife. She had no right to laugh, not when my soul was bleeding in my decomposing body. Often the telephone rang and she talked in a low and hurried voice until I insisted the telephone be unplugged when it wasn't being used for the daily order.

Dr Mallen continued to call regularly. He examined my healing body and gave me a clean bill of health. One morning he sat beside me on my bed, and said: 'There's nothing more I can do for you, Carla. The healing is up to you now, but I think you already know that.'

'Then don't come again. And take Dock with you. I don't like her,' I said.

He smiled indulgently. 'The things we don't like are often the best for us. Don't you remember being forced to eat pumpkin as a child? Or cabbage? I remember specifically hating cabbage.'

I wasn't amused. His smile faded rapidly until he was serious again. 'I want her to stay for another week, at least. Don't worry about the cost. There won't be any.'

I uttered a short, bitter laugh. 'No cost? How very kind, Doctor. Is this the way the town wants to appease me for what they've done to me?'

'No. It's more simple than that. The Johnsons insisted on it.'

'The Johnsons? Why?' I asked suspiciously.

'Because Meryl Johnson was very upset about your . . . the assault. She wants the men brought to trial, but Sheriff Witmore can't do that without your co-operation. I wish you'd reconsider, Carla. You have a strong case.'

'No. He didn't believe me when I told him the truth and I don't want him to believe me now simply because the Johnsons tell him to. I don't need their pity or their money. Tell them that.'

The nights were different now. I took the one pill Dock gave me before leaving each night, and slept painlessly until morning. I would've preferred to stay in bed and sleep the days away too, if only Dock hadn't been so intimidating and demanded that I get up. I hardly spoke to her, but when I did it was in monosyllables or with biting sarcasm. One morning, after I had been particularly nasty towards her, she turned to me angrily.

'Are you going to blame the rest of the world for what happened to you? You're not a child any more, Carla. You know there are evil people and there are good people. God knows you have my sympathy for what they did to you but you have to pull yourself together.'

I glared at her. 'Are you perhaps implying that you're good? While you and everybody else out there are protecting them?'

She sighed. 'I'm a nurse, Carla, not a policeman or a psychiatrist. All I'm interested in is your welfare.'

'What happens when you leave here at night? Do you tell them all about me and laugh with them? Do you report my progress to the Johnsons so that they know they're getting their money's worth?'

'Stop this at once! You're intolerable, questioning my professionalism like this.'

'I don't want you here. You're free to go whenever you please.'

'I'm not ready to go yet. I'll only be ready when you are.'

Towards the end of July the last traces of bruising had disappeared and the physical evidence of my ordeal was finally gone. I desperately wanted to be rid of Dock, to have Eve's Nook to myself again. I started pretending a cheerfulness I didn't feel, and made a point of being up before she arrived in the mornings. I started doing my exercises on the veranda again, I listened to music while she was there and even pretended to work on my book.

One morning Dock announced that I was well enough to

accompany her to town. I had to restrain myself from striking her for suggesting something so grossly insensitive.

'You have to confront them sooner or later,' she said practically, watching me. 'In time people will forget, and so will you.'

'I don't want them to forget, neither will I,' I said firmly.

I started missing Theresa very badly. She was the only sane fragment from my past, the only evidence that once upon a time I'd had a different life – dull, but safe. Dock agreed to go to town alone to empty my mail box, and I hovered near the front door until she returned. There was a cheque from my agent and a separate letter to say that a television network had made a generous offer for the film rights to *The First and the Last*. I couldn't muster any joy at this news which would've elated me only a short while ago. The woman who had opened her heart and shed that sensitive novel no longer existed. I would use her money for my day-to-day needs, grateful to her for supplying a means of financial survival, but I no longer had any connection with her. She had died in the fog with Peter Dreifuss-Jones.

There were three letters from Theresa, mostly about Gavin and the things they did together. She described him as sensitive, honest and adventurous. His parents had simply adored her at first sight and the feeling was mutual. They were unpretentious people who had gone out of their way to make her feel part of their close family circle. Every letter wanted to know when I was planning a trip to Israel, for she missed me very much and also wanted me to meet Gavin. That night I wrote her a long letter, promising to plan a trip to Israel soon. I also told her how very happy I was in the charming town of Oliver Bay. My lies left a bitter taste in my mouth.

Dock left after nursing me for two weeks, convinced that I had been restored to a state of sanity and good health. It was with a great sense of relief that I closed the door behind her for the last time. Now Lulu and I were alone again. Except for the wind, of course. That cursed wind was a living thing, blowing all the time. It howled round the cottage, creaking and moaning, rattling doors and window frames. At night it shrieked and tugged aggressively at the roof. The sea, in unison with the wind, lashed angrily at the coral reefs, spraying white foam a few feet high into the air above. The salt spray clung to the outside of the windows like a misty film until I could hardly see through them.

Sheriff Witmore came one morning and asked if I would reconsider my decision. If I allowed him to pursue the matter he would assist me whole-heartedly to bring the men I had accused to trial.

'Why, Sheriff? Because Meryl Johnson told you to?'

He avoided my eyes. 'Partly, yes. But I want you to know I believe you too. Dr Mallen convinced me you were attacked by more than one man, and his testimony will be invaluable in court.'

'More invaluable than the sworn statements in your possession?' I asked pointedly. 'There will be no trial, Sheriff. Tell Meryl Johnson that. Go now, and don't come back.'

Every day I sat down in front of the typewriter and stared at the blank sheet until my eyes burnt. No words came, no images, no feelings. The hours ticked away on my wall clock, but I had no perception of time. Days and nights merged until I couldn't tell them apart. Weekends were silent too. I no longer saw or heard the picnickers and sunbathers. It was as though they were avoiding the stretch of beach along Eve's Nook. I was their conscience, their guilt, their embarrassment.

Talking to Uncle Billy and the butcher was extremely painful at first. I kept my voice neutral while I rattled off my weekly order. The butcher was by nature an abrupt man, but Uncle Billy was more difficult to handle.

'I'll have the usual order. Delivery to my front door this . . .'

'You know something? I believe you, Carla.'

'Pardon?'

'Them boys are downright mean, I told you so. But not my Ax. He's a . . .'

'That'll be all. Oh, and keep repeating my main order until further notice,' I interrupted him.

'He won't hurt no fly, if it wasn't for them friends of his. His father . . .'

I replaced the receiver. Another morning he said: 'I took the whip to him, I did. But he swore on his father's grave he never touched you, Carla. He said the fog was thick that night, that you was mistaken. But he couldn't speak for them other boys. Always did know they'd go too far . . .'

'Forget it, Uncle Billy. It's over now. Bury the past.'

'If that's what you want, sure thing. But I seen them boys getting outa hand for years now, and nobody . . .'

I replaced the receiver and stared at it. Now that the shock had worn off it was replaced by a deep and terrible anger. I breathed it, ate it, slept it. It lived and thrived inside me and never gave me a moment's peace. While I stared at that receiver it burst from my pores in hot waves. His father's grave, indeed! The devil's spawns had no fathers. They were descended from evil itself and defiled the very air they breathed. They executed their evil deeds in the dark of night, then slithered back to hell, laughing at the destruction they left behind.

One morning I woke to a windless day. The sea lapped gently at the coast, and the only disturbing sound was the soft hum coming from the factory. I had a sudden desire to get out of Eve's Nook. I took the car keys and went to the garage. The car was covered with a layer of sand, and on impulse I decided to wash it. Then, in the dim interior of the garage, my eyes suddenly fell on the two bicycles leaning side by side against a wall. My blood turned cold. They hadn't taken his bicycle and he wouldn't have gone away without it! Here was the evidence I had needed to make Sheriff Witmore believe me, only now it didn't matter any more.

Once again I was struck by the terrible tragedy of his death. In one cruel and senseless hour they had obliterated him from the face of the earth, and continued with their lives as though nothing had happened. The hatred, which had been growing inside me like a cancer, blossomed. Its intensity almost choked me while I stared at the bicycles, remembering how we had cycled together, laughing with the abandon of children, the salty sea breeze in our hair. And how total their destruction of my world had been.

Suddenly it dawned on me what I had to do. I think I had known all along, but hadn't allowed myself to acknowledge it. I had to kill them! All three of them – Ax Reevers and Sam Shroder and Doughie Steyl. They didn't deserve to live, to breathe the air every day, to drink and to laugh as though that night had never happened, snug in the bosom of their community, while Peter's young life had been brutally extinguished and mine irreparably damaged. They had to be squashed underfoot like vermin. I had no immediate idea how I was going to do it, only that I had a driving compulsion to do it. There would be no release from my anger while they lived.

'The law can't punish them, Peter . . . but I can. And I will,' I whispered, my eyes resting on his bicycle. As though in answer to my solemn oath, a freak gust of wind entered the garage and ruffled my hair. It was almost like a caress. Peter's caress.

Now that I had confronted the inevitable and accepted it, I experienced a new surge of life through my veins. Suddenly my existence made sense again, I wasn't merely breathing in a dead body. I washed the car vigorously, then decided not to use it after all. Instead I spent the remainder of the day washing the cottage's windows, enjoying the manual labour and physical exertion.

In the late afternoon I strolled down to the rocks for the first time since that night. I sat down on the spot where we had sat together many times and deliberately relived that night, step by step, moment by terrible moment. It strengthened my resolve to kill them. One by one.

Suddenly I felt strong and invincible – immortal, almost.

11

The car was a late model, white limousine, bumping its way along the uneven surface of the track. It came to a halt in front of Eve's Nook, but I couldn't see anyone through its discreetly tinted windows. After a while a woman got out, stood beside the car and stared fixedly at Eve's Nook. I recognized her immediately. She was the woman with the ash-blonde hair and luminous eyes who had stood beside my hospital bed. It hadn't been an apparition, after all.

From behind the lace curtains I watched her coming towards the front door. Her high-heeled shoes sank into the sandy pathway and she held her hands delicately aloft to maintain her flimsy balance. She was beautiful in a classical way, with a tall, slim figure that would've had Christian Dior raving. Her designer clothes were obviously expensive and she wore them with a natural chic. When the front doorbell rang I deliberately counted to five before opening it. I looked out at her with a neutral expression.

'Oh . . . hello. I'm Meryl Johnson,' she said in a well-modulated voice, extending a manicured, ringed hand. I pretended not to notice.

'You may have heard of me. I'm Cyril Johnson's wife,' she said again, and waited for her announcement to take effect. I raised my eyebrows only slightly. She was clearly taken aback by my lack of response, and I decided that here was a woman living and thriving in the powerful glow of her husband's wealth and power, demanding unearned respect.

'You're Carla Benson,' she continued, rapidly recovering her composure. 'I read your book *The First and the Last*. I was deeply touched by it.'

'Thank you,' I said, unmoved.

'I've tried to get you on the telephone without success. I wanted to know if your cat is all right.'

'My cat?'

'Yes. I fed her while you were away and we became good friends in the process.'

'You? But . . . thank you. I didn't know, otherwise I would've thanked you before.'

'It was entirely my pleasure. I had a cat very much like her when I was a little girl. She used to sleep on the bed with me at night.'

I smiled. 'Lulu does too. Except when the wind blows, then she sleeps under it. She doesn't like the wind.'

'Who does?'

The ice was broken. There was something special about people who liked cats. Cats had free spirits, and anyone who could grant them their freedom with unselfish love had to be admired. Yet I wasn't quite ready to invite her into my home.

'Carla, will you join us for dinner at Pelham's Bluff?' she asked.

'Pelham's Bluff?'

She smiled. 'Yes. That's the family residence. My husband's father named it Pelham's Bluff, but nobody quite knows why.'

I smiled a thin smile, considering the unexpected invitation. To be invited to the Johnson residence was an honour that befell only a select few, and would immediately cast me in a more favourable light. I was an outcast in Oliver Bay now, more so than before, and my every move would be dissected under a magnifying glass. I somehow had to pretend my life was continuing as before, that I had come to terms with the vicious attack and was forgetting it. Then, when the three men felt most complacent, I would strike.

'I'm happy to accept, Meryl,' I answered, putting warmth into my smile. 'Thank you.'

'Will Saturday evening suit you? Say, seven?'

'Perfect. I'll be there.'

Once she had left I carried my canvas chair and beach umbrella onto the beach. I erected the umbrella, sat down in its shade and closed my eyes against the glare of the sun. The rhythmic rolling of the waves had a hypnotic effect and I soon dozed off, only to be plagued by a disturbing dream.

Peter was crawling towards me across the sand, his face a contorted mask of blood, sand and exposed tendon. But instead of fear and pain, his face was twisted in raw hatred – directed at me. 'You let them kill me,' he gasped. Blood bubbled on his swollen lips and dripped onto the white sand with soft, plopping sounds. Horrified, I cringed in the chair. 'Oh, no, Peter . . . no. I couldn't stop them. You know I tried,' I said, but he kept coming. I tried to leave the chair, to flee from this macabre spectacle, but somehow I was glued to the chair, unable to move. He reached me while I watched, horror-struck. Slowly he extended a blood-soaked hand, the nails crushed and bloodied, and clamped it round my ankle. Pulsing blood flowed from his hand onto my leg. It was awfully cold and slimy. 'You must come with me, Carla,' he rasped, and while he spoke the flesh on his face peeled away, exposing a wriggling mass of white maggots feasting inside his skull. I woke screaming.

The sun had moved considerably in the sky and the tide had risen. But I was alone. Directly above me a sea-gull uttered a shrill cry, startling me. Shaken to the core, I dismantled the umbrella, folded the chair and returned to Eve's Nook. I showered and walked back to the bedroom, naked. A shock awaited me in the full-length mirror on the wall. I was painfully thin and looked ten years older. I touched my face in shocked surprise, ran my hand over the lined skin on my neck, over my sagging breasts. It was like touching and examining the body of a stranger. The thin, tired-looking woman who stared back at me from the mirror couldn't possibly muster enough strength to kill three tough, robust fishermen. I had to get to work immediately to regain my former strength and vitality.

My days became occupied with eating and exercising. It was imperative that I regain my lost weight and exercise my sagging muscles. I took infinite care with my diet, adding lots of starch and fat. I jogged up and down the deserted stretch of beach until I felt ready to drop. I reduced my smoking and drank plenty of fresh fruit juice. And in between I visited Pelham's Bluff for dinner, having ensured first that Uncle Billy was aware of the invitation. I knew I could trust him to spread the word through town.

I dressed carefully and purposefully. I wanted to appear both demure and tragic. The dress was plain white with a round collar and with it I wore a single strand of pearls and matching pearl earrings. I brushed my hair away from my face and fastened it at the base of my neck, then added just a touch of lipstick to contrast with the pale of my complexion. The result was perfect, almost Madonna-like. I practised the expression on my face until I was satisfied I exuded just the right air of mystery and tragedy.

They had been expecting me. The electronic gates swung open noiselessly when I stopped the car in front of them. The tree-lined avenue to the mansion was lit by Italian lanterns and life-sized marble statues were placed at regular intervals. It was like entering a fantasy world I had previously only seen in magazines and on the screen. The house was set in a spacious, magnificently landscaped garden. It was ablaze with colour and light. To the left was the glass encased swimming pool, set in a grandiose tropical garden bathed in artificial light.

The Johnsons were practised and excellent hosts. Cyril Johnson was an imposing man with shrewd, intelligent eyes. He was slightly shorter than his wife, Meryl, but appeared taller. His manner was rather aloof and guarded, but as the evening progressed and he realized I wasn't a threat to his self-styled superiority, he became more relaxed and smiled more often.

Meryl Johnson had the mannerisms of a pampered woman. Whenever she spoke her hands fluttered with calculated helplessness, and her liquid eyes often strayed to her husband for approval. It was obvious that Cyril Johnson adored his wife. He was painstakingly polite and attentive towards her, and when he looked at her his eyes shone with a deep-rooted love.

The furniture in the large reception area was ultra-modern and tasteful, that in the dining-room a few decades old, but stately and imposing. I could almost imagine the first Johnson sitting at the head of the long mahogany table, nodding his approval at the maintenance of the original decor. Cyril graced the head of the table, the absolute master of his world, smiling benevolently at his family, sometimes frowning to display his displeasure at an untimely remark. The two boys, home from their private school, joined us for dinner. They were well-mannered, well-spoken boys, who disappeared discreetly after a sumptuous dinner of distinctly French cuisine, served by two liveried servants.

The conversation at the dinner table was light and laced with generalities, but I wasn't fooled. The Johnsons were people who did everything with a purpose and I knew the purpose of this dinner would soon be revealed to me. After dinner Cyril suggested that we take coffee in the adjoining sitting-room, and when Meryl asked to be excused for a short while I knew we had reached the real motive behind the invitation. Cyril offered me a liqueur but I declined. He poured my coffee and a liqueur for himself, then seated himself directly opposite me.

'Carla, we certainly enjoyed your company this evening. Thank you for coming,' he said graciously.

'I enjoyed it too,' I echoed quietly.

'Meryl loved your novel, but I'm sure she told you that. I might add she's very excited about the presence of a writer in Oliver Bay. There is very little cultural stimulation in a town this size, as you very well know. We travel extensively, locally and abroad, but we're compelled to live here for most of the year.'

'I'm hardly an established writer, Cyril. Luck and success are only for the privileged few. People like me have to work that much harder at it. I'm doing my best,' I said.

'Oh, but you're much too modest, Carla,' he objected, and lit a cigar. I took the opportunity to light a badly-needed cigarette. 'Talent and success are synonymous, and you're certainly endowed with the former. The latter follows automatically.'

I inhaled deeply and waited patiently. He cleared his throat and looked at me.

'Carla, I'd like to have a little honest conversation with you.

114

I've heard a lot about you ever since you arrived here, mostly from my secretary. Not that I indulge in small talk, but I like to know what's happening in my town. You'll forgive me then if I say that we're aware of your . . . er . . . misfortune. Meryl was very distressed by it. When she first suggested we invite you here I was very much opposed to the idea. To be frank, I expected to meet a hungry-looking, desperate woman who deserved what she got. I owe you an apology for my misguided conclusions.'

I swallowed back the bitter words that welled up inside me. 'I try to be immune to biased opinions, Cyril,' I said with feigned hurt and just the right touch of sadness.

Immediately he raised a hand. 'Please don't misunderstand me, Carla. Rape is a controversial subject, its authenticity almost always in question. But not in your case. I don't believe you invited the utterly distasteful quality of that attack.'

Do children then? Or old, defenceless ladies? I wondered angrily. I forced myself to lower my eyes, to gaze at the folded hands on my lap.

'The subject is too painful to discuss,' I said and put my cigarette out. 'I have to go.'

'Just a minute, Carla. I raised the subject because I . . . we want to help you. Please hear me out, will you?'

I hesitated, then nodded silently.

'As I said, Meryl was deeply distressed by your case. She had a similar experience in her teens and has never quite come to terms with it. She still suffers the occasional nightmare as a result. I didn't want to mention it but she insisted that I did. She wants to see the man or men responsible brought to trial.'

I waited silently for him to continue.

'If you're willing to discuss your case with me, I'll make sure the guilty person or persons are arrested and prosecuted. We know what you're up against, we know how people here protect each other. I come across it at the factory all the time. If indeed it was the three men you accused, I'll see to it that we have counter witnesses who saw them attack you. If that young man who stayed with you for a while is responsible, I'll use my own resources to trace him. But I need you to be honest with me.'

Honest? Oh, I've been honest, Mr Johnson. They made me a liar and stripped me of my dignity – your town and your sheriff. What is it you want from me? To stand up in court and confess every sexual experience I've ever had so that your judge can decide whether I'm a woman of loose morals or not? Don't you think I know about these trials, how the victims are made to feel on trial instead of the rapists? And how, Mr Johnson, will I prove they killed Peter Dreifuss-Jones when the body disappeared without a trace?

'I appreciate your kindness, Cyril. And Meryl's concern,' I answered simply. 'But please understand, all I want is to forget it ever happened. I want to pick up the pieces of my life and piece them together again. In time the pain will go away and I'll regain my self-respect. Please allow me to do that.'

'Meryl claims it's impossible. She says you never forget. Don't you want to see justice done? Or don't you think I have the power to help you?'

'Power? Oh yes, I believe you have the power. But justice? There's very little justice in anything. For a man who's had everything in life I guess that's hard to understand. Please leave me to overcome my pain my own way. Good-night, Cyril. Please thank Meryl for her hospitality too.'

When I drove away I congratulated myself. I believed I had made the right impression on the Johnsons. I believed I had their sympathy and respect, and when the time came I was going to need their support.

I feared the nights. There were malicious eyes in every shadow, the prospect of danger lurked everywhere. Yet I forced myself to jog along the sand on a moonless night, my dark clothing blending with the blackness, and hiding the holstered gun in the belt round my waist. It was shortly after 1 a.m. and I was heading for the factory. Ax had told us they worked the pet-food section in shifts – he and Sam and Doughie. One of them would be there now. I wanted to see them again, one at a time, wanted to keep the hatred inside me alive while I planned their executions. It had to be done in the cleanest possible way, not that they deserved it but because I couldn't risk discovery until all three had died. I had to do it, both for Peter and myself. One night a young man had simply disappeared from the face of the earth – a young man who had known the art of giving, of laughing, of loving. No one, except me, cared enough to avenge his death, to punish the evil killers. And killing them had become the single most important thing in my life. While they lived I would have no peace again.

I was sheltered by the night until I reached the immediate vicinity of the factory. The strong lights attached to the outside of the buildings were bright and invited hoardes of moths and beetles to bash themselves against the bulbs, singeing their wings and dropping to the ground. The steady hum of machinery travelled from inside. The monster had come alive.

Stealthily I crept along the cement boulders which led to the pier. The voice of Bruce Springsteen blared from a radio on one of the trawlers anchored in the harbour, but there was no one in sight. Bracing myself, I climbed onto the pier and ran towards the shelter of a few oil drums. I crouched behind them, my every sense alert. The huge doors to the factory were agape, waiting like an open mouth to swallow the next catch from the sea. Next to it was the massive warehouse, a few stacks of cartons in front of the open door. I could hear the activity inside and occasionally the sound of men's laughter.

Once I was certain I was still undetected, I moved away from the protection of the drums, ran across the railway lines running parallel to the factory and slipped between the stacks of cartons. They were all labelled 'Johnson Pilchards, Oliver Bay' and provided a perfect hiding place. Once two men emerged from the factory. They stood close to me, lit cigarettes and talked idly. I waited tensely, wondering what I would say if they discovered me here. After a while they threw their cigarette butts to the ground, stepped on the glowing coals and went back inside.

The level of noise here was high enough to drown my footsteps while I ran to the pet-food section. It had a smaller door, the light inside was dimmer. I stood rigidly beside the door, feeling naked in the light of the bare bulb above it. I slipped through the door and immediately hid myself behind a large, rusting piece of machinery just inside the factory space. So far so good.

From the right came a high-pitched whining sound. I peered round the machine. It was the conveyor belt, whining and squeaking its way towards the metal teeth of the mincer. I was dwarfed by the size of the machinery, almost suffocated by the stench wafting from it. There was no one in sight, but I didn't have to wait long. There was a dull thud as someone bumped into something, followed by a string of curses. Doughie Steyl came through another door and walked towards the conveyor belt, carrying a large, metal bucket. While I watched he emptied its bloodied contents onto the conveyor belt, from where it was carried swiftly along to the mincer. Within seconds it had disappeared into the large machine, leaving not even a scrap behind.

And while I stared at the mincer I suddenly knew with sickening certainty how Peter had died and disappeared without a trace. That night they had dragged him here, dumped his unconscious body onto the conveyor belt and watched callously while it was swept along to its horrendous destination – the mincer! What an absolutely perfect way to dispose of any unwanted matter! Peter Dreifuss-Jones had been minced and fed into cans of pet food along with fish heads, tails and inedible innards, small sharks, octopuses and seaweed. The realization was so horrific it stupefied my mind and left me gasping with shock and revulsion.

Sickened, I stumbled away. Blindly I ran back to the oil drums, jumped from the pier and raced across the sand, swallowed by the night again. Bile rose in my throat and dripped from my mouth which was wide open in a soundless scream. By the time I reached Eve's Nook my cheeks were wet with tears, my stomach heaving.

12

Even though he had shared my life for such a short time, there were many things to remind me of Peter. I saw the colour of his hair in the bright yellow of the azaleas in bloom, I heard the whisper of his voice on an evening breeze, smelt his skin in the mists of salt spray, saw the green of his eyes in the clear pools of water at low tide. When summer was at its peak and the wild pomegranates burst open, birds pecked at the blood-red pips and it reminded me of his red blood that had dripped onto the white sand. And my heart bled and my dry eyes wept and there was no escape from the anger that propelled me to survive each lonely day.

Once I debated phoning his father, Gregory Jones, attorney-at-law, Los Angeles, California, but what would I say? Sir, your son was fornicating with me, a forty-year-old writer from Oliver Bay. No, sir, it's a little fishing village on the east coast, as much a part of America as Los Angeles. One night we couldn't sleep because of the heat. We sat on a clump of rocks facing the Atlantic and discussed the paradise we were going to build with that money you married his mother for. And then, sir, we were attacked by three drunken fishermen. They raped and sodomised me . . . that was after they had beaten your son unconscious. But now comes the worst part, sir. They dragged him to the pet-food section at the fish factory and fed his body through the mincer. The horrifying thing is, sir, I think he was still alive when he was minced. Right now he's in cans of Johnson's Pet Food all over the country. Yes, sir, I did report it to the local sheriff but he didn't believe me. And no, sir, I have no proof to substantiate my story. But since Peter is dead now you are free to go ahead and enjoy all that money with your young wife.

I decided against it.

I started going into town again, holding my head erect with a pride born from anger. It was vitally important that I establish a normal routine again, since I wanted people to believe I had recovered fully from my ordeal. Pretending that nothing had happened was one of the hardest things I'd ever had to do, especially since people stared at me as though they were seeing me for the first time. I often heard snide remarks, followed by derisive laughter. They dropped names like floozy and man-eater and brazen slut, which hurt far more than I wanted them to. Uncle Billy was ill-at-ease with me, clearing his throat often and shuffling his feet. His eyes rested on me warily, as though he expected me to hold him personally responsible for his grandson's actions. He was less talkative and clearly relieved when I spoke little and left soon. I had become an innocent victim of small-town prejudices.

Emerging from my self-imposed exile was like rising from the dead. I had the weird sensation that I was living outside my body, a mute observer to the plight of another, most unfortunate woman. Yet the anger inside me continued to grow until it seemed to have a heartbeat of its own. It governed my days and my nights with unrelenting ferocity, and there was no candy in the world that could wash away the bitter taste in my mouth. I hadn't been able to escape sexual abuse in my childhood or in my maturity, and attributed my lack of control over my own body to a curse imposed on womankind by a ruthless God.

My worst moment came when I emptied my cupboard of cans of Johnson's Pet Food. I almost choked on the injustice of it all while digging a shallow grave in the garden and burying the cans. Doing that was like giving Peter the burial he had been denied, laying his soul to rest. Never again would I allow Lulu to eat another can of Johnson's Pet Food. My God, it would be like watching her eat Peter!

'Ashes to ashes, dust to dust,' I intoned, levelling the ground with the spade. 'God giveth and God taketh.' I had once heard a preacher say that at a funeral and it had seemed so dreadfully pat then. Now it seemed apt. God giveth woman a desirable body and man the power of control over it, and He taketh those who aren't strong enough to protect themselves.

Afterwards I strolled aimlessly from room to room, searching for something of Peter – a scent, a blond hair, shavings in the basin, anything. But there was nothing, and I felt terribly empty and alone.

My ill-fated novel continued to gather dust. My creative abilities had been smothered by the unexpected upheaval in my life, and I wondered with indifference if they would ever return. I didn't answer Fran Westcott's letters, only Theresa's. One day Theresa spent the bulk of her small allowance from the kibbutz to phone me. Her voice sounded strange and very far away, and I vaguely wondered what her connection to me was. She spoke mostly of Gavin, and I had trouble associating myself with either of them. I promised again to visit Israel soon and continued to stare at the telephone long after we had said goodbye.

The second call that day came from Meryl Johnson. She had received my 'thank you' card and assured me it had been a pleasure having me, and could we get together again soon? I agreed to spend the coming Saturday with her and a few friends on *Esmerelda*, the family yacht.

On 12 August my fortieth birthday dawned quietly. The day of reckoning had also dawned for one of the three killers. It was now eight weeks since that fateful night, eight weeks during which they had enjoyed a life they had no claim to. I felt remarkably calm as I watched the clock labour its way through each second of the day, ticking away the last hours for one cold-blooded rapist and murderer. I had tried and convicted him, now only the execution remained. Which one would it be?

I had watched them every night for the past five nights, but found it impossible to determine a specific routine. Doughie had worked two nights, Ax one, Sam two, from which I gathered that they swopped shifts with each other as and when it suited them. Each worked alone at the conveyor belt, sometimes just idling the hours away, waiting. On two nights a few laden trawlers were being offloaded. A large, funnel-shaped pipe sucked the fish from the trawlers' holds and I didn't see it again since the funnel disappeared into the factory. The conveyor belt emerged from the factory into the pet-food section, loaded with the offal from inside, while one of the three men ensured the smooth running of the belt's load into the mincer. It was all very efficient and disgustingly smelly.

While I waited patiently for the time to pass, I stared out the window. The sun was setting, bathing the ocean in a deep red glow. It looked like a sea of blood – Peter's blood, spilled by careless men in a drunken stupor. The memory lived like a bogeyman in my spiritual cupboard, very much like the bogeyman Theresa had feared as a child and which I never succeeded in explaining away. When dusk fell I baked a frozen ground beef pie and picked at it absently, with Lulu curled up at my feet.

While darkness crept over the land and invaded Eve's Nook, I watched the minute progress of the clock. For two agonizing hours I checked and rechecked the gun, aimed it and rested my finger on the trigger. I fastened the home-made silencer to the barrel and aimed it again. And again. Now that the fatal hour was approaching, many alarming questions milled about in my head. What if something went wrong and the gun didn't go off? What if someone caught me red-handed? I paced the cottage restlessly, counting my footsteps until I reached a hundred, then starting at one again.

Shortly after midnight I dressed carefully in black trousers, black sweater and the sneakers I had dyed black. Over this gear I

121

wore a camouflage jacket I had picked up for ten bucks in a thrift shop in Greenwich Village. At the time its scruffy appearance had appealed to the rebel in me, the part that refused to grow old. Earlier today I had dipped it into the sea and allowed it to dry, then deliberately smeared it with grease and stale fish, so that now it was revoltingly dirty and stinking. I brushed all my hair back and buried it under the dark woollen cap I had stolen at the factory during one of my nocturnal trips. It was the type worn by most seamen and would make me less conspicuous should I be noticed. With a black eye-line pencil I drew a black moustache on my upper lip, then stood back to survey my reflection. I was every inch the rough fisherman I had wanted to create.

I strapped the holster to my waist. It was perfectly hidden beneath the bulky jacket. I kissed Lulu between her ears, switched all the lights off and left by the french window. The night was cool, the sky clear and star-studded. A half-moon was creeping over the night sky, its light scant enough to conceal my progress.

As I had done on other nights, I jogged along the dark stretch of beach, my sneakers filling with sand as I ran. To my right the ocean roared in timeless motion, and occasionally I felt the cool spray on my face. I reached the cement boulders in eight minutes flat. It was 12.35 a.m. I sat there for a while, regaining my breath and listening to the sounds coming from above. Occasionally I heard men's voices above the din of the factory and the sea, but it was fairly quiet otherwise. My hand strayed to the holster, closed round the cold steel of the gun. I inhaled deeply, then climbed onto the pier and ran to the oil drums, where I crouched.

There were a few trawlers anchored in the murky waters of the harbour. Two men stood idly on the swaying deck of one, their voices carrying to me. I looked towards the factory and saw something that convinced me Lady Luck was smiling on me tonight. The coaches of a train were stationary in front of the factory and I heard the dull thuds as cartons were being loaded onto them. They would protect me from sight for as long as I wanted them to. My immediate concern was the two men on the trawler. I dared not show myself, even in this disguise. My appearance might fool them from afar, but what if they decided to converse with me, mistaking me for one of their own? I couldn't possibly hope to fool them with my voice.

Twenty minutes later they walked down the gangway from the trawler, passed within two feet of my hiding place and walked along the pier towards the factory and out of sight. I emerged from my hiding place, put my hands in my pockets and walked briskly towards the factory. No one cried out or accosted me. I reached the stationary train and crouched beside it. Through the gaps between the metal wheels I saw the moving legs of men working on the other side. Their conversation was laced with vulgarities and they laughed often – coarse laughter that reminded me of that night and made my flesh crawl. I crept along the length of the train towards the pet-food section. When I thought I was directly opposite it, I rolled in under the train and lay flat on my stomach between the railroad lines. My second wait began, since I couldn't act with all that loading activity in progress.

While I waited I had involuntary flashes from happier times in the past. Theresa was a baby again, dressed in frilly pink, smiling a toothless smile. I kissed her rose-bud mouth, which opened instinctively in search of a nipple. We were holidaying on the west coast, and I balanced her between my legs while we glided down a water slide, squealing with delight. The sound of her childish laughter carried to me through the passages of time. She was frolicking in our small garden with Bits, the white Maltese poodle, snapping at her heels. On her tenth birthday she blew out all ten candles on her cake at the same time, while her group of young guests cheered and sang happy birthday. And now she was grown up and someone else shared her intimate moments – a Canadian boy by the name of Gavin who, I prayed to God, wouldn't break her heart.

I thought of Peter too, and how he had thrown his head back whenever he laughed, his teeth snow-white against his tanned face. And how his lips had roused untamed passion in my sleeping body. The deep ache inside me was replaced by a white-hot anger.

The loading ceased at 3.14 a.m. and the men started filing into the factory. Some machinery was switched off and the monster became quieter. I wondered if the shot would be heard above the remaining noise. Only once before had I pulled the trigger to test the gun, and that was on a deserted country road. The dull explosion had been acceptable then, but what if something had gone wrong in the meantime? There was only one way to find out.

I crawled from underneath the train and emerged on the other side. I ran to the pet-food section and slipped inside. The whining conveyor belt was to my right, but no one was there. I still didn't know who would be the first to go, but that was part of the pleasure. A strange excitement coursed through my veins while I ran to the shelter of a drum-like machine with rows of metal protrusions. It stood upright like a gaping jaw and I guessed at some stage in the past it had served a useful purpose in the factory. Now it provided a perfect vantage point for a killer. I settled down to wait for my first victim.

He appeared suddenly from nowhere, carrying a bucket and mop. While I watched he started mopping up the area adjacent to the conveyor belt. Slowly and noiselessly I removed the gun from its holster. My hands were hot and sweaty, but my heart was as cold as ice. I pushed the barrel of the gun through the metal teeth of the machine and waited for the right moment. While I watched him the dreadful events of that night raced through my mind. He was above me again – sweating and panting his stale breath into my face, violating the sanctity of my body, while Peter groaned with his blood-soaked face in the sand.

For a while I just watched him, savouring the power I held over his miserable and worthless life. I would've liked to have seen him crawl and beg for mercy before I shot him, but I couldn't risk discovery if he made too much noise. He was standing directly beside the conveyor belt – a big, dirty and stinking man who didn't deserve to live. He was human trash. I aimed carefully at his head and pulled the trigger. The shot sounded unnaturally loud to my sensitive ears, but it struck its target. A dark hole appeared just above his right temple, blood rapidly spread down the side of his face and ran into his neck. In the yellow glow of the dim light his face acquired a surprised look, then he slowly toppled sideways, grabbing at the air as he fell. The upper part of his body landed on the moving conveyor belt, while the bulk of his torso hung over the edge, keeping him oddly balanced. His head and one outstretched arm flapped rhythmically on the ripples of the belt, and he started sliding from it.

I replaced the gun in its holster and ran towards him. A quick inspection assured me no one was near. I reached him, lifted him from the hips up and shoved. It was no easy feat. He was much heavier than I had anticipated, and I had to strain with every ounce of strength I possessed. Bit by bit his body slipped onto the conveyor belt. A final shove sent him hurtling along the belt towards the mincer, while I watched in cold fascination. His legs reached the mincer first and disappeared rapidly. Blood and fragments of bone sprayed against the metal teeth as it chewed him up. By the time his shoulders reached the mincer, the top of his head burst open like a ripe watermelon, spraying bone and grey matter from his brain, before that too was minced. Within seconds he had disappeared from the face of the earth – sharing the fate they had meted out to Peter.

Before I left I found the spent cartridge in the dust beneath the machine and pocketed it. I hummed to myself while I jogged back to Eve's Nook.

Doughie Steyl would never again commit evil.

13

Esmerelda, the Johnsons' yacht, was an exquisite piece of craftmanship. It lay anchored in the Johnsons' private harbour, ablaze with light, its smooth, sleek shape stretching eighty feet long, its white hull reflected on the oily surface of the water.

Dr Richard Mallen was there, dressed in an open-neck, cream-coloured shirt and Calvin Klein jeans. Removed from his medical surroundings he looked just like any other man one would pass on a pavement without a second glance – dark hair greying at the temples, a non-descript face and a slight air of boredom. I found it impossible to relate to him other than as a doctor and since I wasn't feeling ill, not at all. He had seen me during my worst moments, with blood and semen and sand oozing out of me, and I doubted he had seen anything quite like it in his career.

The only other guests were Frank and Betty Van Schoor, a striking couple from Minneapolis. I didn't know what their connection with the Johnsons was, and didn't particularly care to know. They were the type of people I seldom came in contact with – the idle rich whose lives revolved round jet-setting parties and pointless sea cruises, who disguised their boredom behind fake smiles and trite conversation. Frank drank a lot of expensive champagne while Betty sipped martinis topped with plenty of black olives.

Meryl Johnson was sedately dressed in a pale pink lounging gown, her ash-blonde hair framing her oval-shaped face. Without the overpowering presence of her husband she seemed to radiate a power of her own. Her voice had a firmer quality and she smiled more readily. There was a natural curiosity in her liquid blue eyes and she listened attentively whenever someone spoke, as though what they had to say was of the utmost importance. She was a beautiful woman without using her beauty as a weapon.

Dinner was served on the white deck under a starlit sky by a white-clad Mexican waiter. It consisted of a variety of seafood delicacies, attractively arranged on decorated trays. There was plenty of chilled wine for everyone's taste, and I accepted a glass of white burgundy. The soothing sounds of Richard Clayderman's piano drifted from below deck while we ate. Richard Mallen was seated beside me and made a concerted effort to draw me into conversation.

'I'm glad to see you're looking so much better,' he said softly.

I glanced at him, nodded and sipped the excellent wine. From across the table Meryl tried to watch us unobtrusively but didn't escape my notice.

'You'll enjoy the cruise tomorrow. The Atlantic isn't one of the best places for smooth sailing, but this yacht was built to withstand the roughest seas and provide maximum comfort,' he said again.

'I've never sailed before. I wouldn't know the difference,' I replied.

'I was hoping to join you, but I'm on emergency duty tomorrow. The yacht's skipper is one of the best though, you'll be in the most capable hands.'

I looked away from him, across the dark expanse of water and towards the twinkling lights of Oliver Bay. Those lights sheltered another two vicious killers whose time was running out fast.

'Carla, you're not eating. Would you prefer something else?' Meryl asked from across the table.

I looked at her and smiled. 'Not at all. I'm a slow starter but I improve with time.'

They all laughed politely, as though I had said something very witty. I felt claustrophobic and unduly anxious for most of the evening. I wondered if Lulu was awfully restless being locked up in the cottage, but I couldn't leave a window open for fear my home would be desecrated by strangers again. I also wondered if the travel agent in New York had finalised my trip to Israel and whether I would like Gavin or whether I would feel threatened by him.

'You're so quiet, Carla,' Richard remarked beside me, distracting me from my private world.

'I'm sorry, I was listening to Richard Clayderman.'

'Do you like music?'

'Yes. As long as it isn't loud and abrasive.'

'Same here, but I don't get nearly enough time to enjoy it.'

Across the table the other three were reminiscing over a recent holiday in the Mediterranean, laughing at shared trivialities.

'Are you the only doctor here?' I asked, responding to my social obligations.

'Oh no, there're three of us, but I'm the only Oliver Bay native. The others are from out of town. They come and go as regularly as the seasons.'

'Why is that?'

'One has to have a special kind of love for Oliver Bay to stay. It's isolated and backward and culture-starved. And then there are the factory's noise and smell. It's not easy for someone who wasn't born here,' he said, and offered me a cigarette. I accepted one of his Marlboros and waited for him to light it.

'Were you? Born here?'

'Yes. My grandfather, Thomas Mallen, was the first doctor here. My father followed in his footsteps and I continued the family tradition.'

'Did you ever want to be anything else?'

He smiled reflectively. 'Yes, I would say so. I wanted to build yachts. Like this one. I wanted to challenge the sea, build something that could withstand every nasty trick it could conjure up. The sea has always fascinated me. But instead I built model ships in my spare time and sailed them in the pool at home.'

'The *Titanic* challenged the sea and now it's lying somewhere on its bottom.'

'True,' he conceded. 'But man will always try to outsmart it, no matter what the odds. For some it becomes a way of life.'

'Then what prevented you?'

'Tradition, more than anything else. I didn't want to disappoint my father.'

'Do you regret it now?'

'I don't think so. Healing the victims of the sea is the second best thing to challenging it. Would you like to take a walk round the deck?'

'No, thanks. Not right now.'

'Later, perhaps?'

'Perhaps.'

I turned away from him and feigned an interest in the conversation taking place between the other three. I was relieved when the hospital paged him shortly after 10 p.m. and he left. The Van Schoors retired soon afterwards, leaving me alone with Meryl in the cosy saloon below deck. She stretched herself on the sofa with cat-like grace, then looked across at me.

'A night-cap?'

'No, thank you. I've had enough for one night,' I said, feeling light-headed from the four glasses of burgundy.

'I think Richard is still very concerned about you, Carla. I think in a way he feels personally responsible for what happened.'

I stiffened. 'Why should he?'

'The guilt weighs heavily on all our minds. You're a guest here . . . and instead of hospitality you got . . .'

'Please, Meryl . . . you don't have to say anything. It really doesn't matter.'

What else could I say? I'm grateful, Meryl, that someone still thinks of me as a human being. Mighty generous, you know, like being kind to a poor relative. Extend a few alms and perhaps she'll go away peacefully.

'Will you have coffee instead?'

'I don't think so. If you'll excuse me . . .' I said, getting to my feet.

'Carla, don't go, just yet,' she said hurriedly. 'I've been wanting a quiet moment with you, like this.'

I tensed. 'I don't want to discuss it, Meryl. Please try to understand. It's too soon.'

'It's never too soon!' she said sharply. I looked at her. Her eyes burnt with an intense light, her delicate hands were drawn into tight little fists. 'I made the same mistake, Carla. I refused to discuss it, refused to share my shame and hurt, and it almost destroyed me. The anger was the worst thing. For many years I was so angry it suffocated me. I know now it was a mistake, that I should've discussed it, dissected it and come to terms with it. I understand what you've suffered, Carla. I'm in a position to help you . . . if you'll let me.'

'Why? For my sake, or your own?'

'For both of us! And for all the other women out there who've suffered the same fate. Bring them to justice, Carla. You'll have more power behind you than you can possibly imagine. I'm not a defenceless teenager anymore. I'm strong, I can fight them!' she said, her liquid eyes aglow.

'Meryl, have you any idea how merciless the defence is with a rape victim? Have you any idea how utterly degrading and humiliating it is?' I asked. 'Do you know how the victim is made to feel on trial, how they portray every relationship you've ever had as seedy, how grossly vulgar every sexual experience? I've read about it, Meryl. Haven't you?'

'You don't seem to understand, Carla. I'll be there, right beside you, protecting you. And Cyril will be there, and Richard. We all care about this case, we all share your anger,' she persisted.

'You're mistaken, Meryl. I'm not angry. Not any more. I only want to forget it ever happened. Please allow me to do that,' I said.

She jumped to her feet. 'Don't you care about the fact that they're free? What are you? Some kind of a saint?'

I stared at her coldly. 'I'm no more a saint than you are, Meryl, but I don't want to be an instrument for your old grudges, or a spectacle for the town's amusement. Men have violated women throughout the ages and they'll continue to do so. The law in this town is male, the judge is male, the witnesses are male. Don't you know that they protect each other because they understand each other's sexual urges? Don't you know that each and everyone of them wishes they had the guts to do it themselves? There are those who rape their girlfriends, their mothers, their wives, their sisters. It's safer that way.'

'Oh Carla, I don't believe you mean that. There are kind men and loving men, there are men who write the most thought-provoking poetry about women and love. Don't allow this single incident to embitter you so. Let the culprits be punished.'

'No!' I said harshly. 'It wasn't a single incident. My father abused me from the age of nine, my ex-husband continued the tradition. My world's been a much tougher one than yours, Meryl. Please don't ask me to do something I don't believe in.'

Her expression was one of sadness while she looked at me. 'Oh, Carla, I'm so sorry. I had no idea. Your book . . . the love you described is so pure and so innocent.'

'That's because I still believed in fairy tales,' I said, giving a short, bitter laugh. 'I created a fantasy world in which to function, but now even that has been taken away from me.'

'That young man . . .'

'Peter? He was part of the fantasy. He was one of my characters come to life and performing on cue. I might've written the words myself. When they killed him they destroyed my fantasy world. Like Cinderella I became a hag again, scrubbing hearths. I can't write anymore, Meryl. That's the worst part,' I said, my voice thick with suppressed emotion.

Meryl came towards me, her eyes brimming with tears. And in spite of my inner resistance I allowed her to embrace me. I wished desperately that I could weep, as she was, but my eyes remained dry, the coldness in my heart thoroughly set.

'Please allow me to help you,' she urged softly.

'No!' I cried, and fled from her.

Saturday passed in a trance-like state. We sailed on a vast expanse of water, swaying with the wind and the motion of the sea, sunbathing on the deck and sipping martinis. I joined in the light-hearted conversation and laughter without realizing what I was saying or why I was laughing. I had the odd sensation that I wasn't there at all, that I was merely a transparent observer. I avoided being alone with Meryl again, but her manner towards me remained warm and spontaneous. When we docked back in the harbour shortly before sunset I was glad to get away. I thanked her for a most pleasant interlude and drove home to Eve's Nook.

Lulu was pleased to see me and some of my old warmth towards her returned. She was the only good thing left in my life, the only thing that didn't suck me dry of energy. Yet the moment I opened the bathroom window she disappeared through it, no doubt to the fascination of the surrounding bush. I couldn't compete with that.

On Sunday morning I cycled into town where I bought the weekly *Oliver Post*; a four-page local publication. It was a poor example of a newspaper, its contents confined to the dull events of Oliver Bay, which centred mostly round the factory and its production achievements. Doughie Steyl's disappearance was front-page news. His mother's picture was there, dressed in black, her hands outstretched in a silent plea. The article underneath said Doughie had been missing for five days and if anyone knew his whereabouts would they please contact Sheriff Witmore without delay. His family was sick with worry, since Doughie was an only child and had never left home in twenty-eight years. I smiled to myself. I was the only one who knew his whereabouts, and I wasn't telling. Doughie Steyl shared the same fate as Peter Dreifuss-Jones. This very minute he too was being eaten by domestic pets all over the state! A knot of laughter started deep inside me, rose through my chest and bubbled over my lips. It had a sick, disjointed quality to it, but relieved some of the bitterness.

During the afternoon I sat in the window seat of my bedroom and stared vacantly at the scene beyond. The odd picknicker had returned. A few people strolled along the stretch of beach, dogs trailing behind them. They barked at sea-gulls who fluttered into the air with shrill cries of alarm. When they left during the late afternoon I went for a stroll too, enjoying the feel of the fine, warm sand beneath my bare feet. I climbed onto the rocks, which were still warm from the day's heat, and sat down in my favourite spot, the spot Peter had shared with me for a few weeks. I stroked the surface of the rock where he used to sit, trying to imagine the feel of his firm young skin under my touch. Instead I felt the hard muscles of drunk men while they deliberately hurt me and laughed at my degradation. A terrible ache settled in my heart while I stared out across the ocean. I wanted to scream my anger to the sea, curse God for my fate, demand an explanation from the universe. Instead I sat very still, like a statue, suspended in time.

The telephone was ringing when I got back to the cottage. It was Richard Mallen, wanting to know if I had enjoyed the previous day's sailing. I assured him I had.

'Carla, I have one of those rare free evenings tonight. Will you join me for dinner? At my house?' he asked tentatively.

'Thank you, but no. I've already eaten. And I rarely have free time myself. My novel takes precedence over everything else, and I want to complete another chapter before I leave,' I lied smoothly.

'Leave? You're leaving?'

'For a short holiday,' I said. 'I'll be back early next month.'

'Oh. Could we have dinner together when you get back?'

'I doubt it, Richard. I don't want to be pitied. I'm no longer the battered patient you sewed back together in hospital.'

'Is that it? Is that what you thought this was? Pity?' he asked, surprised.

'What else?'

'You're wrong, Carla. I . . . I like you for yourself. I know it's much too soon after your . . . er . . . unfortunate experience, but I'd like to be your friend. If you'll let me, of course,' he replied.

Unfortunate experience? Was that all he thought it was – an unfortunate experience?

'You're right. It's much too soon, even for friendship,' I agreed.

'Will you at least think about it while you're away?'

'Perhaps. Goodbye, Richard.'

I replaced the receiver and kept staring at the instrument with resentment. I should have it disconnected before I left and learn to live without it, like before. Telephones allowed people to intrude on your private world at random, and you were obliged by a mute instrument to respond. Yes, I would arrange that tomorrow, but there was one more call I had to make.

The butler at Pelham's Bluff answered at the second ring and promised to call Mrs Johnson. When Meryl came on to the line I pretended a heartiness I didn't feel, and assured her that the cruise had been a most enjoyable experience. When I finally got round to the purpose of my call she immediately agreed to feed Lulu during my absence.

I had a temporary respite from my murderous task, and for the first time since Peter's death I slept well that night.

14

The plane landed at Ben-Gurion Airport at 3.20 p.m. I disembarked with the other passengers, trying to subdue the unreasonable fear inside me. I'd had enough time on the plane to wonder if the stress of my ordeal still showed on my face or in my eyes. Would Theresa sense the contamination of the rape and my first act of revenge with the same uncanny perception with which we had sensed each other's moods for years? Had I changed physically as well as psychologically?

She was there, in the airport lounge, waving her arms and squealing with delight when she spotted me. We struggled through the thronging crowd to reach each other, and fell into each other's arms. Her body against mine felt strange, grown-up. And had she always been this tall and this pretty? We kissed and laughed and kissed again and laughed again. We bombarded each other with questions and feasted our eyes on each other. Then I became aware of the tall and dark-haired young man standing just behind her, smiling indulgently at our joy. I drew away from her and smiled at him.

'Gavin?'

'Ms Benson?'

We shook hands, our eyes examining and appraising each other. He was attractive in a rugged way, with broad shoulders and dark, curly hair. His dark eyes were warm and alive, his smile contagious.

'Terry's spoken of nothing else these past few weeks. I'm glad you're finally here,' he said.

Terry? She used to hate me calling her that. Did it have a different ring to it when he called her that?

'And I'm glad to be here, Gavin. Shall we get my luggage?'

133

Theresa hooked onto my arm possessively. Her joy at being with me was child-like, and some of my earlier fear dissipated. She was a little girl again, her small hand buried tightly in mine, smiling up at me. My dormant protective instinct came to the fore and I showered her with questions. Did she eat regularly? Did she rest enough, exercise enough? Was she happy?

'See? What did I tell you?' she asked, turning to Gavin. 'My mother can't believe I can function without her.'

We all laughed. 'Don't all mothers?' I countered.

It was twenty minutes before we emerged from the airport building. Gavin owned a dust-covered, rusting jeep with graffiti all over the bodywork – some in English, some in Hebrew. The seats were torn and dusty, the dashboard littered with protruding wires. It was a practical vehicle for country roads, he explained laughingly. Its suspension was shot too and we bumped our way along the country roads towards Haifa in the north.

Theresa chatted incessantly, pointing out various places of historical interest on the route. We passed mile after mile of alternately barren landscape and fertile valleys. It was a strangely contradictory countryside, but I was more interested in Theresa. She had been a shy, pale and intense child, now she had a carefree, confident air about her. Her blonde hair blew carelessly in the hot afternoon air, reminding me of Peter. She looked healthy and suntanned, a new light shone in her hazel eyes. If I'd had any doubts about her happiness they disappeared rapidly as I watched her. Occasionally she laid a hand on Gavin's thigh and he clasped a strong, brown hand over hers with an intimacy born from mutual love. I was happy for her. No, for both of them.

Naharim, at the foot of Mount Carmel, was the kibbutz inn on the fringe of the Kibbutz Aliyni. Theresa and Gavin had chosen it so that I could be near them and see them while they worked. It was also close enough to the city of Haifa if I cared to wander off by myself. We reached it shortly before sunset, and it was a blessed relief to remove my protesting muscles from the confines of the jeep.

Naharim was an old but charming, double-storeyed building with a lush display of tropical plants in its small garden and foyer. After checking in, Gavin carried my bags to the small room on the upper floor which I was going to occupy for the next two weeks. It was a cosy, friendly room, despite its size, with a colourful, hand-knitted bedspread and Oriental rugs on the floor. Gavin was doing a spell in the kibbutz inn kitchen and excused himself shortly after our arrival. The moment we were alone Theresa and I embraced again. We sat on the bed and shared a cigarette, the way we used to, while a warm breeze blew through the open french window.

'So, what do you think of Gavin?' she asked eagerly.

'Gavin? He seems a nice enough boy,' I responded.

'Is that all? Nice enough?' she asked, her eyes pleading for more. My approval had always been so vital to her and it was the one thing she hadn't outgrown.

I laughed and ruffled her straight, blonde hair. 'More than nice enough. He's everything you said he was – adventurous, warm, sincere. Are you very happy?'

'Oh, yes. Very.'

'I'm thrilled, darling. I look forward to seeing you both back in the States by the end of the year.'

'Oh, Mom . . . we're not sure yet if we want to go back. We're both so happy here in Israel, we're seriously considering staying. At the kibbutz, of course. At least until we know what we want to do,' she said, her eyes shining with a contented glow. 'Will you be very upset if we do?'

'Upset? Good heavens, no. This is all I've ever wanted from life – your happiness. God knows happiness is elusive enough. If this is the life you want you must grasp it with both hands,' I assured her.

'But what about you? Sometimes when I think of how you live all alone in that obscure little town called Oliver Bay I feel like getting on the first plane back home.'

'I absolutely forbid you to. I like Oliver Bay. It's my home now, and I'm happy there,' I said, almost choking on the words. 'I miss you and I'm sure you miss me too, but we'll see each other as often as we can.'

'You're so unselfish, Mom,' she said, putting her arms round me and leaning her head on my shoulder. 'And I love you so very much.'

'I love you so very much too, honey.'

She joined me for dinner in the small, crowded dining-room. Gavin had arranged to serve our table and went about his task with a display of affected professionalism. He bowed when he

135

handed us the menu and gave each simple dish an exotic French title. We giggled like schoolgirls and teased him about the quality of the service, which we claimed was atrocious.

'Everybody's equal on a kibbutz, there's no class distinction here. That's what I like most about Israel,' Theresa said. 'I don't know if I could live in a different society again. I don't know if I'd want to.'

'It sounds like a good way of life,' I agreed, realizing she had already made up her mind and was merely preparing me for the punch line. 'We live in a world of such extremities – extreme wealth and extreme poverty, and from either side there's little tolerance for the other. Sharing is one of man's dismal failures.'

Theresa watched me over a glass of semi-sweet Israeli wine, her expression pensive.

'You've changed, Mom. You're . . . different somehow,' she said.

'In what way?' I asked, immediately on guard.

'I can't quite put my finger on it. There's something in your eyes that wasn't there before . . . a sort of lost look. Why don't you tell me how awful it is in Oliver Bay, how much you hate it?'

I forced myself to laugh lightly. 'Oh, but I don't. What you see in my eyes right now is a blend of fatigue and alcohol sedation. I've just travelled half-way across the earth. Do you blame me?'

'I'm a total beast, for sure. Let's have coffee, then I'll help you unpack. I have to be back by eight, so you're welcome to an early night. Okay?'

'Okay. But when will I see you?'

'Every day. My shift finishes at three in the afternoon and I promise to come right over. Gavin's going to swop his shift so we can show you around. There's so much I want you to see and so little time. Can't you stay longer than two weeks?'

I shook my head. 'I'm afraid not. My second novel's nearing completion now and I have to rush home to finish it.'

'When are you going to tell me about it?'

'When it's published. You know how superstitious I am about discussing unfinished novels,' I said.

I hadn't brought much clothing with me and the unpacking was done in no time. When Gavin called for Theresa shortly before eight they left immediately. In spite of my fatigue, I suddenly felt wide awake and deeply alone. I walked out the door leading onto the balcony and stood against the railing, listening to the night sounds. Downstairs a bus drew up and released a handful of tourists carrying suitcases and overnight bags. They conversed in many foreign tongues and disappeared into the foyer. The bus driver left and silence settled over the rural scene again.

I was half-way across the earth and should've felt far removed from Oliver Bay and Peter. But I didn't. His voice carried to me along the corridors of space and time and when I closed my eyes I could hear the waves breaking against the rocks below Eve's Nook. Peter and Oliver Bay were part of my destiny and would beckon wherever I went. As long as there was unfinished business, as long as two killers still lived.

The two weeks became a whirlwind of sight-seeing, to which I was partly deaf and blind. Israel rang with historical and archaeological echoes of ancient civilizations, and was an inexhaustible source of contrasts. Eastern faces mingled with western faces – skullcapped, veiled, uncovered, cowled. And running through it all was a current of religion so strong it dominated everything else. People seemed to flock here from all over the world, in search of God and identity. Walking the paths where Jesus had walked might somehow give meaning to an aimless life, visiting the places where God had appeared to the ancient prophets might wash away the sins of the past. Israel brought reality to the Bible stories they had read as children, and the dying embers of their childhood faith were rekindled.

I tramped the same paths as other tourists, with a cold heart and feigned interest. In a cave on Mount Carmel I vaguely heard the guide explain how the prophet Elijah had found refuge from King Ahab. I stood mutely on Massada where King Herod had built his fortress overlooking the Dead Sea, impervious to the breathtaking view of the pink mountains of Moab in the background.

It was at the Sea of Galilee that I suddenly realized why I had come to Israel. It dawned on me while I watched Gavin and Theresa at play – two young lovers as yet untouched by the eroding emotions of disillusionment and disappointment. I had come to Israel to say goodbye to her, to reassure myself that she was adequately equipped to continue life without me, that she was happy. Not for one moment did I fool myself that I would get away with killing three men. In fact, once they were all dead, I would want the world to know why I had killed them. Theresa would have to understand why I had brought such shame on her, and I believed Gavin was strong enough to support her through the confusion and grief that were sure to follow.

In the ancient city of Jerusalem I remembered Peter's expressed wish to visit it. I stood in front of the Wailing Wall, suddenly in awe of the powerful presence of history, yet resentful of the God who had afflicted me with such tragedy. I was an emotional leper, sentenced to die a slow death behind the walls of obscurity. Peter was beside me while we retraced the footsteps of Jesus through arches and alleys, cupolas and columns. He was sitting beside me in street cafés, thronging market places for souvenirs. And Jerusalem was where I came closest to weeping. For him and for myself.

I had a hidden source of laughter, and for the sake of Theresa and Gavin, I drew on it often. I threw my head back and laughed on the wobbly back of an old camel, laughed at the antics of a comedian on a cabaret floor, at the haggling merchants in the oriental markets, at the witty remarks Gavin dropped from time to time. If Oscars were awarded for human endurance I would've qualified.

During the mornings I often hired a horse and trotted with other tourists through the green fields of the kibbutz, hoping to get a glimpse of Theresa at work. We had very little time alone. Gavin was our constant companion, eager to amuse and to please, but in spite of my initial fear I neither resented nor disliked him. He was a strong, well-adjusted young man, and when the time came he would be her rock of strength.

The two weeks were up before we realized it, and the day before my departure Theresa arrived alone for our evening date. She wanted to spend the last evening alone with me, she explained shyly, and I was grateful for this private interlude. In Haifa we visited a restaurant which looked like an old stone castle from the outside. It was a quiet place with relaxing background music and excellent food. We sat under a straw canopy at a lavishly decorated table, lit by an oil lamp which threw oddly-shaped shadows across the stone walls. We enjoyed traditional Jewish cuisine – chicken soup, stuffed carp with horseradish, chopped liver with onions, kugel and cholent, washed down with an excellent house wine. Yet my departure hung heavily between us.

'Mom . . . I don't know what happened to you in Oliver Bay, but whatever it is, it's bad enough to show in your eyes. You're hiding something,' Theresa said seriously.

I reached for her hand across the table. 'I'm okay, really I am. I have the cottage by the sea I've always wanted, my second novel is nearing completion and you're happy. What more could I want?'

'Love and companionship. Everybody needs somebody.'

'Will you stop worrying about me? I'm fine. Just fine.'

'I don't believe you. You raised me to believe that honesty is the most important virtue, now you're being dishonest,' she persisted. 'Gavin and I have been discussing you. I told him how you struggled to raise me, to give me the best you could, and he agrees that you shouldn't have to live alone. No, Mom . . . let me finish. You've always said I owe you nothing for what you've done for me, that it's every parent's duty to do the best they can for their children, but I didn't grow up with blinkers on my eyes. I saw the relationships my friends had with their parents and I always compared it with ours. They always fell short. You were more than a mother. You were my friend, my sister, my soulmate. You never tired of giving.'

There were tears in her eyes and I felt a lump in my own throat – rising and swelling. My main aim in life had been to protect her from the ugly side of life, to send her into the world without terror and hatred as foundations.

'I only did what came naturally,' I said.

'You like to pretend you're such a tough cookie, but you've always been a sucker for the underdog – beggars and stray animals and abused people. You fed and clothed and loved anything that needed you. My father must've been a real bastard to have treated you badly.'

'That doesn't matter anymore. It belongs to the past,' I said, stroking her hand.

'We want you to come to Israel. The three of us could get a little place of our own. We'll continue to work on the kibbutz while you write. We're so close to the sea here, you can go there whenever you feel like it,' she appealed.

'Does that mean you and Gavin intend getting married?' I asked.

'Not right away. We don't need a piece of paper to bind us together. Maybe later.'

'Whatever decision you make will be the right one,' I assured her.

'You haven't answered me, Mom. Surely you can write anywhere, it doesn't have to be Oliver Bay.'

'Maybe so, but right now Oliver Bay suits my mood. Also . . . I have unfinished business there,' I replied, staring at the flickering flame of the oil lamp. 'Very important business. Besides, I couldn't possibly live with you and Gavin, you know that. Mothers-in-law tend to get in the way.'

'Then get a place nearby. Like in Haifa,' she said.

I shook my head. 'I'm not even sure I like Israel. Two weeks are hardly enough to make such an important decision,' I fenced.

'Mom, you're the one who said one shouldn't examine anything too closely, that sometimes it's better to plunge headlong into an adventure. Remember how terrified I was of coming to a strange country and meeting strange people with strange customs? Remember how you made it seem so damn easy I couldn't wait to get on a plane?'

'I wanted you to grow feathers and spread your wings,' I said. 'The world you shared with me was much too small for a young girl on the threshold of life. And if things went wrong I was always going to be there to cushion the blow. You even had a return air ticket. What could be safer? Aren't you glad you did come?'

'Oh yes, but I'd be even gladder if you joined us here. You're the only family I have and you're right on the other side of the earth. It's just not right.'

'It's right as long as we love each other.'

'Does that mean you won't even consider it?' she asked unhappily, blinking away the tears that gathered on her lashes.

'I promise to. Can we leave it at that for the time being?'

'Okay. As long as it isn't a definite no,' she agreed reluctantly.

We had more and returned to Naharim slightly intoxicated. We fell on the bed tiredly and talked for a while. She lay in my arms like she used to when she was a little girl, and at that moment I wanted to be nothing other than a mother and she nothing other than a little girl. We fell asleep like that.

Gavin kissed my cheek at the airport, then stood aside while Theresa and I embraced.

'Darling, whatever happens . . . remember I love you very dearly,' I said, touching her tender, young cheek. 'You've always been the most important person in my life, but sometimes there are things we have to do which transgress the bounds of acceptable behaviour. It's so that we can continue to live with ourselves.'

'Mom, what you are trying to say?'

'I don't have time to explain. Be happy. Youth is so terribly short,' I said and broke away from her.

I didn't look back for fear of acknowledging her confusion. The pain I would cause her later weighed heavily on my mind when I boarded the plane.

And then I was on my way back to Oliver Bay. And the second execution.

15

I arrived back in Oliver Bay in early September. The days were still pleasantly warm, but a chill was creeping into the nights. More often now there was a thick blanket of fog in the mornings which took longer to clear as the season progressed towards winter. The sun rose later every day and so did I, but I used the extra time in bed to nurse my anger and plan my next strike. Soon after my return I resumed my gruelling exercise schedule and started feeling fit and well again. I was steadily gaining each lost pound and my face seemed fuller, my colour more healthy. Lulu was well-fed and had glossy fur. After a spate of turning her nose up at the ground meat and raw eggs I offered her she settled down to her old diet again. When I learnt from Meryl that she'd been fed rare steaks and fresh fish during my absence I understood why.

One morning, four days after my return, Meryl arrived in her chauffeur-driven limousine. The uniformed chauffeur remained in the car while she joined me on the patio for tea. She was casually dressed but somehow managed to retain that natural elegance that was characteristic of her.

'Did you enjoy your trip to Israel?' she asked, lighting a Cameo.

'Very much. It wasn't nearly long enough though.'

'What holiday ever is?' she quipped.

For a while we sat quietly. I was glad she had come. I was beginning to like Meryl Johnson, not only because she was a gracious and friendly person but also because she seemed so genuinely interested in me. Whenever I spoke she listened closely and made me feel I was important to her. It also amazed me how perfectly at ease she could be wherever she was, like now. She lazed back in the cushioned cane chair, staring out to sea, her beautiful face serene. Suddenly she looked at me and caught me staring at her.

'Carla, aren't you afraid to live here alone . . . after what happened?' she wanted to know.

'Yes,' I answered honestly. 'I am afraid. Every sound in the cottage frightens me, even in broad daylight. Some nights I hardly sleep at all.'

'Then why on earth do you stay?' she asked, surprised.

'Where else should I go? Back to New York where I'd never had an identity . . . where I was merely another nameless face in the milling crowds? Or should I slither away to another town like Oliver Bay and exist by constantly looking over my shoulder?' I asked, unable to conceal my bitterness.

'You could find someone to share your life with . . . a friend, or a lover. And in a less isolated spot. It can't possibly be healthy living alone like this.'

'Why can't a woman live alone wherever she wants to or whenever she wants to without falling prey to human vultures? Why is it that we are always intimidated by the threat of violence, victimized for our individuality?'

'Carla, Carla, I'm not attacking you. I understand what you're saying, but unfortunately men have been endowed with superior strength and there'll always be those who enjoy using it against weaker people. Do you know that for many years I actually believed I couldn't live with a man? I found them so overpoweringly physical, it offended me. Until I married Cyril. He's kind and considerate and protective. He makes me feel so valuable . . . so very unique. His love for me has never faltered through sixteen years of marriage. Sometimes I think I don't deserve him.'

I watched her silently.

'I didn't love him when I married him, you know,' she continued lazily. 'I thought he was a fool, that he was weak, that I could manipulate him. It was the Johnson name and wealth that attracted me to him in the first place. Does that shock you?'

'No.'

'I was such a screwed-up kid I needed to function behind the protection of the Johnson name. Cyril knew it but wanted me anyway. With patience he won me over and changed my distorted views, now I can't imagine a life without him.'

'Did he know about the rape when he married you?' I asked.

'Who didn't? It happened right here in Oliver Bay. At the cemetery, to be exact. I was only fifteen years old.'

'The cemetery?' I asked, immediately recalling the story Richard had told me at the hospital.

'Yes. My father was a public accountant who had the nasty habit of stealing from his employers and getting fired. He served a short spell in prison in Salt Lake City but it didn't cure him. We moved often, sometimes living under false names in little hick towns in no-man's-land. We moved to Oliver Bay when he got a job in the factory here. They gave us one of the better company houses at the top end of town and for a while we were actually happy. I was praying that Dad would keep his fingers out of the petty cash box, that we wouldn't have to move again. But other things started happening to mar my happiness. I couldn't make friends at school. The children kept me at bay, made me feel as though I didn't belong here. My mother told me to be patient, that they'd eventually come round to accepting us.'

She replaced her empty teacup on the tray and lit another cigarette from the last.

'At that time Cyril was away at a private school in Switzerland and I didn't meet him until we'd been here for five months. He was the only child and heir to the Johnson fortune and that alone

143

fascinated me. Money meant security. When you're rich you don't have to steal other people's and move every few months. We met at the factory one day. I was visiting my father and he was making the grand tour of his future domain. He was so awkward then . . . all ears and eyes and teeth, but I was struck by his easy manner with the staff – management and factory alike. I remember my father saying he was a humane boy, unlike old man Johnson, who was a real tyrant, even towards his own family.'

She inhaled and let the smoke escape through her nose.

'I was a pretty girl and I knew he fell for me that day. Most boys did. It was in their eyes when they looked at me, but no one wanted to be the first to date me. So I started going out alone, to movies mostly, or strolled along the beach with my dog, Caspar. It never occurred to me that I could be in physical danger, not in a town this size. One night I returned from the movies . . . I remember seeing Clint Eastwood in *A Fistful of Dollars*. The street to our house was dark and quiet, my footsteps echoed in the silence. The car came from nowhere and stopped next to me with screeching tyres. I smiled and called hello. How stupidly naïve I was! They bundled me into the car, gagged me with a greasy rag and drove out to the cemetery. They were disgustingly drunk and rowdy, and all the way there they discussed me as though I was a piece of prime meat . . . who would go first, and so on.'

Her liquid eyes had gone hard, her lips were merely a thin line in her pale face.

'Who were they?' I asked.

'One of them was a class ahead of me, but he dropped out and was helping in the school's tuck-shop. His name was Carl Flagg, the son of a local fisherman. The other was Ray Bremmer. He worked in the factory as a machine-hand. They raped me for six hours on a mound of earth, right beside a freshly dug grave. They threatened to bury me alive if I screamed and that gaping hole next to me terrified me even more than they did. They . . . they made me do things that haunted me for years afterwards. And they beat me – savagely. I was so battered my mother fled the hospital in hysterics when she saw me. The factory paid for a plastic surgeon to come out here to reconstruct my face.'

'And the rapists?' I asked, but I already knew the answer.

'All their friends swore under oath that they'd been drinking at the Oyster Inn that night, that they never left before closing time.

144

One claimed to have given them a ride home, and their parents swore they'd never left their homes again. There wasn't even a trial. But through it all I made one good friend in Oliver Bay. Richard Mallen. His father treated me in hospital. Richard was a year younger than me, but he visited me in hospital every day. He brought chocolates and magazines, or sometimes just sat there without speaking.'

I wondered why she put herself through the agony of remembering when it had all happened so long ago. Or did the memories always stay this fresh?

'What happened then?'

'I couldn't go back to school. Nasty rumours spread through town. They said I was an easy lay who'd asked for it, then blamed it on innocent boys. The people hated me and made no secret of it. I refused to leave my room and my mother cried most of the time. My father resigned and we moved on to Louisville. I met Cyril again at a youth leadership seminar in Washington four years later. I was working as a counsellor at a summer camp, trying to figure out what to do with my life. We got married two years later and I came back here with him. Carl and Ray had both left town by then, nobody knew where to. Cyril's father had died, and his mother was so incensed by his "unsuitable" marriage she moved to Miami and refused to speak to me.'

'And you've lived with the anger for so long?' I asked.

'I thought the anger had died . . . until I heard what had happened to you. It brought the past back so vividly it could've been me all over again.'

'Meryl, I remember seeing you at my bedside in the hospital. I have a vague recollection that you kept saying the same thing over and over, but I can't remember what it was.'

'Oh, you do? I didn't think you would. You were still pretty groggy from the sedatives,' she said casually.

'What was it you said?'

'Gosh, I can't say I remember. I was very upset at the time. I saw myself in that bed, all those years back. I believe I cried when I first saw you. I so much wanted to tell you that I knew exactly what you were suffering, but first Richard and then Ella Murdock kept me away from you. They said you had to forget, not be reminded of it. I disagreed, but what could I do?'

'It was kind of you to care. It felt as though no one did,' I said.

'I wasn't the only one. Richard cared very much, and still does. It was the first time I'd seen him lose his cool. He demanded that Sheriff Witmore bring those men in and lock them up like the wild animals they are, but the Sheriff couldn't without a formal complaint from you.'

'It doesn't matter any more, Meryl. I want to forget about it.'

'Carla, did you know that one of your attackers disappeared?'

'Oh?'

'Yes. Doughie Steyl went missing a few weeks back. They haven't been able to trace him. His parents insist he's had an accident somewhere, that he wouldn't have left Oliver Bay,' she said, watching me closely.

I shrugged my shoulders. 'That's totally immaterial to me, Meryl. My attackers don't have identities for me any more. They could've been any number of men going under any number of names, living in any number of towns.'

'If he left town he didn't take any of his personal belongings with him. His room was untouched, he didn't even take his mouth-organ. His mother said he never went anywhere without it.'

'Why are you telling me this?' I asked carefully.

'I just thought you'd like to know. What do you think happened to him, Carla?'

Our eyes met and what I saw in hers made my blood run cold. Did she know?

'Your guess is as good as mine, Meryl. I'm not particularly interested,' I said evenly. 'More tea?'

The spell was broken. 'No, thank you. It's time for me to go. Will you come for dinner soon?'

'I'd love to,' I said and accompanied her to the car.

I felt slightly sick when I returned to the veranda to collect the tea tray. For a few brief seconds Meryl Johnson had looked right into my core and read the truth there. I had seen it in her eyes, the knowledge. What would she do? Point a finger of accusation at me? But how could she? There was nothing to link me to Doughie Steyl's disappearance. Nothing whatsoever. But then, even if she did know, would she want to do something? Somehow I very much doubted that.

Only once since that night did I come face to face with one of my attackers again. One morning I emerged from Bay Traders and bumped into Ax, who was just coming into the store. My reaction was startling. I recoiled as though struck by a rattlesnake, my entire body went into a rigid spasm, my gut contracted painfully.

'Hi, there, Carla,' he greeted, a daring smile curving his fleshy lips.

I brushed past him, my skin crawling with a thousand worms directly from the pits of hell.

'Hey! You're stuck-up now you mix with the Johnsons!' he called after me, then laughed mockingly.

'Hey, you! Shut your trap!' Uncle Billy barked from inside the store. I slammed the car door behind me and drove away, shaking with the aftermath of shock and revulsion.

Two weeks after my return from Israel I accepted an invitation to dine with Richard Mallen, not because I wanted to but because I needed to continue the pretence that I had recovered fully.

Richard's house came as a total surprise. It was double-storeyed and almost completely covered with ivy. The heavy oak front door was patterned with artistic symbols and had a heavy brass knocker and big brass handle. The entire house oozed character and style without being overbearing. The paintings adorning the walls were tasteful, the carpeting rich, and a pleasant aroma of pipe smoke hung inside. A small and frail-looking coloured woman met me at the front door and introduced herself as Rita. She was almost completely grey but with a surprisingly unlined face and lively black eyes.

'I'm sure glad to meet you, Miss Benson. The doctor don't nearly have enough visitors,' she greeted me, then lowered her voice. 'Not that he's home that much, mind. Lives for that hospital and those people who don't even know how to thank him for it. You come right on in and make yourself at home.'

'Thank you, Rita.'

Richard met us in the sitting-room, casually dressed in an open-neck shirt and grey slacks. He took my hand.

'I would've fetched you, Carla,' he said.

'I told you it wasn't necessary.'

'I'm glad you came. Allow me to take your coat,' he offered.

I stood stiffly while he removed it and handed it to the smiling Rita, who left the room with it. The sitting-room was cosy, with some beautiful pieces of furniture that looked hand-crafted. It was the kind of room where a close family would spend a pleasant evening, discussing the events of the past day over a cup of steaming milo. I accepted his invitation to sit down, feeling like an intruder.

'Will you have a glass of wine before dinner? Or a martini?' he asked.

'A martini will do.'

He walked over to the corner bar, opened a small refrigerator and mixed a martini with practised skill, then poured a Scotch for himself. When he handed me mine I drained it much too fast, trying to remember why I had come here. Was I merely taking refuge with Oliver Bay's most prominent citizens as a safety precaution, or was I searching for a flicker of warmth in a world that had gone insane? I didn't know.

Richard was an excellent host, but I couldn't relax. I sat on the edge of the easy chair, tongue-tied and ill-at-ease, telling myself that his manner was solicitous. This could very well have been a waiting-room, I the patient with a mysterious ailment, and he the doctor on duty. Being with him reminded me vividly of how I had lain in a hospital room, my body battered and bleeding, my spirit broken.

Rita served dinner in the dining-room, proudly presenting her thick vegetable broth with fresh rolls, then crisply grilled fish and fresh salad. At first I was too tense to appreciate her meal and had to force myself to eat and pretend an interest in the conversation. But after a few glasses of dry white wine the tension gradually eased and I started responding to his questions about my writing, about Theresa, about my past life in New York. I managed to forget that he was the doctor who had sewn me back together, and related my life in New York with nostalgia. What had seemed an utterly dreary existence a few months ago now sounded like a haven of safety and obscurity.

When we left the table an hour later, he put a protective arm round my waist and guided me to the sitting-room. The casual touch brought me back to reality, reminded me of who I was and the purpose of my visit here. Rita served percolated coffee from a silver pot with a family crest on it, adding fresh cream and fussing over us like a mother-hen. There was an easy camaraderie between her and Richard, like that of mother and son, and I asked him about it once we were alone.

'Rita's been with the family for as long as I can remember. When my mother died she just assumed the role, and I'm too fond of her to object.'

He sat so close to me I could smell the faint aroma of his aftershave lotion. I found his proximity disquieting, his gentle manner disarming. Not only was he a man but a native of Oliver Bay too, and I shouldn't let my guard slip. Ever again.

'Carla, in the hospital you were very distressed about Peter. Are you still convinced that he died that night?'

The reference to Peter almost had me choking on the coffee. Peter was my private pain, not to be shared with anyone.

'Yes. But I prefer to believe that night never happened. Will you indulge me?'

'I don't think it's healthy to, Carla. It's like covering a festering wound so the pus won't escape. The result could be detrimental to your health.'

'The wound has healed,' I said abruptly.

After a short silence he asked: 'Did you love him?'

I looked at him, an angry retort on my lips. I bit it back when I noticed the genuine interest in his eyes, and the compassion that was always present there.

'Does it matter? If I didn't would it justify what they did?'

'No, of course not. I didn't mean it to sound like that.'

'You're a product of the sixties too. You know how much garbage about love was fed to us by the movie-makers in Hollywood during the fifties and sixties.'

'Garbage?'

'Yes. I think those were the worst years to grow up in. For women, at least. Love was one big lie presented to us by those dream-makers of Hollywood. We were transported through the magic of legendary romances that always ended with marriage – the ultimate state of bliss. According to the movie-makers, that is. We sat mesmerized by each passionate kiss, hung onto the lips of tall, dark and handsome heroes who courted women with fault-less chivalry. Alas, reality was a rude awakening. Instead of passionate kisses that accompanied pledges of undying love, we had to suffer the clumsy fumbles on the back seats of cars from immature boys with bad breath and wet lips.'

He laughed softly. 'Immature boys with bad breath grew up too, didn't they?'

'Yes, but I don't think we ever recovered from the shock. When no tall, dark and handsome heroes presented themselves, we married those immature boys with the bad breath and discovered that the happy-ever-after was a vicious circle of pregnant bellies hanging over hot stoves and screaming toddlers littering the floors and making unreasonable demands. The ''boys'' didn't flush the toilet after using it, they farted in bed, they broke wind at the dinner table, they didn't shave over weekends. They cursed us for burning their dinner and for ruining their lives by producing those screaming brats, all by ourselves, in a deliberate plot to deprive them of sleep.'

'You're much too cynical, Carla. Surely some things were good.'

'Cynical? For me Rock Hudson in *Giant* was the personification of the perfect man. We all know he died from AIDS, an over-sexed homosexual. And what about Richard Burton as the strong and silent Anthony in *Cleopatra*? He died a hopeless alcoholic. But worst of all, Elvis Presley, that idol who had us swooning with his oozing sensuality – he died from drug abuse. What went wrong? Am I just being cynical, or were we led by the nose by shrewd agents and money-grabbing producers?'

'Perhaps you should try and see it in more perspective, Carla. After the Second World War people were battle-weary, caught in the clutches of depression, recession, unemployment, hunger. The movies provided an hour or two of escapist entertainment, gave people the courage to continue and to hope for a better tomorrow. Shouldn't they be credited with that, at least?'

I looked at him. 'It wasn't fair. We clung to illusions and reality became a farce, until they started making those movies that shocked. Suddenly we could identify with real people in real situations and that's where the cynicism crept in.'

'I didn't go to the movies much. But then . . . I haven't done much of anything. There is enough reality in illness and injury. I don't think I could've handled any more.'

Rita entered with a fresh pot of coffee, then bade us good-night.

'Have you never married?' I asked once we were alone again.

'Never. All the girls I fancied tended to regard me as their big brother,' he replied casually, and offered me a cigarette. I accepted and waited for him to light it. I poured the coffee while he lit his pipe.

'Wasn't it perhaps safer to hide behind that guise of big brother and doctor?' I asked again.

He chuckled softly, sucking on the pipe. 'Are you always this analytical?'

'No,' I said, smiling for the first time. I was beginning to enjoy this evening more than I had bargained for, and it disturbed me. What disturbed me even more was that I found it so easy to talk to him, that with him I had a desire to take my shoes off and curl my legs on the settee. But I had no right to these forbidden fruits. I was a killer.

'Will you have a liqueur?'

'No, thank you. It's late,' I said and got to my feet. A look of disappointment crossed his face, and I suddenly realized that Richard Mallen was a very lonely man.

'It's only just gone nine. Wouldn't you like to listen to some music? Richard Clayderman, perhaps?'

'Not tonight, Richard,' I said, suddenly anxious to leave. He had invited me here because he felt sorry for me, not because he was lonely. I was the underdog, qualifying for his inherently sympathetic nature. I wanted none of it.

He fetched my coat and helped me into it. For a few seconds his hands rested on my shoulders while I stood rigidly.

'Carla, is something wrong? Did I offend you in some way?' he asked, frowning.

I moved away. 'Not at all,' I said, my voice falsely cheerful.

'For a while this evening you dropped your guard and actually opened up a little. Now it's back in full force. Can't you learn to trust someone again? Just a little at a time?'

Without replying I walked to the front door, and he followed me.

'Thank you for dinner, Richard. My compliments to Rita. Good-night,' I said, avoiding his eyes.

'Good-night, Carla.'

That weekend I joined Meryl at Pelham's Bluff. Cyril was in Canada, attending an international fishing convention. The boys were away at boarding school and we had the large mansion to ourselves.

On Saturday we swam in the heated pool and sipped cocktails and discussed feminine matters such as fashion and men and women's contributions to the twentieth century. I hadn't had a female friend since primary school and was surprised to find that I enjoyed the frank discussions and shared confidences. We both felt that male chauvinism was still alive and well and thriving in America, but that the initial hysteria of the sixties woman had been replaced by a more subtle tenacity to succeed in a man's world and retain a good measure of femininity at the same time.

'Cyril claims a woman's place in society is unique and can't be filled by anything else, that by usurping man's place we are leaving a gap in the social structure and that the family unit will eventually collapse. But then Cyril's always been conservative to the point of being irritating. Do you know that he wouldn't make love to me until our wedding-night? And that he'd only had one prior sexual encounter before that night? With a high-class prostitute in Dallas. His father arranged it, telling Cyril he wasn't going to be a man until he'd tasted the ancient pleasures of copulating. As it turned out, poor Cyril ejaculated while she was still undressing him and couldn't get it up again. So the last of the red-hot lovers bit the dust.'

We laughed hilariously. No doubt the subject of our laughter would've been indignant had he known. Saturday evening we watched two old movies on television, toasted marshmallows and retired early. We started Sunday by having a lavish breakfast in the garden under a large umbrella, then Meryl suggested that she show me the estate on horseback.

The mare assigned to me was a proud, chestnut-brown animal with a surprisingly gentle nature. She watched me patiently while I ran a hand over her powerful frame. We trotted away from the house, a cool sea breeze in our hair. Meryl was relaxed and seemed to flow with the graceful movements of her horse, and for one fleeting moment I wondered what she would say if she knew she was riding with a killer planning another two murders.

The estate was enormous, the scenery uncluttered. Sand dunes, almost symmetrical, rose and fell for miles, with the sea in the background. On the crest of the highest dune we drew the horses in and sat there quietly, our eyes roaming across the deserted coastline. Then Meryl spoke.

'When I first came to Pelham's Bluff I regularly raced my horse along the beach there and screamed as loud as I could. The sensation was absolutely exhilarating, the effect more beneficial than a year on an analyst's couch. I was so damned intimidated by the Johnsons and their way of life. I still do it sometimes when my emotions are in a turmoil and I can't express them. Cyril loathes emotionalism and absolutely forbids what he calls tantrums, and you won't believe how much of a strain that can be. Perhaps you should try it.'

'What? Screaming?'

'Yes.'

'Oh no, I couldn't.'

'Why not?' she challenged. 'You're a very disciplined person, Carla. Perhaps too disciplined. I haven't once heard you curse those men, or seen you cry, or demand justice. Are you keeping it all bottled up inside, or are you really as cool and calm as you pretend to be?'

I turned away. 'I don't want to discuss it, Meryl.'

'God, I'm sorry. I just don't know how to mind my own business. Will you promise me one thing, though?'

'What?'

'If you ever need me . . . in any way, will you tell me?'

I looked at her. 'I think I can manage, Meryl, but I appreciate your interest . . . more than I can say.'

'It's more than just an interest. I relate to you, Carla,' she said sincerely.

'Thank you,' I said simply, and steered my horse away. She followed.

A mile further we unexpectedly came across a little log cabin facing the sea. It seemed very old and was badly neglected.

'That used to be my father-in-law's cottage,' Meryl explained. 'Gerald often withdrew from the world of high finance and frozen fish to lock himself away here, and nobody was allowed to disturb him. About ten years ago Cyril had it renovated and we decided to spend a weekend of solitude here. But the floor creaked most eerily when we walked across it, the wind whistled through the gaps in the logs, and all night long it sounded like human cries. We fled back to the house in the middle of the night, convinced the place was haunted.'

'What was he like? Gerald Johnson?'

'He was a sour old man who couldn't tolerate weaknesses in others, yet frequently indulged his own. When he was younger he was the supreme law in Oliver Bay, and any misdemeanour was punishable by public lynchings . . . administered by himself, of course. He mellowed during the last two years of his life, but even then he used to fly into uncontrollable rages which had his family thoroughly cowed. A tyrant like him couldn't survive today, not with unions and protective legislation.'

We dismounted, held the horses' reins and strolled along the lonely stretch of beach.

'Carla, do you like Richard?' she asked casually.

I continued to stare at the sea. 'Richard is a good doctor and a kind man, Meryl,' I answered evasively.

'I have an admission to make. I used to be in love with him. Very much so. There was a time when I could've responded to the loneliness in his eyes. It was when Cyril and I were still dating and Cyril brought me home for weekends and holidays. But Richard was a medical student then and penniless. He didn't fit into my scheme of things. Later, after I'd married Cyril, I realized that it was Richard I really wanted. There was a time when I would've gladly surrendered my world of luxury for his love, but by then he was treating me like a sister. Do you know that the most sensual experience I've ever had was when Richard delivered my eldest son? The blend of pain and pleasure was so exquisite it made me cry, and Richard thought I was crying from happiness at the sight of my son.'

For a while I was speechless and somewhat embarrassed at this peep into her deepest recesses. It was like seeing her naked. 'Isn't the grass always greener on the other side?' I asked then, staring out at the sea.

'I suppose so. My infatuation with Richard eventually burnt itself out and I learnt to love him like a brother. I would've liked to see him settled, with a family of his own.'

'I'm sure he never lacked opportunities.'

'In Oliver Bay? Are you kidding?' she laughed. 'Years ago I tried to play Cupid by inviting some of my eligible friends for holidays and introducing them to Richard. One night he called me into the study, thanked me politely for my subtle but transparent efforts, and asked me not to do it again. He never gave me a reason for his lack of interest.'

'Perhaps he's gay. Ever considered that?' I asked bluntly.

'Oh, Carla! How outrageous! He's anything but gay, believe me. He had a long-standing affair with Ella Murdock. Everyone thought he would marry her, then they just seemed to drift apart. It happens sometimes when people grow up together. I think Ella still loves him. She never got married herself.'

I remembered the immaculate, efficient nurse who had shared my life at Eve's Nook for a few weeks, tried to imagine her in a passionate embrace with Richard Mallen, and failed.

The weekend finally drew to a close, and I had to continue with the life that had been carved for me by fate. When I thanked Meryl for her hospitality and companionship, I meant it sincerely. For two days she had allowed me to forget the cobwebs of intrigue in which I was caught, and to share her uncomplicated and placid world.

16

With cold logic I scheduled the second execution for the first day of October. Too much time was elapsing since their crime and I didn't want them to think they could erase one night of brutal violence with a mere shrug. In spite of my friendship with the Johnsons and Richard Mallen the town's attitude towards me didn't change. They no longer sneered openly but avoided eye-contact with me and sniggered behind my back. I went about my business ignoring them and hiding my anger.

I woke that morning with an awareness of a different smell in the air. It was a sharp, salty scent, and when I went outside I saw why. The sun was obscured by a bank of cumulus cloud, their dome-shaped crests expanding rapidly across the sky. There was a cold dampness in the air and the sea, as though sensing the pending storm, roared in angry retaliation.

I strolled in the small garden, remembering how Peter had enjoyed working here, his chest bare, his sculptured body glistening with a thin layer of perspiration. The weeds were thriving again, spreading their ugly tentacles against the north wall of Eve's Nook. We had wanted to plant something exotic there, something that would sprout bright, colourful flowers in spring and summer, instead the weeds resembled the evil that had crept into our lives and torn us apart.

A gale-force wind started blowing during mid-morning, screamed its way along the coast and showered the cottage with sand. By lunch time the storm broke loose in all its fury. Rain pelted the windows with frightening force and Lulu decided the safest place was under the bed. I remained sitting at the window seat, watching the malevolence of nature and preparing myself for the coming night. After tonight the gun and my nocturnal clothing would have to be concealed in a safe place. Suspicion was bound to be aroused after the second disappearance and I didn't want any conclusive evidence lying around. I also decided I didn't like the gun as an executioner's tool. Being shot was by far too quick and painless a death. Take Doughie Steyl, for instance. He had never even known what hit him, and why. His execution had lacked the brutality, the shame, the humiliation, the pain of Peter's, and after killing him I had felt strangely let down. Doughie Steyl hadn't suffered. Yet, after many sleepless nights and restless days I failed to invent a more savage and prolonged execution without attracting attention. What if the next one should call out and alert others? I couldn't risk discovery until all three had died, and by then it wouldn't matter. The third one, I decided, would suffer the full brunt of my anger and compensate for the easy deaths of the others.

When the sun set I ate my dinner of cold tuna and salad without feeling hunger or tasting the unappetizing food. I swallowed mechanically and washed it down with two cups of strong, black coffee. Eating had become purely an act of fuel injection for a body that needed to survive until its predetermined tasks were complete. As I had done the first time, I watched the clock and paced the cottage restlessly until it was time to prepare myself. The ritual was more familiar now. Dark, stinking clothing, hair hidden inside a seaman's cap, a black moustache drawn on my upper lip, the gun in its holster around my waist.

By midnight the rain had settled down to a fine drizzle. I left the cottage and started my jog across the sand, while gusts of wind plucked at my body and stung my cheeks with icy drops. The night was very cold and pitch-dark. My sneakers sank into the soggy sand and soon my clothing was soaked right through to the skin. To my right the sea battered the shore with angry waves, leaving a ragged line of frothing foam behind. Once I stumbled over a dead log and fell sprawling onto a pile of slimy seaweed. The gun dug painfully into my right hip, but I got up and continued the unpleasant journey.

The cement boulders were wet and slippery tonight, and I had to climb carefully, making sure I had a good grip before taking the next step. In the harbour the anchored trawlers creaked loudly in the strong wind and bashed noisily against the tyres along the pier. It looked as though the entire fleet was anchored here tonight. Obviously the weather had prevented them from going out to sea today. For a while I crouched behind the oil drums, ensuring there was no one in sight, then walked hurriedly along the pier towards the factory.

The large doors of the factory were tightly shut tonight, but there were lights on inside and I could hear the hum of machinery. The warehouse door and the one leading to the pet-food section were shut too. There were no coaches on the railroad lines to afford me shelter tonight, but visibility was restricted and no one would recognize me. I walked with my hands buried in my pockets, my head down against the driving rain. I ran across the railroad tracks towards the pet-food section. There was no fear or anxiety in my heart, only a cold determination to conclude my task, in spite of the odds.

I reached the door to the pet-food section and tried it. It was locked from the inside. I stood in the pale light of the bare bulb burning just above it, shivering in the fine drizzle and cold wind. Unable to accept defeat, I decided to wait. I sat down with my back against the wall, drawing negligible shelter from a rusty canopy above the door.

The hours passed slowly and the rain kept falling – sometimes hardly above a drizzle, at other times pouring heavily. Water ran from my woollen cap into my eyes, blinding me. Streams of muddy water washed against my buttocks and over my legs, and soon a cold numbness set into my muscles. After a while it got so

157

cold my teeth started chattering, my nose running. The wind was howling furiously round the brick monster, plucking mercilessly at my wet body. I deliberately shut my mind off from the cold and discomfort and continued my solitary wait.

While I waited I remembered my father – a short, stocky man with cold blue eyes and thin, bloodless lips. I was only nine years old when he first took my hand, unzipped his pants and ordered me to play with him. I was too young to grasp the significance of the strange request, but my fear of him had been too ingrained to query the order. His soft, pasty phallus slowly hardened into a rigid appendage, his breath racing through his wet lips, his eyes cloudy. When my thin arm got tired he shouted for me to go faster and faster, until I sobbed with fear and discomfort. When a warm, milky fluid suddenly squirted over my hand, I backed away in terror, convinced I had done something awfully wrong and would be punished for it. Instead he snapped at me to bugger off, and I fled, sobbing. That was only the first of many such nights, nights during which he cursed me and slapped me when my movements weren't fast enough. Later he demanded that I take him in my mouth, and hit me with his fists when I gagged.

For the first time I admitted to myself that the night I killed Doughie I had also killed my father, that tonight he would die again, and that he would die a third time with the third victim. He and Arthur Benson and all the men who had ever subjected women to fear and humiliation. Perhaps by killing them I could erase the past and regain a vestige of human dignity.

The factory fell silent at 3.47 a.m. From past observation I knew the shifts changed at 4 a.m., and I waited patiently for the minutes to pass. I frequently shifted position to ease the advancing cramps, but the numbness was spreading rapidly throughout my body. For a while the only sounds were those of the wind and the rain and the sea, and from the harbour the creaking of the tugs. Then, shortly after 4 a.m., the din of machinery inside the factory increased in volume. Once I heard men talking nearby, heard someone run in the rain, then the human sounds faded while I remained sitting in the steady downpour.

'What the fuck you doing out here?'

Admittedly my guard had slipped, but he had appeared so suddenly through the door I'd had no warning. One moment all was quiet, then the door next to me had been flung open and he was standing there, silhouetted against the light inside – Sam Shroder. His bulky frame towered above me, his huge hands swaying at his sides. He wore a dirty brown raincoat, the collar up against his neck.

I struggled stiffly to my feet, watching him with mounting alarm. His mean eyes were narrowed against the rain.

'You deaf, or what?' he snarled. I was on my feet, but my legs were so numb I had to lean against the wall for support. I waited tensely for him to recognize me. The terror of that night was welling up inside me again and I had to refrain from screaming.

'No,' I croaked, deepening my voice.

'Who the hell are you and what're you doing out here?'

'I . . . I'm looking for work,' I said hurriedly. My hand slipped in under the jacket and found the clasp of the holster.

'Work? At four o' fucking clock in the morning? You gone mad, boy?' he barked, stabbing his head with a forefinger.

My wet fingers closed round the cold steel of the gun. He was standing too close to me. If I produced the gun now he could overpower me before I had time to pull the trigger.

'I been waiting since last night,' I said, keeping my voice low.

'For what?'

'I didn't know where to go.'

'Where you from, boy?' he asked suspiciously.

'Down south. Heard there was work up here,' I said, and moved away to the left.

'Fucking arsehole. You think someone's gonna give you a job if you sit out here in the pissing rain? Get your arse outa here and come back in the morning. The office's at the other side of the building. Now go on! Get the hell out!'

I backed away, feeling faint with relief.

'What's that black muck on your face?' he asked again, approaching me.

The rain had smeared the black moustache! I wiped at it with the sleeve of my jacket.

'Dunno. Musta got grease on my face,' I said hurriedly.

'Punk! Now get the hell outa here,' he ordered, turned his back to me, and walked away in the rain.

I hesitated only briefly, then followed him at a safe distance. He heard me and swung round.

'Don't ya hear too well, boy?'

159

I stopped. 'Can I watch you work? I once worked in a fish factory out in Atlanta . . . just been wondering if it's all the same here.'

His eyes swept over my dripping wet body and I wondered if the outline of my breasts showed through the wet jacket.

'You hang round here one more second and I'm gonna kick your arse from here to hell and back. You hear me, boy?'

He meant it. Of my three attackers he had been the most vicious. He had almost killed me with his bare fists that night, indifferent to my screams of agony. Suddenly the fear inside me was replaced by seething anger and a cold hatred. I withdrew the gun from its holster, held it in both hands and pointed it at his chest. He didn't notice it at first.

'Remember me, Sam?' I hissed through clenched teeth, blinking my eyes against the rain.

'What? What did ya say, boy?'

I pulled the trigger. There was a click and nothing else. He advanced on me, his bulky arms swaying at his sides.

'Hey! What're you doing? What you got there?'

I backed away and stumbled over something at my feet. I struggled frantically to regain my balance, and succeeded. He was almost upon me. Panic-stricken I raised the gun and fired again. The shot was muffled and should've hit him, but he kept coming. I shot him again, holding my breath. Abruptly he stopped, a mere two feet away from me. His hand went to his chest and came away bloodied. Immediately the rain washed the red liquid from his hand. He looked at me, his eyes stretched wide with disbelief.

'Jesus God . . . you shot me,' he said, his mouth falling slack.

'Remember me now, Sam?' I asked again and waited, the gun levelled at his chest. Yet this was all wrong, I thought. This wasn't how it was supposed to have been. He wasn't supposed to die out here in the open.

'What . . . did . . . you . . . do . . . that . . . for?' he gasped, clutching his chest with both hands, his face a mask of shock and pain. I pulled the cap from my head. My hair fell in wet strands to my shoulders. 'Remember me, Sam? Remember a young man named Peter? Remember a foggy night in June?' I asked, smiling a sick smile that twisted my face.

Slowly recognition registered on his stunned features. He

opened his mouth to say something, but instead blood gushed onto his lower lip, mixed with the rain and dripped onto his chest.

'Oh, Jesus . . .' he muttered, turned away and staggered towards the side door.

I aimed carefully and shot him a third time. His body jerked violently when the bullet hit him between the shoulder blades, but he kept going. I aimed again, excitement pulsing through my veins. I'm doing this for us, Peter! Can you see me? Can you see me right now killing them for us? My finger was closing round the trigger again when his legs suddenly buckled and he crumpled to the ground. He fell heavily and lay still in the rain.

My breath was wheezing through my throat while I searched the ground for the spent cartridges. It felt as though I had just run fifty miles. It took a minute or two but I found all three and pocketed them. I replaced the knitted cap on my head, then ran to his still form. He lay close to the door, face up in the rain. Any moment now someone could come along and discover me here. I had to work fast.

I opened the door to the pet-food section, went inside and looked around. There was no one, the belt was switched off. I returned to him, grabbed hold of both his ankles and pulled. He was heavier than Doughie Steyl, but I'd had more time to regain my strength. Little by little I dragged him to the conveyor belt. A trail of blood followed him, but I would worry about that afterwards.

When I reached the conveyor belt I sank to my knees, totally exhausted. I leaned with my face against the belt, my heart pounding in my ears. My body had taken as much abuse as it possibly could, but my task had hardly begun. I looked at him. His face was turned to the side, wet and bloodied, his raincoat torn and drenched with blood. In the pale light his complexion was a sickly grey. I felt nothing – no remorse, no revulsion, no association with him.

After a while I forced myself to get up. I gripped him under the armpits and heaved with all my remaining strength. His head fell precariously to one side, but I managed to lift him high enough to drop the upper part of his body onto the edge of the belt. I balanced him there with my hip while pulling at the lower part of his body. My muscles screamed in protest, but I managed to lift him inch by inch until the lower part of his body was on the edge of the belt too. Then his head slipped over the side and he started falling to the ground again. I caught him and shoved, groaning deep in my throat with the effort. Finally he rolled over the edge and fell heavily onto the belt.

And then, to my horror, he groaned. I stared at him in ghastly fascination. Dear God, he was still alive! What was he? An immortal monster? Was he going to get up now and say he's tired of playing this boring game and can we knock it off? Totally exhausted I leaned against the belt and watched him. The fingers on his right hand twitched, he moved his head slightly. His mouth opened like a fish out of water and blood gushed from it.

I stumbled towards the control box, my breath whistling through my parched throat. I reached it and searched for the control lever, driven by a need to hurry. I couldn't see it in the dim light, yet it had to be here! I had watched them starting the conveyor belt from here many times! Then, from somewhere close by, someone suddenly called out. I froze.

'Hey, Sam! You out there?'

I waited, my eyes riveted on the bloodied figure stirring on the belt. Slowly his one bloodied hand crept over the edge.

'Sam!' the voice called again. I sat rigidly, my hand on the gun. Suddenly there was the dull bang of a door being slammed shut, followed by silence.

I resumed my search, found the control lever and moved it to the 'on' position. There was a shrill squeak and the conveyor belt sprang into action. I turned back to watch. He had raised himself over the edge, but the pull of the belt was too strong. He fell back onto it and rapidly moved towards the mincer. Just before he reached it he uttered a long, low cry, and in a last desperate attempt to evade death he gripped the edge of the belt. While his body disappeared into the mincer with amazing speed, the hand remained clutching the edge, blood spraying from the severed wrist. I approached it, resisting the nausea that threatened me. I couldn't leave it there. They had left nothing of Peter's behind, I would leave nothing of theirs behind. I gripped it by the wrist and pulled. It twitched in my hand before it came away. The fingers curled inwards and touched the palm of my hand. Repulsed, I threw it into the mincer. It disappeared in a flash.

His death hadn't been nearly as easy as Doughie's, but then I

162

hadn't wanted it to be easy. During his final moments on earth Sam Shroder had known he was going to die, and why. I switched the belt off again and listened for any unusual sounds. There were none. I fetched the bucket and mop I had seen them use many times, filled it with water from a tap above a cement basin and proceeded to mop up the trail of blood leading to the conveyor belt.

Weak and utterly exhausted, I stumbled out of the building and ran through the driving rain back to Eve's Nook. But my task wasn't complete yet. At the cottage I stripped off the bloodied clothing, rolled it into a bundle and put it into two empty shoe boxes lined with plastic. The gun and holster went into another shoe box. I carried both boxes out into the rain, fetched the spade from the garage and proceeded to dig a hole in the soggy garden. From the sitting-room window Lulu watched me mutely, the only witness to my crime.

I buried the boxes approximately two feet deep, grateful for the rain which immediately washed away all traces of digging. When I went back into the cottage the first light of dawn was turning the overcast sky grey. I ran a shower as hot as my body could take it, and allowed the blessed warmth to seep back through my pores and into my bloodstream. I soaped myself again and again, washing away the traces of the past night – the contamination of his wicked blood, the after-taste of fear and hatred that still clung to my skin. I stepped out of the shower, feeling purged.

I had killed Sam Shroder and Doughie Steyl with the same lack of emotion with which I would've swatted a fly. Now only one remained – Ax Reevers. For the first time I admitted to myself that it was Ax's death I most looked forward to. Ax had been the leader, the instigator of their evil deeds. Without him I doubted the others would've had the courage to act.

I enjoyed a glass of chilled, dry wine before going to bed.

17

I woke with a burning fever and dry, racking cough, and when I moved every muscle in my body hurt, even those I never knew I had. This was the penalty I'd have to pay for the long, cold hours I had spent in the rain, stalking a killer. It was still raining outside, but the angry wind had died down. Water dripped from the leaking gutter to a spot just below my bedroom window with a regular plop-plop which sounded almost like a heartbeat. For a while I just lay there, listening to its monotonous beat, trying to remember what day it was. My mind was fogged with fever and I soon abandoned the effort. Lulu, who was sitting at the foot of the bed, was startled when I coughed. With lightning speed she jumped off the bed and fled from the room.

I struggled out of the bed and walked drunkenly to the bathroom. My head hurt so badly I was convinced there was a brick inside, and all hell's fires burnt in my bronchial tubes. In the medicine chest I discovered an old bottle of cough mixture but couldn't open it. The sugary substance had calcified round the lid and nothing short of breaking it would release its much needed contents. I sat down on the edge of the bath, feeling miserable and sick and alone.

Outside a car stopped, and I listened while wet footsteps approached Eve's Nook. Were they coming to question me already? Had they found something at the factory to connect me to Sam's bizarre death? I inspected my face in the mirror above the basin, looking for tell-tale signs of last night's deed. Or was it the night before? I hadn't grown fangs or devilish horns or hair on my cheeks. The face staring back at me was flushed with fever, the eyes bloodshot, the lips dry. I looked like a sick woman, not a cold-blooded executioner.

It was Meryl, standing under a black umbrella. As soon as I opened the door she brushed past me.

'God, what frightful weather! Whoever said earth is a friendly planet?'

I coughed drily, leaning against the door. 'Yes, it's pretty awful,' I croaked.

She turned to me. 'Carla! You're ill.'

'Just a lousy chill.'

'It sounds far worse than a lousy chill. Get right back to bed. I'll send Paul to fetch Richard at once.'

'No,' I objected feebly. 'I'll be fine. A day in bed . . .'

'Don't be so damn stubborn, Carla. Do as I say,' she ordered, and I obeyed meekly.

While we waited for Richard to arrive she made tea and shared a cup with me sitting curled up at the foot of the bed. Her eyes never left my face and she winced every time I coughed.

'I want you to come back to Pelham's Bluff with me, Carla. You can't stay here alone,' she said.

'Oh, no,' I said, shaking my head. 'I'll be fine. Really.'

'Why can't you accept some goodwill? Why be so bloody independent?' she asked heatedly.

When Richard arrived she took the tea cups to the kitchen, leaving us alone. His manner was gentle but faultlessly professional.

'How long have you been ill, Carla?' he wanted to know, sitting down beside me. I got a whiff of pipe smoke.

'I don't know. What day is it?'

'It's Wednesday, the 3rd.'

I had slept for over twenty-four hours. 'Since yesterday, I guess.'

'You guess? You mean you don't know?'

'I feel a bit confused. My head . . .'

'What more do you want to subject yourself to before you leave this isolated cottage?' he asked brusquely.

I stared at him silently. His cool fingers touched me. The examination that followed was detached and quick, yet for me it had a personal quality. When he listened to my chest with a stethoscope I shifted uncomfortably on the bed, acutely aware of my naked breasts with the criss-cross scars where Doughie's teeth had sunk in. He didn't seem to notice and kept his face discreetly turned away.

He left enough medication to cure an army and promised to call again. Meryl fed Lulu that day and returned the next with a flask of thick broth and fresh rolls. I felt well enough to sit up and we ate it sitting on the bed like old and trusted friends.

'Carla, I think it's time I told you how very much I admire you. You're so positive, so sure of yourself. You're a survivor. You've overcome that ghastly attack and continue living here as though nothing has happened. You've written a book and raised a child alone while you kept a career going. You're the kind of woman I've always wanted to be.'

Meryl Johnson admiring me? Meryl who had everything – from a doting husband and two sons to beauty, wealth and respect? I tried to reply but a fit of coughing left me drained.

'Sometimes I feel there should be more to life than just being Cyril's wife and the mother of his children,' she continued. 'I would like to have an identity of my own. Something that's as unique to me as yours is to you.'

'More often than not I doubt that I have one at all,' I said.

'Carla . . . a while ago, when we were sitting outside talking, I wasn't totally honest with you. One of the reasons I married Cyril was to have a seat of power in Oliver Bay. These very people were the ones who had ostracized me as a child, laughed at my misfortune, protected those boys from the law. I never forgave them for it. I wanted to have their fates in my hands, play God with their lives. And for a while I did. The families of those boys have long since left Oliver Bay, driven away by me. I persecuted them in every possible way, made sure they couldn't work anywhere in this town. Over the years I've decided the fate of other families connected with that rape too, but once the sweet taste of revenge was expended, I started searching for something more. Only, there doesn't appear to be more.'

'It's because there isn't more, Meryl. If you search too hard for meaning to life it'll only depress you, so why bother?'

'Are you happy, Carla?'

'No.'

'What is it you want from life? Fame and fortune? Recognition? Love?'

'The right to be myself and to live without anxieties, mostly. And to die without pain, and at all times . . . to have dignity.' And to kill one more rapist who had deprived me of all those qualities, I wanted to add, but didn't.

166

To my surprise her liquid eyes filled with tears, but I didn't know if they were for me or herself.

The weather didn't improve for days. It continued to rain and the air I breathed remained damp and salty. I was confined to the cottage, wheezing and coughing, unaware of the passage of time. I slept most of the time and when awake stared at the rivulets of water running down the window panes. Richard's calls were regular but professional, and on the third day I asked him not to return. He looked at me searchingly, but didn't comment.

As soon as I felt better I started spending long hours sitting in front of the typewriter, printing words that formed disjointed sentences with distorted meanings. Sometimes I laughed out loud and sometimes I felt like weeping bitterly, only I couldn't. I tore the pages up and tried again. And again. Somewhere, buried beneath all the anger and hatred lay my dormant creative powers, straining to be released. All I had to do was unlock the door and set them free. It seemed so goddamn simple if only it wasn't so goddamn complicated. There was order in the universe but not in my life.

I was lonely. It was a loneliness that had little to do with being alone. It was a deep-rooted ache – a longing for the love I had been denied as a child and for most of my adult life. I was constantly aware of the emptiness of my double bed, the solitary seclusion of Eve's Nook. The teddy bears stared at me with their lifeless, glassy eyes, their fixed grins mocking me. While I stood in front of the window staring out at the rain, I felt like the last person left on a desolate earth, and I started wishing I had never come to Oliver Bay.

One evening, when the night sky was clear and the moon threw its pale light over the earth, Richard came without his medical bag. I watched him through the window of the darkened sitting-room. He was clutching a neat bunch of red carnations in one hand, and almost slipped on the wet stairs leading to my front door. His knock reverberated through Eve's Nook, while I remained standing rigidly in the dark. He left after the third knock, still clutching the flowers, and I felt strangely sad while I watched him go.

Cyril and Meryl Johnson had gone to Europe for two weeks. She sent me a postcard from Paris with a few short sentences scribbled on the back, inviting me to attend Cyril's birthday party at Pelham's Bluff on the 4th of November.

Sheriff Witmore called exactly ten days after Sam Shroder's disappearance, which had been reported in the *Oliver Post* with more fanfare than Doughie Steyl's. He was hailed as the hero of the 1981 sea disaster when two trawlers had run aground on the reefs at Jutters Point, leaving sixteen men drowned and many more injured. Sam Shroder had single-handedly braved the raging sea to rescue five men with an inflatable dinghy. He had also been the man who had sodomised me and battered me with brutal disregard.

I had been expecting Sheriff Witmore. If he hadn't come he would've been a worse policeman than I believed. He politely removed his hat after entering the cottage. I invited him to sit and offered him something to drink, but he declined. His manner was guarded, his eyes roamed over the room, inspecting and examining.

'Are you still living here alone?' he asked.

'No. I live with my cat, Lulu,' I replied.

He smiled patiently. 'That wasn't what I meant.'

'I know what you meant, Sheriff. If you want to know if I've picked up any more drifters . . . the answer is no. I live alone,' I said levelly, meeting his gaze squarely.

'You ever heard from that young fella again?' he asked.

'No.'

'Hmm. What did you say his last name was?'

'I didn't say. I don't know, and it doesn't matter at all. He is dead.'

'How do you know that, Miss Benson? You seen a body?'

'No.'

'Then what do you base your assumption on?'

'I told you at the hospital. Why did you come here, Sheriff?'

He looked at his notebook before replying. 'Where were you on the night of the first, Miss Benson?'

'The first? Why the first?'

'Just answer my question,' he said shortly.

'Where I am every day and every night. Here, at Eve's Nook.'
'Alone?'
'What else?' I asked before succumbing to a fit of coughing.
'Then I suppose you have the same answer for the night of the 12th of August?'
'You suppose right, Sheriff.'
He looked at me, drumming his fingers on the armrest of the chair.
'Something mighty strange is happening right here in my town and I don't like it one bit,' he said slowly, his eyes boring into mine.
I raised my eyebrows. 'Oh?'
'A few weeks back, on the night of the twelfth of August, Doughie Steyl disappeared like a puff of smoke in the air. He left for work as usual, carrying a pack of sandwiches and a flask of coffee. No one remembers seeing him arrive at the factory and he never got back home. It seems that somewhere between his house and the factory he simply vanished off the face of the earth. Weird, ain't it?'
I held his gaze. 'I would say so, yes. Unless he left town without telling anyone,' I said, and coughed again.
'With what? His folks say he had two dollars in his pocket, no clothes, no nothing,' he said, watching me. I gazed at him silently, totally unruffled.
'And now, what's even more weird, is that Sam Shroder disappeared too,' he continued. 'On the morning of the second he arrived at the factory for his 4 a.m. shift. A co-worker saw him going out into the rain to take a leak and that's the last anyone's seen of him. Just like Doughie he disappeared into thin air too.'
I lit a cigarette with steady hands and succumbed to a fit of coughing when the smoke reached my congested lungs.
'I don't understand why you're telling me this, Sheriff,' I said once I regained my breath.
'I'll tell you why, Miss Benson. Because I think you know what happened to those boys,' he said, his eyes suddenly hard.
'And what do you base that assumption on?' I countered evenly.
He leaned forward in the chair, his eyes cold. 'It took me a while to make the connection. You were raped and beaten and accused three local boys of the crime – Sam Shroder, Doughie

Steyl and Ax Reevers. The same night your young boyfriend disappeared and you claimed they killed him. Now the boys you accused are disappearing one by one. Coincidence, Miss Benson?'

'Yes, Sheriff. I haven't seen any of those men since . . . since that night.'

'I think you're lying, Miss Benson. I think you know what happened to them,' he said, stabbing the armrest with his index finger.

I stared at him. When the time was right I would tell him everything, give him all the gory details of the boys' disappearances. But not while Ax was still alive. He would have to wait a while longer.

'I'm inclined to take offence at your insinuation, Sheriff, but I realize you're only doing your duty. I'm afraid I can't help you,' I said, then coughed into a tissue.

'Pretty nasty cough you have there, Miss Benson. You been out in the rain? On, say, the night of the first?'

I smiled. 'No, Sheriff. I don't like being wet.'

He shuffled on the couch and consulted his notebook again.

'I'll tell you what else I'm thinking, Miss Benson. I think you're protecting that young drifter. I think he's hiding out here somewhere, knocking the boys off one by one. I believe they knocked him about that night, he recovered somewhere else and came back here, taking revenge. Where is he, Miss Benson?'

'Peter died that night, Sheriff. Please go now. I can't help you with your investigation.'

'Not so fast. I have a warrant here authorizing me to search these premises,' he said, pulled a folded sheet of paper from his shirt pocket and handed it to me. I read the typewritten words. It was a search-warrant, signed by Judge H. J. Vanhess.

'This wasn't necessary, you know. All you had to do was ask me. I have nothing to hide. Be my guest,' I said and handed him the warrant. 'I'll be outside if you need me.'

'Kidnapping and murder are capital crimes, Miss Benson. You wouldn't make yourself guilty to being an accessory?'

'No, Sheriff.'

He watched me silently while I put on a cardigan. I left the cottage and walked towards the rocks. The beach was strewn with rotting seaweed that had washed out during the storm and the stench was bad. The cold wind tore at my flimsy dress and stung my eyes. I climbed to my favourite spot and sat down facing the sea. It was high tide and the waves broke against the rocks with such fury that white foam sprayed a few feet high into the air and splashed through crevices. I sat very still, watching a large oil tanker passing slowly on the horizon.

A sea-gull landed on the rocks beside me and watched me with its red, beady eyes. It was so close I could reach out and touch it, but I didn't move. Reassured that I posed no danger it started grooming itself. I wondered for the umpteenth time about the hostility between the earth's creatures. Every species mistrusted the other, with man the universal enemy. Yet, man's cruelty to man far outweighed that of man to God's other creatures.

Once I looked back and saw Sheriff Witmore climb the stairs to the attic. He would find nothing there, just as he had found nothing inside Eve's Nook. There was no trace of Peter, just as there was no trace of Sam and Doughie. He was groping round in the dark and would continue to do so until my task was complete. Just lately I had been having a vague desire to die. I had been feeling bone-tired, my life seemed utterly purposeless. I couldn't think of a reason for living apart from killing Ax Reevers, and once that was done – none.

Sheriff Witmore came walking across the damp stretch of beach, his hands in his trouser pockets, his shoes leaving deep indents on the damp sand. I climbed down the rocks and met him half-way.

'Satisfied, Sheriff?'

'There are two bicycles in the garage,' he said, making it sound like an accusation.

'I know. One belonged to Peter. When the killers removed his belongings from the cottage, they forgot the bicycle. They wanted to make it look as though he bolted, but he wouldn't have left without the bicycle. It was his only means of transport.'

'I want you to tell me about this Peter. Everything you know,' he said, his hard eyes challenging me to refuse.

'Why?'

'Because I don't believe he's dead.'

I started walking back to the cottage. He was right beside me.

'I know very little about him. I was driving along the coast one day when I offered him a ride. The wind was strong that day and he was pushing the bicycle along. He said he'd been cycling along the coast for five months.'

'And you invited him to stay here with you?'

'No. He was sleeping down there by the rocks. He needed a break, he said. I invited him into the cottage one night when it rained. He made himself useful . . . did some work round the cottage – gardening, painting and so on. We didn't talk much . . . about ourselves.'

'Did you sleep with him?' he asked bluntly.

I fixed him with a cold stare. 'I don't believe that's any of your business, Sheriff.'

'Fair enough. So he said his name was Peter. What else did he say?'

'What about?'

'About where he came from, where he was going to?'

'I never asked him about his past, or his future plans.'

'You mean to tell me he lived here with you for weeks and never told you a damn thing about himself? Come on, Miss Benson, you don't expect me to believe that,' he said impatiently.

'I don't care what you believe,' I said indifferently. We reached Eve's Nook. 'Will you have something to drink now?' I asked, pausing on the steps.

'Coffee, yes. Then I want you to give me a full description of this boy,' he said.

No description on earth would help you, Sheriff. Peter Dreifuss-Jones doesn't exist anymore.

He followed me into the kitchen. 'I don't believe that boy didn't have family expecting him home. I'm going to feed his description into the local computer for nation-wide distribution. We'll soon know if anyone by that description has been reported missing.'

His mother is dead and his father doesn't care, I thought dully.

I described Peter objectively while we waited for the kettle to boil. I didn't tell him how the sun had danced on Peter's corn-coloured hair, how his long fingers had left me trembling with pleasure at the slightest touch, how the nights had been filled with love and passion. It all seemed so long ago now, as though it had merely been a dream, dispelled by the bright morning light.

I handed him the mug of steaming coffee and sat down opposite him. For a while we sat in silence, then he broke it.

172

'This young boy . . . this Peter . . . is he threatening you in any way?'

'No.' The dead cannot threaten us, only the living, Sheriff.

I drove into town the next morning. Most people were kept indoors by the weather, and the streets were deserted, the shop doors closed with signs saying 'open'. Even the factory stood silently in the background, its long chimneys empty for once. I pushed open the door to the drugstore and went inside. There were a few customers waiting for medicine, chatting idly. When they noticed me a deadly hush fell. They watched me approach with open hostility in their eyes, and I realized that Sheriff Witmore's suspicions were shared by the town. It left me cold. These were the people who had protected their own, irrespective of the gravity of their crimes.

I bought a few personal toiletries, ignoring the hostile stares. I paid, took the small parcel and left the drugstore, aware of their eyes boring into my back. I held myself erect, my head raised proudly. Once outside I glanced back. Through the glass door I saw their lips moving in hurried conversation, their eyes darting hatred at me.

Two blocks further I stopped at Bay Traders. Here too the front door was closed, and when I pulled it open the warm air from inside rushed past me. The store was empty except for Uncle Billy leaning over the counter, counting nails. For the first time he didn't smile when he saw me. There was hostility in his manner when he greeted me. He made me stand there for a full two minutes before putting the nails into a small drawer and turning to me.

'You heard 'bout them boys disappearing?' he asked gruffly.

'Yes. Sheriff Witmore came out to my place yesterday, asking about them. Somehow he thinks I had something to do with it,' I said frankly, since I suspected everyone knew that much anyway.

'And you didn't?' he asked, his toothless mouth pursed while he watched me closely.

'I can't imagine what he thinks I did with them. Can you?'

'It sure is damn funny, the way them boys just up and disappeared like that. And that after what happened to you. What

173

worries me is now there's only Ax left. He ain't much of a grandson, but he's all the fam'ly I have left. I'd sure hate for something real nasty to happen to him.'

'I don't understand. What could happen to Ax?'

'Ain't Ax also one of them boys you accused? Folks round here says you had somethin' to do with the other two. They says that young scoundrel's still hiding up there at your place, doing somethin' to our boys,' he said, his manner becoming more accusatory and aggressive.

'Sheriff Witmore also thought that, Uncle Billy. He brought a search-warrant and didn't find anything. Are you going to serve me now or do I go elsewhere?' I asked coldly.

For a few minutes we glared at each other, then suddenly his shoulders slumped.

'Ax never was no bad boy till that Doughie and Sam put a spell on him. Did I ever tell you I raised that boy alone? Me, old Billy Reevers,' he said, stabbing his chest for emphasis. 'He'll come right now the other boys . . . eh . . . are gone.'

There was a naked plea in his eyes, and I smiled reassuringly. I reached over and patted his gnarled hand.

'Ax is going to be just fine, Uncle Billy. You worry unnecessarily.'

Didn't the snake assure Eve that everything was going to be just fine once she had eaten the apple?

The hostility of a small town is a nasty thing to experience. They came in the dead of night and pelted my windows with stones the size of bricks. After a while I didn't bother replacing them. They brought garbage cans and emptied them on my veranda, someone sprayed the word 'whore' on an outside wall with black paint, notes were stuck to my front door, asking where Sam and Doughie were. They urinated and excreted on my front steps and threw dead rats through the broken windows. One morning I got to my car and found all four tyres slashed and the windscreen broken. The word 'bitch' was sprayed on the roof and sides. I excavated the gun from its burial place and sat up all night waiting for them to enter the cottage, but at least they stopped short at that. A few times I thought I noticed Sheriff Witmore among them, his badge of justice shining dully in the night light.

One morning I became aware of the lone figure of a middle-aged woman standing on the beach a few feet away from my gate. She was dressed in black, her face deeply lined, her hair almost completely grey. She stood very still, staring at Eve's Nook. It unnerved me. Whichever way I turned I saw her there, silently staring. There was something so utterly pathetic about her it drove me out onto the veranda.

'What do you want?' I called.

The tell-tale signs of a hard life were etched on her face, in her slumped posture. The wind tugged at her thin grey hair.

'Where's my boy?' she asked with the flat accent of the villagers.

'Who's your boy?' I asked, but I think I already knew.

'Sam's my boy. You accused him of something he never done. Now he's gone, just like the other one . . . Doughie.'

We stared at each other for a while. They hadn't cared about the fate that had befallen me, yet they were quick to react when their own were affected.

'I can't help you. Now please go away.'

'He never touched you! He had a girl, was gonna be married next year. You killed him! You and that no-good drifter!'

'If he did nothing wrong, why would we harm him?'

'A woman living alone never done no good to nobody! You was asking for trouble flaunting yourself with that boy. You'll rot in hell, the both of you!'

I went back inside and slammed the door behind me. Later, when I looked out the window, she was gone. But the worst episode was when Lulu disappeared. I circled the cottage for two days calling out to her, with no success. On the third day I went into the adjacent bush and found her carcass there, crawling with ants. Her throat had been crudely slit, her fangs exposed in a death grimace. The ants had devoured her eyes, leaving only rotting sockets behind. There were traces of dried blood on her paws, evidence that she had struggled fiercely for her life. I sat beside her, sick with shock and horror and anger.

'Do pets go to heaven too, Mom?' Theresa's voice came to me through the years. 'Of course, darling. I'm sure God has a special place for them in His heaven.'

'I'm sorry, Lulu,' I mumbled brokenly. 'So very, very sorry. You were an innocent victim of my private war.'

When I stumbled away my eyes burnt with unshed tears. For the second time in five months I had lost something I loved and treasured.

One morning Uncle Billy arrived at Eve's Nook on his Vespa scooter. His pallor was a sickly grey, his ragged breath wheezed from his toothless mouth. He had aged visibly in a matter of days. I invited him into the warm kitchen and made two cups of hot chocolate. He didn't speak until he had taken a sip of it.

'The folks says you dabble in witchcraft. A voodoo type thing, they says,' he announced, holding the cup with both hands to warm them.

'I don't care what the folks say, Uncle Billy. They've hated me from the start.'

For a long time we sat quietly by the kitchen table, sipping hot chocolate and listening to the howling wind outside. Then he spoke, hardly above a whisper.

'My son, Trevor, died in early '69, exactly seven months after the wife. A big chunk of me died with the both of them. I cursed America and I cursed God and I cried like a woman. Then Ax's mother ran off and left the boy with me. He called me pa and he loved me and I started living again. I wanted him to get educated and leave this hick town where a man's got no future. But he fell into bad company and ended up in the factory, same's everybody else. But you know something? He loved me and gave me money every month, and I guessed God wanted me to be there for the boy to love, not have him alone in a big city far away.'

Tears trickled down his leathery cheeks and dripped onto his brown cardigan with the leather elbow patches. He blinked at the tears and looked at me – an old man clinging to an illusion. For a man like Ax had no capacity to love.

'He's a bad boy, just like his pa, but I love him all the same. I can't make him better, but I don't have nothing else to live for,' he said again, his voice quivering.

'What is it you want from me, Uncle Billy?'

'I want for you to forgive my boy for what he done to you. It was madness, brought on by drink and bad company.'

'Did Ax ask you to come here, Uncle Billy?' I asked carefully. The answer was of the utmost importance. If by some miracle Ax had a heart left in that obscene body and regretted the injustice perpetrated on me and Peter, perhaps I'd be able to pick up the pieces of my life and start believing in the human race again.

'He don't know I came here, Carla. He'd be mighty angry if he knew. Never did like me meddling in his 'fairs. You won't tell him, will you?'

I sighed. 'No, Uncle Billy. I won't tell him.' I should've known better than to have hoped for a slice of humanity in the heart of a lethal snake.

'You're a fine woman, Carla,' he said, wiping at his eyes with the back of a gnarled hand. 'Folks been treating you wrong. Don't bring no harm to my boy. He won't do nothing bad now the other two are gone. Let him be.'

I didn't reply, just sat there staring into the empty cup in my hands. Sometime later he got up and shuffled out of the kitchen. He closed the front door behind him.

As October drew to a close, I was constantly aware of being watched. At night there were invisible eyes at the windows, whispers outside the front and back doors. They were deliberately and methodically destroying my property and trying to intimidate me with their hate-campaign. Sheriff Witmore was snooping round the cottage too – watching and waiting. I hardened my heart against Uncle Billy's appeal and strengthened my resolve to complete the task I had set for myself.

Time was running out for both Ax Reevers and myself.

18

One day, just as suddenly as the victimization had begun, it stopped. The night visitors ceased to torment me, Sheriff Witmore stopped snooping and silence fell over Eve's Nook again. I knew then that the Johnsons had a hand in this respite and that my friendship with them was finally paying off.

The fourth of November arrived, and I dressed carefully for Cyril Johnson's birthday party. It was an old-fashioned dress with a high neck and long sleeves, and was totally black. It was one of those dresses every woman owns but never wears. I deliberately made no attempt to break its sombreness. Black stockings and black high-heeled shoes completed my outfit. I knew I was dressed for a funeral rather than for a party, but for the last time I needed to blend with the night, for tonight Ax Reevers was going to die. It was now almost five months since the attack he had instigated, and already he had lived far too long.

I intended shooting Ax in front of witnesses tonight. At least he would be spared the indignity of being measured into cans of Johnson's Pet Food. It was going to be my grand exit from the double life I had been leading for the past few months. I had executed American justice in my own way and wanted the world to know about it. I wanted to serve as the living warning to other men that they could no longer get away with violating women to satisfy their vulgar lust. They couldn't sexually abuse their children and their wives and strangers without inviting retaliation. We were tired of being the weaker sex, the victims of man's uncontrolled hunger, while laws made by men protected men and left women exposed. I wanted to be remembered as the pioneer for revenge by abused women the world over.

There was a nervous tension in me tonight that hadn't been present with the other two. The palms of my hands remained damp, there was a tight feeling in my chest and my stomach contracted painfully. Reluctantly I admitted to myself that I lacked the blind courage that had propelled me before. Was it because I feared Ax more than I had the others? I asked myself, wiping my damp hands with a tissue. No, perhaps I had just grown weary of the bloodshed. Already three men and one animal had died violently. Yet, I couldn't retreat now, not when the end was so close. I put the gun into my handbag before leaving the cottage. I wasn't going to need the silencer tonight.

The eye of the swivelling camera rested on the car, then the electronic gates swung open. I drove through and along the tree-lined avenue towards the house. Pelham's Bluff was aglow tonight, standing splendidly in its magnificent garden. Colourful lanterns bathed the spacious grounds with their exotic shrubs in varying colours of purple, red and blue.

I stopped in front of the mansion, where the uniformed butler and chauffeur waited. The butler opened the car door for me and bowed when I got out.

'Good evening, Miss Benson. Welcome to Pelham's Bluff.'

'Good evening,' I replied.

'Paul will park the car. Please allow me to escort you,' he said pompously, his eyes lingering disapprovingly on my black outfit.

He led the way up the stairs and to the front door. When he opened it the busy hum of conversation came to me from inside, the clink of glasses, the sounds of laughter. He closed the door softly behind him, leaving me alone. I took a deep breath before proceeding down the short passage and through the double-door leading into the main sitting-room. I'd had only a glimpse of this stately room during my previous visits. Now it was abuzz with guests – sitting or standing in groups – talking, laughing or looking fashionably bored. Liveried waiters moved among them, carrying trays of champagne and hors-d'oeuvres. The glitter of delicate crystal and polished silver competed with the brilliance of diamonds and gold designer jewellery, and the reek of money surrounded the idle rich in this room.

'Carla! How wonderful to see you again!'

Meryl had materialized through the sea of faces and embraced me warmly. The fragrance of expensive perfume hung about her, and she looked stunning in a creation of white silk which caressed and complimented the subtle lines of her lithe body. Her eyes travelled briefly over my sombre outfit, but she was too polite to show her dismay. I was grateful that she didn't pretend I was devastating. She took both my hands in hers.

'I'm frightfully sorry about those awful incidents at your cottage. We didn't know for a while,' she whispered, her eyes resting on me anxiously.

'It's all right, Meryl. I survived.'

'It should never have happened. Cyril was livid when I told him. He called the men together and threatened to fire everyone who had the vaguest connection with it. And he meant it.'

'Thank you, Meryl,' I said and withdrew my hands from hers. I was afraid she would feel them tremble.

She hooked into my arm and steered me into the crowded room. She stopped a passing waiter and offered me a glass of champagne. I took one and immediately spilled some of it all over the front of my dress. When I laughed it had a hollow ring to it. Meryl inspected my face, an enquiring frown between her delicate eyebrows.

179

'Carla, are you all right?' she whispered.

'Oh, yes! I'm just being clumsy,' I assured her, but my voice was unnaturally loud.

And then Cyril was there with his unmistakable aura of authority. How could Meryl ever have thought him weak? I wondered. He shook my hand politely, while his eyes travelled discreetly over my black outfit.

'Best wishes for your birthday,' I said, falsely cheerful.

'Why, thank you, Carla. And thank you for coming tonight. We are honoured by your presence. Please go right ahead and have a great evening,' he said jovially, then turned towards Meryl. 'Darling, I see Frank Ottoman has just arrived. Will you excuse us, Carla?'

'Of course.'

'Please make yourself at home, Carla. And don't be shy. Introduce yourself as you go along,' Meryl said before being swallowed by the guests.

I stood awkwardly in one spot, feeling conspicuous and wondering what to do next. As a rule I hated parties and this one wasn't going to be an exception.

'I don't believe we've met,' someone said, touching my elbow with a hot, clammy hand.

I turned to him. He was overweight, with a bloated face and soft, red lips. His nostrils were flared, his greying hair sparse. His bold eyes devoured me hungrily.

'No, I don't believe we have,' I replied coolly, cursing my luck.

'I'm Cedric Thompson, at your service,' he smiled, reaching for my hand.

'Carla Benson.'

His hand was soft, the handshake effeminate. His eyes were slightly unfocused from an over-indulgence in champagne.

'Ah . . . Carla. What an unusual name,' he breathed, then leaned closer. 'For an unusual lady. Anyone ever told you black suits you?'

'No.'

'Well, believe you me it does. It takes a lot of courage to wear black, and if there's something I admire about a woman it's courage. Where did you fly in from, Carla? New York? Houston? Dallas?'

'None. I live right here in Oliver Bay,' I said, and hurriedly gulped more champagne. It was going to be a long night.

'Oliver Bay? Good gracious, girl! You mean to tell me you're one of these provincial people?'

'Yes,' I answered, wondering how soon I could escape his hungry look and slobbering eyes without being downright rude.

When he laughed his red lips were wet. 'Forgive my bad manners, but I thought the Johnsons were the only crazy people here tonight. But perhaps, like them, you're stuck here through business interests?'

'What's so amusing, Cedric?'

Richard Mallen appeared beside him, his eyes on me.

'Hi, Richard! What a pleasant surprise!' Cedric laughed and slapped Richard playfully on the back.

'Good evening, Carla,' Richard greeted formally.

'Hello, Richard,' I replied, grateful for the distraction. He was immaculately dressed in a dark suit with pale yellow shirt and matching tie.

'You two know each other?' Cedric asked superfluously, then slapped his ample thigh. 'But of course! Carla was just telling me she lives in this one-horse town too. Are you hanging onto your sanity, pal?'

'Only too well, Cedric,' Richard smiled. 'Oliver Bay guarantees the lowest incidence of heart attacks and ulcers. You should try it some time.'

'No bloody chance! Hard living's my idea of a good time, not choking on the stench of fish,' Cedric said and laughed uproariously.

A tall, striking woman with straight black hair suddenly appeared next to Richard. Her ruby-red dress clung to her body like a second skin, the low neckline revealing the creamy cleavage of her well-endowed bosom. She oozed sensuality and cat-like grace.

'Richard, darling! You shouldn't disappear like that,' she pouted, hooked an arm through his and leaned heavily against him. He smiled down at her.

'I had to rescue a damsel in distress. I don't think she appreciated Cedric's dubious charms. Andrina, meet Carla Benson. She's an author, a great contribution to our culture-starved society. Carla . . . meet Andrina Richter. Andrina grew up here, then married a Texas oil millionaire and deprived us of her beauty. We only see her once a year on Cyril's birthday.'

Her green eyes flashed over my black dress and I recognized a blend of disdain and pity in them.

'My pleasure, Carla,' she murmured. 'An author hiding away in Oliver Bay? How very interesting. What have you written?' she asked condescendingly.

'Nothing much. I'm still working on the great American novel.' My voice sounded flat even to my own ears.

'Carla's being extremely modest. You should read *The First and the Last*,' Richard said. 'It's a great novel.'

'Maybe I will, darling. Oh, look who's here! Natasha, darling! How long has it been?'

The group increased in size as more people joined in, kissing each other and discussing people and events I knew nothing of. I felt claustrophobic and moved away. I sauntered through a door and into the adjoining dining-room with its lavish displays of food. The sight of the rich cuisine made me nauseous and I slipped through a side door. The patio was large, overlooking the glass-enclosed swimming pool. I stood there, inhaling the cold night air, aware of the increasing noise coming from inside. I didn't know if I had the courage to go back in there. The events of the past few months were taking their toll on my scant reserves, and I was beginning to walk the tightrope of collapse.

I heard Richard approach and sensed his identity before he reached me. I felt myself stiffen.

'Carla? The one moment you were there, the next you were gone. What are you doing out here?'

'I don't like parties,' I answered without looking at him.

'Neither do I. I only come every year as a matter of courtesy and because I like the Johnsons.'

He stood so close I could smell his aftershave lotion. It simultaneously excited and offended me. I moved away and pretended to admire the cactus-like plants along the patio. He followed me.

'Shall I get you another drink?' he asked.

I realized I was still carrying the empty champagne glass. 'Yes, please. Champagne,' I said.

He took the glass and disappeared inside. I found a wrought-iron bench just below the patio and sat down. A cold breeze was blowing from the Atlantic and I shivered. A short while later he returned with two glasses of champagne, handed me one and sat down beside me. I wished he would go away and leave me alone.

'Thank you,' I said absently.

'A toast,' he said, raising his glass. 'To the success of your next book.'

'I didn't know you'd read the first.'

'I did. And enjoyed it.'

'Thank you,' I said simply. Our glasses clinked and I took a large sip. The champagne rushed to my head and brought a numbing warmth to my tense muscles.

For a while we sat in silence, drinking champagne and staring at nothing in particular. Crickets were chirping all round us, to the left frogs were croaking on the edge of the fish pond.

'Carla . . . you're very far away. May I share whatever it is?' he asked softly.

Share? What would he say if I told him I was a cold-blooded killer, that within the next few hours I would commit the third murder in as many months? Would he recoil in horror? Despise me? His world was an ordered and sane one, it had no room for madness, the kind I was afflicted with.

'Some things can't be shared, Richard.'

He reached out and took one of my cold hands in his. I sat rigidly.

'Carla . . . my anger at what happened to you goes much deeper than you can possibly imagine. No human being should have to suffer such degradation. It makes me deeply ashamed to be associated with a town that shares that guilt. Can you forgive me . . . us . . . for what happened?'

I looked at him. His eyes were merely two dark pools behind the spectacles. How very simple things were to him, I thought. Everything fitted into pigeon-holes. If you misplaced something you merely shifted it to the correct slot. He expected me to say yes, I forgave them, to continue with my life as though nothing had happened.

'Can we change the subject?' I asked and withdrew my hand from his. I got up and walked towards the fish pond. The surface of the water reflected all the colours of the burning lanterns. Richard was next to me.

'Carla, I'm aware of the things that have happened to you lately

183

– the victimization, the unfair suspicions. I had a word with Sheriff Witmore, told him you've suffered enough. I have his assurance that it won't happen again. There's another side to Oliver Bay I think you should get to know. There are real caring people, unrivalled scenery and a peace and tranquillity you won't find anywhere else on this continent. If you could open your heart just a little I'll show you the true face of Oliver Bay.'

I have seen it's true face, in all its ugliness. 'It doesn't matter any more, Richard. I'm a big girl now. I can take care of myself.'

He laid a hand on my shoulder. I shrank away from the intimate touch, but he didn't seem to notice.

'Carla, I knew you before you came to the hospital as my patient. Twice I saw you at Wreckers Strand, enjoying the scenery and your lone lunches. I often drive out there on a Sunday. I watched you through my binoculars, saw you scribbling in your notebook, saw the expression of peace on your face. I would like you to become that person again.'

'Why should it matter to you what I am? Your obligation ended when you discharged me from hospital.'

'I wish it did, but unfortunately it isn't that simple. You've made me aware of the cesspit we're trying to bury in Oliver Bay. Everybody turns a blind eye as long as it doesn't affect them personally. I'm guilty of that too. I grew up here and accepted the closeness of the community, which is noble in times of tragedy but misplaced when we try to cover up a crime. I would like you to give us all a second chance.'

From inside the house the band started playing. There were loud cheers and spontaneous applause.

'Carla! Richard! I've looked everywhere for you!'

Meryl was coming down the stairs towards us. 'How very naughty of you to hide her away here,' she chided Richard playfully. 'There are so many people I want you both to meet. Come on inside.'

She took my hand on the one side and Richard's on the other.

'And I thought we were safe,' Richard said, winking at me.

There were faces with names that held no meaning. I saw their lips move with meaningless utterances and I couldn't help wondering what they would say once the truth about me became known. Would they tell their acquaintances that they had met this avenging Amazon, but gosh, she had appeared so plain, dressed in black at Cyril's birthday party, for Pete's sake. Nothing about her to hint at the murderous intentions. My, she'd even smiled a lot, and drank at least five glasses of champagne in quick succession. And yes, she had danced with that charming Dr Richard Mallen, allowing him to hold her close during that old Frank Sinatra number – 'Strangers in the Night'.

He steered me expertly through the dancing couples and for a short while I allowed myself to forget my mission for tonight. I closed my eyes and pretended I was merely a woman and he merely a man, that there had been no Peter, no rape, no murders. I had no past, only a present and a future. When I mentioned the heat, he steered me through the dancing couples, through the double-doors, and out onto the patio. His hand was still on my upper arm when I leaned against a pillar, taking deep breaths of the cold night air. I felt heady and tired, perhaps that was why I didn't object when he pulled me closer until I was leaning my head against his broad chest. His arms crept round me and stroked my back. I felt his face in my hair, heard him whisper my name. Then he lifted my face to his and for a few moments our eyes held. His lips touched mine. They were soft and cool. I closed my eyes, trying to shut out the fearful beat of my heart.

'Carla,' he whispered again, his breath against my cheek. And suddenly the spell was broken and it was that night again. There was heavy breathing on my face and callous hands bruising my body and groans of lust piercing my ears and my body cringed again at the pain. I recoiled at the memory and strained against him to free myself.

'Carla, no! This is right. Don't fight it,' he urged, trying to hold me against him.

I threw my head back and screamed with all the terror in my heart. It was a raw, agonized scream that released some of the accumulated anger and fear I had harboured for so long. And then I was free and running. I ran through shrubs, bumped into statues, stumbled over flower beds. He caught me from behind.

'Carla!'

I fought like a wild cat, slapping at his face, slamming my fists against his chest, scratching at his eyes, all the while grunting like a demented animal. He overpowered me easily and forcibly twisted my hands behind my back. I bent my body backwards, my screams drowned by the volume of the music inside. And then, dear God, the dam finally burst and I was weeping with the abandon of an injured child. Great, heaving sobs racked my body, bringing blessed release to the pain that had eaten into my soul like a cancer since that night.

'It's all right, perfectly all right . . . just let it go,' he soothed, holding me against his chest. 'Carla, Carla . . . you're going to be all right now.'

My grief was so great it sapped me of my remaining strength. My knees buckled and I collapsed onto the damp grass. He supported me and went down with me. He held me close, uttering comforting words and stroking my hair. For a long time it kept coming – wave upon wave of grief that drained me until I felt like an empty shell – dry and brittle. He wiped at my face and nose and talked to me as though I were a child, and I was too weak to object.

When the flood finally subsided, I continued to lean against him, totally exhausted.

'It's over now . . . all those bad feelings,' he whispered. 'You'll never have to cry again. I want to make you happy, more happy than you've ever been.'

Peter too had said those words not so long ago, but perhaps not for the same reason. Now that I saw it in perspective, I realized he had been infatuated with an older woman who had responded to him with the love and passion his mother had denied him. He had expressed his need the only way he had known how to – in the form of searing passion. Remembering Peter also reminded me of what I had done and what I still had to do. I broke free from him.

'Thank you . . . for being here when I needed you,' I said, suddenly remote again.

'I've seen it festering inside you for months. I'm glad you've allowed it to come to the surface. It's over now. You can start afresh,' he said gently.

Dear God, he didn't understand anything! Ax Reevers was still alive! I had a mission to complete. And afterwards . . . afterwards I had to give myself up . . . explain why I had done it. There would be no new life for me, now or ever.

I allowed him to help me to my feet. 'I don't want you to be alone tonight. I want you to come home with me.'

I shook my head tiredly. 'No. There's something I still have to do. Tonight.'

'What is so important it can't wait until tomorrow?'

'You won't understand,' I said, avoiding his eyes.

'Try me, Carla.'

'No. Please don't insist,' I said, turning away from him.

'Carla, look at me,' he urged. 'All you have to do now is forget. I know it's still painful and will be for a while longer, but together we can conquer it. Come home with me. I promise I won't make demands on you. You're safe with me. Trust me.'

'Not tonight, Richard.'

'Why not?'

'Please . . . I can't tell you. Tomorrow . . . you'll know tomorrow,' I said, backing away.

'Will I see you tomorrow?' he asked hopefully.

I smiled weakly. 'Sure, Richard. Tomorrow I'll come to you and then I'll explain everything. Please give me this one last night.'

Without waiting for a reply I ran through the garden towards the parking area. In my car my hand slipped into my handbag and closed round the butt of the gun. Tonight I would use it for the last time, then hand it over to Sheriff Witmore. It would be the final chapter to the saga that had started the night my father had taken my small hand and cupped it round his testicles.

I started the car and drove away.

19

At the factory I pulled into a parking bay reserved for managerial staff and switched off the engine. My heart sounded in my ears with a dull refrain, my hands shook visibly while I fumbled in my bag for the gun. I found it, lifted it out and rested it on my lap. It should've felt good but tonight it didn't. It was a cold, lethal weapon, designed to penetrate the soft flesh of a human body and create havoc there. And I remembered that he called Uncle Billy 'pa' and gave him money every month.

Deliberately I pushed my thoughts aside and got out of the car. For a while I stood there, swallowed by the giant shadow of the factory. From this angle the noise was louder, the stench more acute. I closed the car door, then ran towards the brick wall of the factory. My black clothing blended perfectly with the shadows. The gun lay heavily in my cold, clammy hand, perspiration drenched my dress in spite of the cold of the night. I leaned against the wall, waiting. For what? I asked myself. Why wasn't I elated that the last of the three rapists and killers was going to die tonight? Why was I shaking like a leaf in a strong wind?

I looked ahead. All I had to do now was walk twenty yards, round the corner and enter the pet-food section. Ax would be there. I had been watching the shifts carefully for the past twelve nights. They were rotating shifts regularly – he and the two new men who had replaced Sam and Doughie. I would walk up to him, call out his name and smile when I saw his shocked surprise turning gradually to naked fear. I would keep the gun aimed at his chest and give him an opportunity to raise the alarm. Once there were witnesses I would empty the gun into his chest, but the first shot had to hit him in the face. Neither Sam nor Doughie had had their faces marred before dying, unlike Peter's face that had dripped blood onto the sand, and mine which had been beyond recognition. Once he was dead I would wait calmly for Sheriff Witmore to arrive and arrest me. For so many countless sleepless nights I had planned it all to the finest detail, visualizing each moment, the resultant horror, the publicity, my statement.

And Holy Christ, I just couldn't go ahead with it. I stood there rooted to one spot, lacking the anger that had propelled me before. The hatred had sapped me dry, the anger was spent. I could no longer be a pioneer for violated women the world over. It wasn't hatred that had conquered me, but Uncle Billy's pathetic request that I spare his grandson, and the hand of friendship extended to me by the Johnsons and Richard. Even if it was too late for me to take that hand. I was tainted, my hands already drenched with the blood of two men.

I slumped against the wall. Ax Reevers would live, not because he loved his grandfather and gave him money, but because I no longer possessed the desire to kill him. All that remained now was to surrender to the law. I looked up, and in the shadows saw the faint outline of a slender young man standing a few yards away. His corn-coloured hair glowed in the dark, his green eyes seemed to shine with a pale light.

'I'm so sorry, Peter. So very sorry. I can't do it,' I muttered before stumbling back to the car.

Eve's Nook stood isolated in the ghostly light of the full moon, a cottage that had indulged my dreams for the future. For a while I remained sitting in the car, remembering with how much breathless anticipation I had arrived here. It seemed like so many years ago now, not a mere eight months. Like a naïve fool I had believed I could function in the world I had created for myself, a world that wasn't going to allow strangers in, a world that would've protected and sheltered me in my old age. It had been nothing but an illusion, shattered the day I allowed Peter to enter it.

My hands were still trembling and I struggled with the front-door key. It finally turned and I entered the dark and silent cottage. I locked the door behind me and reached for the light switch. The room flooded with light, then I drew my breath in sharply. Ax Reevers had been waiting for me. He was sitting on my settee, chewing gum, wearing his faded denim outfit, his check shirt open to the waist.

'So you're back,' he smiled, getting up. 'You're early, Carla. Didn't you like the Johnsons' party?'

I stood paralysed, my face drained of blood. He strolled towards me, his eyes cold and calculating.

'Ain't you gonna speak to me? Where's your manners, Carla? I'm a guest in your home,' he drawled, smiling the evil smile I remembered from that fateful night.

The blood that had drained from my head rushed back. I turned towards the front door and frantically tried to insert the key, but he was too fast for me. In a split-second he reached me, roughly pulled me away from it and slammed me against the wall. My handbag fell to the floor. I shot forward, reaching for it, but he kicked it out of reach.

'Bitch! There's nowhere to run to. It's only you and me now . . . alone,' he smiled, his fleshy face close to mine.

I found my voice. 'What do you want, Ax?'

'What do I want? Cut the crap, bitch! You know goddamn well

what I want. But before we get to that, you're gonna tell me a little story.'

'A story?'

'Yes. You're gonna tell me what you did to make my friends disappear. Get that?'

'I don't know what you mean,' I croaked, my throat tight. 'I haven't seen them since . . . since that night.'

'You're a fuckin' liar!' he snarled viciously, slapping the wall beside my face. I cringed as though the blow had struck me. 'They made one goddamn big fucking mistake, and you know what that is? They turned their backs to you! I ain't gonna be a sitting duck for you. You want me, you're gonna look me right in the face and do what you have to do. Wanna get on with it?'

His hot and sour breath was on my face, his jaws working mechanically on the gum. Bile rose in my constricted throat.

'I don't know what you mean,' I repeated hoarsely. 'Why don't you leave now, Ax? You can't possibly get away with it a second time.'

'You wanna bet? Hey? You wanna bet? You also wanna bet before this night's out you're gonna tell me everything I wanna know?'

Suddenly the knife was in his hand, its razor-sharp point pricking the soft skin on my neck. He grabbed a fistful of my hair and slammed my head against the wall, sending darts of agonizing pain through to my eyes. His face was directly above mine, a vicious sneer on it. I recognized the madness in his eyes and knew I had made a terrible mistake. I should've killed him first.

'I been watching you, bitch. I seen you snooping round that factory at night. You're a shit-stirrer, knew that the minute I laid eyes on you. What did you do with Sam and Doughie?'

I uttered a strangled cry when the knife pierced my skin. Warm blood ran down my neck and soaked the neckline of my dress. I closed my eyes, waiting for death, praying it would be quick and merciful when it came.

'Look at me!' he snarled, banging my head against the wall. I opened my eyes. 'You're gonna talk to me, you hear? You're gonna talk so much I'm gonna have to shut you up. Yeah, shut you up for good! I shoulda killed you that night. You ain't gonna sneak up on me some dark night and make me disappear like you did those arseholes. No, sirree! Ax Reevers is one step ahead of you all the time.'

As he did that other night, he licked my face. I squirmed in disgust.

'But first we're gonna have some fun . . . you and me.'

With his fist still entangled in my hair, he dragged me towards the bedroom. I was no match for his brute strength and knew there was no point in resisting him. He was going to kill me, but suddenly it didn't matter any more. Now that the anger and hatred had left me there was no fear either. I would feel no pain tonight, and that would be my triumph over him.

In the bedroom he threw me roughly onto the bed. I fell sprawling and lay still, looking up at him. He stood silhouetted against the light penetrating from the sitting-room, an ape-like man clutching a deadly knife. With a quick jerk of the hand he unzipped his jeans and struggled from them, his small eyes watching me hungrily. In the dim light his face changed shape until it was my father standing there, staring at me hungrily. And then it changed again and he was Arthur Benson. His underpants followed, then he unbuttoned his shirt and threw it aside. He stood there naked, his frame covered in black, curly hair. While I watched he caressed himself, chuckling softly.

'You ain't had a man for months now, bitch. You missed me, didn't you? You missed me real bad, didn't you?' he said, his breath coming fast over his wet lips. 'I'm gonna give it to you. Oh yeah, I'm gonna give it to you so good and hard you're gonna beg me to stop.'

I watched him, emotionless. He got onto the bed and straddled me like a horse, the knife in his right hand. He grabbed the front of my dress and with a few quick strokes cut it open with the razor-sharp blade. It fell away from my body. Another quick snip and my bra fell away, then he reached for my panties. When I finally lay naked beneath him, he took a handful of my pubic hair and tugged viciously.

'Hey! Look happy, bitch!' he snarled. When I didn't respond he put the knife's point against my right eye. 'Come on! Liven up!'

I lay motionless, like a rag doll. When he slapped me with the back of his hand my head fell sideways and remained like that. I waited indifferently for the next blow, but it never came. Instead he began twisting oddly above me, uttering short, strangled cries. The hairy legs beside me stiffened, his body jerked backwards. I turned my head and looked at him. His hands were clutching at his throat, his mouth wide open, his eyes stretched wide. In the dim light I saw the figure of someone behind him, strangling him slowly and methodically.

I struggled to get away from him and into a sitting position. There was something round his neck, cutting deeply into his skin and tendons. Blood squirted from his neck and down his hairy shoulders and chest. The gum fell from his open mouth, his tongue came through his fleshy lips, while he uttered horrible, wet sounds. After an eternity his body went rigid, gripped in a dying spasm. His clawed hands came away from his neck and clutched the air.

There was more blood now, gallons of it. It sprayed over the bedding like red rain and onto my cold legs. Suddenly his body slumped, he rattled once, then fell backwards and off the bed. His head hit the floor with a sickening crunch, while his feet remained on the edge of the bed, the toes curled inwards. The sweetish reek of fresh blood hung in the room.

I looked up. Meryl Johnson was standing over his slain body, breathing heavily. Her white silk dress was splattered with fresh blood, her ash-blonde hair dishevelled. In the dim light her liquid eyes emitted an unnatural glow.

'Meryl? What, in the name of God . . .?'

'You slipped up with the third one, Carla,' she said. 'You shouldn't have allowed him to creep up on you like that. You grew complacent.'

'You . . . you know?' I gasped.

'About the other two? Oh, yes. I've been watching your every move for the past five months. I was there when you fed Doughie Steyl into the mincer. I was there when you shot Sam Shroder outside in the rain and had to drag him to the belt. I was tempted to help you that night, Carla, but you seemed to manage so well. God, how I admired you for what you did! You have the courage of your convictions. I knew you were a winner the first time I met you.'

I stared at her in shocked silence. My own and Ax's blood was congealing on my chest and legs. I looked down at him. She had strangled him with a length of fishing reel. It had cut right into his neck, exposing his trachea and jugulars. His swollen tongue protruded from his thick lips, congealing blood glistened in the hair on his chest. In death Ax Reevers was even more repulsive than he had been in life. I looked at Meryl again. She was taking leather gloves off her delicate hands and dropping them to the floor.

'I've lain awake for years imagining how I was killing them – Carl Flagg and Ray Bremmer,' she said, her voice thick. Her tongue flicked over her dry lips, she brushed strands of hair from her face with a blood-splattered arm. 'I used to have this recurring dream, you know . . . of being buried alive while I was being raped. I could taste the gritty soil in my mouth, feel it clogging my nose, filling my lungs, until I couldn't breathe anymore. I used to wake screaming in the dead of the night, soaked with perspiration, and I used to wonder what it would feel like killing them. Now I know. It feels good, Carla. Very, very good.'

'Oh, Meryl . . . you shouldn't have. This was my private war, not yours. You have so much to lose,' I said shakily.

'Nobody's going to lose anything. Get dressed now. You're coming home with me.'

'But . . . what about him?' I asked, looking at the gruesome remains of Ax Reevers.

'He'll be taken care of. Do as I say. And hurry.'

I climbed off the bed, suddenly aware of my nudity. She watched me when I left the room and disappeared into the bathroom. I closed the door behind me and leaned against it, my eyes tightly shut. Waves of nausea passed through me, made me shudder. I had to force myself to think clearly. It was imperative that I protect Meryl, take responsibility for that god-awful mess out there in the bedroom.

I washed in the handbasin and watched indifferently as the water turned red and disappeared down the drain. There was a small cut on my neck, still oozing blood. I dabbed at it with a tissue, feeling dreadfully tired. I leaned heavily over the basin. When I looked ahead there was no future for me, when I looked behind there was no past. Only the present strewn with bloodied corpses. And suddenly I knew I had to go ahead with my original plan. I had to tell the world what I had done, justify the carefully plotted executions. I owed it to other victims – past, present and future. I had to tell of the many sleepless nights when each shadow posed danger, of the days when the sun seemed to expose your pain for all to see and there was nowhere to hide, how you loathed to look at your naked flesh because it brought back the pain inflicted on it.. The world had to know about the shame and the anger and the hatred that gnawed at your guts day and night. Of the deep feeling of aloneness, when no one could share your suffering because all you wanted was to be left alone to nurse your bleeding wounds.

I put on my bathrobe and returned to the bedroom, switching the light on as I entered. She was sitting on the edge of the bed, staring at Ax's corpse, her face flushed with excitement.

'God, it tastes so wonderfully sweet. I don't feel so helpless and vulnerable anymore. I feel strong and in control. I don't ever want the taste to go away,' she said, her face shining.

Tiredly I laid a hand on her shoulder. 'I'll handle this, Meryl. Go home now.'

She rose and faced me. Her eyes were glazed, like one with fever. 'We proved we can fight back and win, Carla,' she said, then threw her head back and laughed shrilly.

'Go home, Meryl,' I repeated.

'Yes! Let's go home! We're done with them now. The last one is dead, we're both free,' she said eagerly, taking me by the hand.

I drew away from her. 'No, Meryl. I'm staying here. Go now.'

'No! I won't leave you here with him! You're coming with me!' she cried.

And I was just too goddamn tired to argue. I allowed her to drag me through the cottage like a child, out the front door and to the limousine parked in front of it. Paul, the uniformed chauffeur, got out of the car, walked round and held the rear door open for us. I was still dressed in my bathrobe, but if he noticed either that or Meryl's blood-stained dress he gave no indication. His face was expressionless, his eyes focused on a spot just above our heads.

In the car Meryl took my hand and smiled at me companionably. I looked away from her, at Eve's Nook. It stood forlornly on its sand dune, guarding the awful evidence of the past night. A shiver passed through me.

It was shortly after midnight when we pulled into the four-car garage at Pelham's Bluff. The party was still in full swing. Music blared through the open windows, competing for prominence with the chatter and laughter of the guests. I wondered how we were going to get into the house unnoticed.

'Thank you, Paul. You know what to do next,' Meryl said, addressing the chauffeur. He nodded his head in acknowledgement. 'Come, Carla.'

We kept to the shadows close to the house until we reached a balustraded patio. Meryl climbed over it and beckoned me to follow. I obeyed meekly. She opened a french window and we entered a dark room. I heard her move about the room, then the light came on, illuminating a classical, *belle époque* bedroom with a huge four-poster bed. Two doors led from the room – one to a bathroom, the other to a small sitting-room.

'This used to be Heather's quarters. My mother-in-law, you know. Before she fled to Miami to escape my offending presence,' Meryl explained, smiling and patting the bed. Her face was still flushed with excitement, as though we were children who had just returned from a successful treasure hunt.

'I want you to have it. For as long as you want it,' she said generously, put her arms round me and hugged me. 'We're blood sisters now, Carla. We share a deadly secret and from now on we'll share everything else. I'll never deny you anything.'

Unexpectedly she kissed me on the lips, unaware of my resultant revulsion.

'You must never be afraid again. From now on you'll be under my protection. No one will ever dare touch you again, not unless you want them to. You're going to stay right here at Pelham's Bluff and be my sister. My real sister.'

I stared at her. Had that madness always lurked behind those liquid eyes, or had she only just lost her grip on reality? Had the festering wound she had kept covered for years only just erupted, releasing its pus? Unlike her, I felt deflated, as though I had taken part in an arduous stage play and there was no applause when the curtain fell.

'I have to change now. Cyril won't start the fireworks without me. Sleep well, little sister,' she said, and was gone.

I sat down on the *chaise-longue*. Meryl had no idea of the seriousness of tonight's events. She acted as though it was purely a game we had both enjoyed. Didn't she realize that her doting husband would be aghast by her participation in my acts of revenge? That neither he nor the Johnson money could protect her from the consequences? I would protect her, of course. She had saved my life tonight, for whatever it was worth, and I owed her that, at least.

I switched off the light and lay back against the luxuriously deep cushion. Shortly afterwards there were cracks and hisses outside, and the room was illuminated with flashing lights. The fireworks signified the end of the Johnsons' party and the guests would leave soon.

I didn't see Meryl again that night. Some time after 3 a.m. the noise finally subsided and silence fell over the large estate. I lay back against the cushion and wondered about Heather Johnson and the reason behind her intense dislike of Meryl. It was a triviality that steered my mind away from the visions that assailed it, and which were threatening to destroy the last remnants of my sanity.

20

The light of dawn was accompanied by rays of weak winter sunshine beaming through the lace-curtained windows. For a while I just lay there on the *chaise-longue*, cold and stiff, listening to the silence of the big house. From here one couldn't hear the sea or the factory, and a silence this absolute was unknown to me.

I got up, still clad in my bathrobe, and sauntered onto the small, private patio. The early morning air was bitingly cold, reminding me that winter was creeping up fast. I leaned against the ornamental railing, shivering in the lukewarm sun. In the stark morning light there were no rainbow colours dancing on the fish pond, the statues that had witnessed the release of my grief last night stood cold and impersonal, their faces fixed with frozen smiles. This was the last morning I had woken a free woman, yet free only in a physical sense. I had already been imprisoned within myself for forty years, traipsing through life like a branded steer, too afraid to draw attention to myself and have my shame exposed. The shame that should've been my father's but which became mine. I had taken the law into my own hands and now I was ready to pay the penalty. Revenge had been a sweet fruit that had turned bitter as gall, but then, nothing in life came without a price tag.

Absently I touched my neck, felt the dried blood on the superficial cut. I suppose I should've been grateful to be alive, but I simply didn't care one way or the other. Meryl should've allowed me to die last night. She'd had no right to partake in my private war and play God with my life. I had recognized the raw evil in Ax Reevers the first time I laid eyes on him, and the hidden anger inside me had responded to it. For a while I had actually been vibrantly alive with that evil force. I had never really lived except within myself. I was bone-tired of standing on the outside, looking in, occasionally getting a whiff of happiness that only increased my hunger for life. Perhaps I had loved Peter, perhaps merely been infatuated with his fresh youth and vitality, and his naked, unadulterated need for me. I couldn't remember now exactly what I had felt for him except that he had given me a glimpse of what it was like on the inside. Which was frightfully symbolic of my life. Everything happened at the wrong place and the wrong time.

When I returned to the room, a young black girl was laying an outfit of clothing on the bed, complete with underwear and stockings.

'Good morning, Miss Benson,' she greeted me shyly, her large, black eyes full of natural curiosity.

'Good morning,' I returned, then inspected the clothes.

'Mrs Johnson says to give you these. There's cosmetics on the dressing table, she says. And breakfast will be served on the main patio at eight.'

So Meryl was determined to sustain the act. Did she think by doing so Ax's corpse would conveniently disappear from Eve's Nook? Could she really be that naïve?

'Please thank Mrs Johnson, but tell her I won't be staying for breakfast,' I replied. 'And . . . thank you.'

When she smiled her white teeth contrasted sharply with the raven–black of her skin. She was very pretty, her dark eyes full of the innocence of youth. How long would it be before someone destroyed that open trust in them, made them wary and suspicious?

Meryl's clothes were a size too large for me, but it didn't matter when the expensive material flowed with the lines of my thin body. In the adjoining bathroom I splashed my face with cold water, brushed my teeth and then my hair. I was deathly pale this morning, but the hard lines of the past few months were gone, there was resignation in my previously tortured eyes.

I powdered my wax-like complexion, put a shade of lipstick on my bloodless lips. If I was going in I might as well go in with style and dignity. Soon there would be reporters, scribbling down every word I uttered for the world to read, and cameras flashing. I tried to imagine the courtroom scene. I would stand proudly erect, explaining the motive behind my actions in a carefully controlled voice, while an absolute silence hung in the courtroom. All eyes would be focused on me, tongues would click in sympathy, heads would nod their approval at what I had done.

Then why didn't I experience a measure of happiness at the vision? Why did that courtroom scene seem like a bizarre pantomime with hollow laughter ringing in my ears? Would the world really care about my motives, or would they merely make sensational headlines for propaganda-starved Sunday newspapers? 'Ruthless woman slays three men! Read all about it!' Wouldn't it be like hanging my dirty laundry in public for all to see? Did anyone have the right to take a glimpse at my inner soul, to share the anger, the hatred, the pain? Perhaps not, but there was no alternative route to take. I had come to the end of my worthless life.

I left by the french window, suddenly aware of the perfect beauty of nature all round me. In future there would only be grim prison walls and a bleak yard. I inhaled the fresh air, touched the velvety leaves of shrubs, paused at the fish pond to watch the darting movements of the goldfish. The garden was a paradise, lush and green, and I felt serenely happy while strolling through it. No one accosted me while I walked down the long, tree-lined driveway, relishing the crispness of the cold morning air. The only thing I was going to miss in prison was nature and its tranquil effect on me. And Lulu, of course. I would always remember how soft her fur was under my touch, how warm her body, how yellow her eyes.

I reached the electronically-controlled gates and stopped. There was no button in sight and I didn't know what to do next. Suddenly the closed circuit television hissed as it turned towards me. There was a crackle of static, then Meryl's voice came through the speaker mounted next to the gate.

'Good morning, Carla. I was hoping you'd have breakfast with us.'

It was an eerie sensation being seen by Meryl and not being able to see her. I stared at the instrument, feeling conspicuous.

'Why are you leaving, Carla?' she asked again.

'There's something important I have to do, Meryl,' I answered. 'And it can't wait. Please open the gate.'

'There's nothing important left to do, Carla. It has all been done. Don't you trust me? Didn't I tell you last night that we're sisters now?'

I wondered if she was alone or if Cyril was there, sharing our monstrous secret. Did he love his wife enough to indulge her to the extent of murder?

'Please come back, Carla. I'd like you to stay here at Pelham's Bluff for a while. The house is enormous, you can have your own wing and all the privacy you need.'

'Please open the gate, Meryl. I wouldn't like to climb over it, but I will if I have to.'

'Don't go, Carla. Don't do whatever it is you're planning to do. It isn't necessary, believe me. You're under our protection now,' she urged.

Our protection? Then Cyril had become party to our secret?

'Open the gate, Meryl.'

There was a short silence. 'Very well. I'll send Paul to drive you.'

The speaker clicked off. I waited. A short while later the drone of a car engine approached, then the limousine came round a bend. He stopped next to me and prepared to get out. I got into the back seat without waiting for him to open the door. His face was as expressionless as it had been last night. He was like a programmable robot, executing his duties mechanically. The wrought-iron gates swung open silently and he drove through.

It was Sunday morning and Oliver Bay was still asleep. The church bell tolled its monotonous summons, which reverberated through the quiet town as it had for generations. Soon people would make their way to the impressive stone church, dressed in their Sunday best, their expressions pious. God would smile benevolently at them from His heaven and magnanimously for-

199

give them their multiple sins. They would emerge, cleansed and ready to indulge in another week of sin, safe in the knowledge that next Sunday He would forgive them yet again. Why, didn't the Bible say so?

'Please take me to the police headquarters,' I said tonelessly. The chauffeur gave no indication that he had heard, but a minute later he drew up in front of a small brick building where a limp American flag hung from a pole. There was no sign of life here either.

'Thank you, Paul,' I said and got out of the car.

'I'll wait,' he said through the open window.

'That won't be necessary. You may go back.'

'I'll wait,' he repeated.

Ignoring him I entered the building and found myself inside a small, badly-lit office. A large, cluttered desk occupied most of the space, the walls were covered with newspaper clippings, some yellowed with age. There was a closed door leading to another room. A seductive poster of a nude girl was pasted to it, the edges curling outwards. She was clutching her over-ripe breasts with both hands, her pink tongue playing on the cherry-red lips in a provocative pose. I could just imagine Sheriff Witmore sitting behind this desk, feasting his eyes on her while he jerked himself off. Would men ever think of women as people and not as bodies?

'Hello!' I called, and rapped the desk with my knuckles. A few moments later there was shuffling behind the closed door, then it opened. Sheriff Witmore filled the doorway, yawning. His unbuttoned shirt hung loosely over his creased trousers, his face was covered in stubble.

'Miss Benson? Anything wrong?' he asked, coming into the office.

'Good morning, Sheriff. I didn't expect you to be sleeping still.'

He glanced at his watch and yawned again. 'Wasn't exactly sleeping. There ain't much to do here on Sundays. Or any other day, for that matter.'

Suddenly he remembered his attire and started buttoning his shirt. I noticed that his fingernails were dirty.

'You've got any trouble out there at the cottage?' he asked.

I took a deep breath. 'No. I've come here to report three murders.'

200

He stopped midway to the next button, raising an eyebrow. 'Three murders, you say?'

'Yes.'

'That's a helluva lot of murders, Miss Benson. Sit down, will you? How about some coffee?'

'Yes, thank you,' I replied and sat down on the worn leather chair in front of the desk. I removed my cigarettes from my handbag and lit one. Did they allow one to smoke in prison? I wondered absently.

He filled the kettle with water at the basin behind the desk, plugged it in and switched it on. I watched him silently. Perhaps he hadn't fully grasped the significance of my statement. If he had he wouldn't be doing something as insanely ordinary as making coffee. He measured the coffee carefully into the cups.

'Sugar?'

'Two.'

Surely only in a place like Oliver Bay could a confessing killer be served coffee instead of being handcuffed. While he waited for the kettle to boil he leaned with his back against the wall, folded his arms and looked across at me.

'Do you want to tell me who was murdered, and by whom?'

'Yes. Sam Shroder, Doughie Steyl and Ax Reevers. I killed them, Sheriff.'

His expression didn't change. For a few moments I thought I detected a trace of amusement in his eyes, but that was impossible, of course.

'And you feel you have to confess?' he asked matter-of-factly.

'Yes. I'll tell you everything – how it was done, where and when. And most importantly – why.'

'It doesn't call for much imagination to guess that, Miss Benson. You're still smarting about that attack on you. Not that I blame you, mind. It was one of the worst I'd seen.'

He was supposed to handcuff me now, switch on a tape recorder, focus a glaring light on my face and interrogate me. That was how they did it in the movies. Perhaps I would get the electric chair. Or had they invented a more civilized method to rid society of killers like me? I had once seen a movie called *Daniel*, and the execution in the electric chair of Daniel's parents had horrified me. It had seemed so barbaric and sadistic, like medieval torture. But then, hadn't my killings been barbaric too?

The kettle boiled. He turned away and proceeded to make the coffee.

'I'm sure you killed them many times over . . . in your mind,' he said conversationally, his back to me. 'Milk?'

'Yes.' What did he mean – in my mind?

He carried the cups to the desk, sat down and pushed one across to me. I stirred it absently, then took a sip. He watched me pensively from across the desk, but didn't speak.

'You questioned me about Sam and Doughie a while back, Sheriff. I'll tell you exactly what happened to them.'

He slurped his coffee, watching me over the rim of the cup. 'I already know that,' he said, and sniffed loudly.

'You do? Then why didn't you arrest me?'

'Arrest you? There was no need for that, Miss Benson. I agree for a while I was worried about those boys, but as it turned out . . . they're just fine. Sam's gone to Canada, heard they pay better in the fish factories there. Doughie . . . well, he's living in Miami with a tart he picked up along the way.'

I stared at him. What was this? His idea of a joke? But this wasn't April Fool's day.

'It's impossible for those men to be where you say they are,' I said. 'I fed both of them into the mincer at the factory. Right this minute they're in cans of Johnson's Pet Food all over the country.'

'Phew!' he whistled. 'That's some fertile imagination you got there, Miss Benson. You using that line in your latest book?'

'This isn't fiction, Sheriff. I killed those men. I shot both of them before putting them on the conveyor belt which fed them into the mincer. And last night I killed Ax in my cottage. I . . . I strangled him with a length of fishing reel.'

He laughed shortly, but the humour was lacking in his eyes. 'I wish you could hear yourself. A skimpy woman like you overpowered a beefy guy like Ax and strangled him while he lay still for you to polish him off. You don't think that's nonsensical?'

'No.'

He lit a cigarette and watched me through the smoke swirling round his head. 'Ax Reevers is dead, all right. There was an accident at sea early this morning. He did a shift on one of the harbour tugs last night. Seems he slipped on the deck this morning and fell overboard. His body hasn't washed up yet, but we'll be combing the beach for it today. I remember years back, when I was still with the San Francisco police department, we used to get a lot of cranks coming in regularly, confessing to the most macabre crimes. This is the first time it's happened in Oliver Bay.'

'I'm not a crank,' I said, fixing him with a cold stare. 'Who paid you to disbelieve me? Meryl Johnson?'

'Meryl Johnson? What's she got to do with this?' he asked, suddenly impatient.

'What was your price, Sheriff? A hundred? A thousand? One hundred thousand?' I asked in a clipped voice.

His eyes suddenly became hard. 'That's enough, Miss Benson. You fantasize all you like about killing men you believe raped you and killed your boyfriend, but keep your fantasies to paper. I'm satisfied those boys are where they're supposed to be. Their folks confirmed hearing from them. As for Ax . . . his body will wash up later today. They always do.'

'Yes. With a nasty wound that runs all the way round his neck. How are you going to explain that to the coroner?'

'Go home, Miss Benson. I promise to read your book when it's published. Sounds gruesome enough, but that's what sells these days, judging by all the garbage on the bookshelves,' he said abruptly.

We glared at each other across the desk. I had believed Meryl when she told me she had power, but not for one ridiculous moment had I imagined the extent of her power. This town truly belonged to the Johnsons, they owned each man, woman and child – body and soul.

'I can prove I killed those men,' I persisted. 'You may have removed Ax's body from my cottage, but the bloodstains are all over the carpet and bedding. The gun with which I shot the other two is there too. And my blood-soaked clothing is buried in the garden.'

He ran a hand through his thinning hair. 'Miss Benson, I sympathize with your obsession with those men. But for Christ's sake, they've left town 'cept for Ax, who's dead. They'll never bother you again. Let it drop, you hear? You don't want people to think you're ready for the loony bin, now do you?'

'I want you to come to the cottage with me, Sheriff,' I said. I know it sounds as though I was trying to commit hara-kiri, but I desperately needed to be believed, to pay the price for my crimes. I could no longer carry the burden of my dark and terrible secrets alone.

He sighed exasperatedly. 'Okay, okay. I don't understand why you're doing this to yourself, but I'll indulge you. Please wait outside, I'll be out in a minute.'

I knew he wanted to make a phone call to the Johnsons now, getting instructions on how to explain the bloodstains. Perhaps he would demand more money for his part in this farce.

Paul, Meryl's chauffeur, was still sitting stony-faced in the limousine. When he saw me emerge from the building, he got out of the car and held the rear door open for me.

'I won't be going with you, Paul. You may go now.'

He nodded and got back into the car, but remained sitting with his hands on the steering wheel. Suddenly I remembered something from last night. I leaned towards the open window, and said: 'Paul . . . last night, after you dropped me and Mrs Johnson off, she said you knew what you had to do. What was it you had to do, Paul?'

His fixed expression didn't change while he looked at me with his lifeless eyes.

'I don't recall, Miss Benson.'

'I think you do, Paul,' I insisted. 'I think you had to go back to my cottage and remove something from it.'

'Something, Miss Benson?'

'Yes, something. Something that resembled a corpse with a length of fishing reel buried in its neck. You had to take it out to sea on a harbour tug and drop it overboard. Do you recall now, Paul?'

A tiny muscle twitched just below his right eye, but his gaze was unwavering.

'I can't say that I do, Miss Benson.'

'You then had to clean the room of blood and remove all evidence of what happened there. How much did Mrs Johnson pay you to do all that, Paul?'

Sheriff Witmore emerged from the building. 'Are you going with Paul?' he wanted to know.

I turned away from the limousine, recognizing the futility of my interrogation. 'No. I'm going with you.'

I accompanied him to the black and white police car parked in front of the limousine. He started the engine and drove off without speaking. Once I looked back and noticed the limousine following us. Paul was determined to execute Meryl's orders to the last letter. Was it money alone that demanded such loyalty?

Eve's Nook stood mutely on its sand dune, its doors and windows tightly shut. I noticed that the pale yellow paint Peter had so diligently applied was starting to look faded. It was no longer a place of pleasure for me. All my bitter and conflicting emotions of the past six months were entombed in that cottage, it was the epitome of all my shattered dreams.

I felt uneasy while unlocking the front door. What if Ax was still in that blood-smeared bedroom? Did I have the courage to see him again, to be reminded of last night and everything that had preceded it? I soon learnt that Meryl had gone to great extremes to remove every shred of evidence. I reached the bedroom first and stopped dead in my tracks. The room was immaculate, the bed neatly made. There were no bloodstains on the walls or on the carpet. I stared at the carpet. It wasn't mine. The shade of beige was slightly lighter than the old one, the pile thicker.

I ran to the bed and ripped the bedding off in layers. Nothing. Then I noticed that the bedding was fresh, not that which had been on the bed last night. I had to congratulate Meryl. Whoever she had hired to do the job was a true professional. There was nothing here to give the slightest indication of the violence of the past night.

'So, where's all the blood, Miss Benson?' Sheriff Witmore asked from the doorway, an expression of ridicule on his face.

'This is not my carpet. Someone replaced this carpet. He was lying here on the floor . . . his feet up on the bed.'

The sheriff grinned. 'You sure he didn't do a tap dance while he was at it?' he asked sarcastically.

'Sheriff . . .'

'Miss Benson, why don't you take a few weeks off and go away for a holiday?' he asked impatiently. 'Living alone like this was bound to twist your mind sooner or later. When you come back I'm sure the realtor can find something closer to town for you.'

I grabbed my handbag from the dressing table and feverishly emptied its contents on the bed. The usual paraphernalia spilled from it – keys, face powder, hairbrush, bills. The gun was gone. I swung round.

'The clothes are buried in the garden.'

'Where in the garden, miss?' he asked, suddenly alert.

I opened my mouth to reply, then hesitated. 'Oh no. I'm not going to tell you. You'll only make it disappear like you've made everything else disappear. Get out of my house, Sheriff.'

Suddenly there were hurried footsteps coming along the corridor, then Meryl burst into the room, with Cyril close on her heels.

'Carla! Whatever's come over you?' she cried, approaching me with outstretched arms.

'Congratulations, Meryl. It's a cinch,' I said, backing away from her.

'Is she still persisting with that ridiculous story?' Cyril asked, addressing the sheriff.

''Fraid so,' he confirmed.

'Oh, Carla . . . we understand how you've suffered,' Meryl said. 'Richard says this is a kind of delayed shock. Come home with us. You need plenty of rest and we don't want you to stay here alone.'

'Yes, Carla,' Cyril echoed authoritatively. 'You must come with us. We'll take care of you.'

'I'm not going anywhere. Please go now and leave me alone,' I said.

'Carla, darling . . . we all love you, don't you see that? We want to help you. Right now you're not well,' Meryl said soothingly, coming closer.

Behind her the two men spoke in hushed whispers. My eyes darted from her to them and back to her.

'Don't come any closer, Meryl. There's nothing wrong with me, you know that. Go away. All of you.'

She reached me. 'You won't get well if you stay here alone. Be reasonable, Carla.'

'Get out! Get out of my house!' I hissed.

At the same moment Richard rushed into the room with his medical bag.

'Thank God you could come, Richard. She's very upset, as you can see,' Cyril said hurriedly.

Richard's eyes were on me, examining, questioning. 'Carla?'

'She tells the craziest stories. She actually believes she killed the three men who attacked her,' Sheriff Witmore explained. 'She

206

brought me here convinced there was a corpse in this room and blood all over.'

'What's worse is that she believes she fed them into the mincer at the factory. Please help her, Richard,' Meryl appealed to him.

They were discussing me as though I weren't there. My eyes were riveted on Richard. Was he party to this? Would the next step be to certify me insane and conveniently spirit me away to an institution for the mentally unbalanced?

'There's nothing wrong with me, Richard,' I said calmly, holding his gaze. 'I agree I had an insane vision that I killed those men, but I've come to my senses now. I apologize . . . to all of you, for causing you this inconvenience. It's over now. Please leave me alone.'

He looked uncertainly from me to the Johnsons. Would they insist? I wondered. Would they decide that even in an institution I would be too much of a risk? Would I too be thrown overboard from a harbour tug?

'We want her to come to Pelham's Bluff, Richard,' Meryl said firmly. 'We'll take care of her there.'

'I'm not going anywhere. Is that clear? I've apologized. What more do you want from me?' I cried.

'Carla, you can't stay here. Isn't it wonderful to know you have so many friends who care about you?' Richard asked.

He was party to this plot! They wanted to remove me from Eve's Nook so that they could complete their work here. I had told Sheriff Witmore about the clothing buried in the garden and I had no doubt it wouldn't be there when I returned from wherever they decided to take me. If I returned.

'Come with us, Carla,' Meryl urged, touching my elbow.

Sheriff Witmore was coming towards me. 'I think you should go with the Johnsons now,' he said, his voice and manner threatening. Cyril was advancing on me too, his expression determined. They were closing in on me while Richard watched.

On the spur of the moment I decided to run. I bumped Meryl out of my way and made for the opening between the two men, but they caught me expertly. I kicked and screamed and tried to bite them, but they held me fast. Richard was opening his medical bag and filling a syringe from an ampoule. No! No! I couldn't allow them to do this!

He reached me, holding the needle aloft. Don't do this, Richard! my eyes pleaded with him. I was helpless in their grip while he plunged the syringe into my upper arm and emptied its contents. I searched his face desperately for a sign of compassion but found none. Perhaps even now they were killing me, and there was no one to witness it.

And then a paralysis affected my muscles and I slumped between my captors. Or murderers.

21

I woke from a deep sleep to find myself in a strange room. What was even more strange was that my personal belongings were there too. I recognized my teddy bears, my potplants, my wind chimes, my desk and typewriter. Bewildered I sat up in bed and looked around me. It was a room filled with old but highly-polished furniture. The ceiling was richly panelled in wood, there was a fireplace against the opposite wall with a rocking chair in front of it, the dying embers of a fire still glowing in the grate. Then, with startling clarity, I remembered the faces of my captors and Richard plunging the syringe into my arm. Where was I? Did rooms in mental institutions have this much character?

From outside came the sounds of fluttering wings and the shrill, almost human, cries of sea-gulls. I got out of the bed, walked across to the window and looked out. I was on the upper floor of a house, looking out on a small, paved courtyard with ivy on the walls. Richard, wearing a thick cardigan, was standing on the steps leading to the courtyard, throwing bits of fresh fish to a flock of sea-gulls. His breath made puffs of steam in the cold morning air.

I watched him for a while, ready to withdraw should he look up and see me. What was I doing here? Had he been appointed my jailor, instructed to keep me prisoner until they were satisfied I posed no threat to them? I was convinced that if I went to the door now I would find it securely locked. When I turned back I caught my reflection in a copper-framed mirror on the opposite wall. I was wearing my warm winter pyjamas, the ones I had bought at Bloomingdale's last year and never worn. On impulse I went across to the dark mahogany wardrobe and opened it. I stared at its contents. All my clothes were there, neatly hung. In a chest of drawers I found my underwear. I turned, went to the door and tried the handle. It opened silently onto a long corridor. I closed it again softly and dressed hurriedly in corduroy slacks and warm jersey. There was no time to waste. I had to get out of this house and out of this town. There was a madness in Oliver Bay that far outweighed my own, and I had to distance myself from this menagerie, start afresh somewhere else, somewhere where no one knew me and where the past wouldn't haunt me like a menacing shadow.

Suddenly I stopped, struck by panic and the blackest despair. Where would I go? Back to New York where I'd be swallowed by the indifference of a metropolis and drowned in noise and pollution? Or to another city or town, perhaps? Or could I join Theresa and Gavin in Israel and pretend Oliver Bay never happened? None of these options appealed to me. They simply called for too much energy and right now I had none left.

Dejectedly I sank onto the edge of the bed. Dear God, I just didn't have the strength to start all over again in my quest for identity and peace of mind. Not in any other city or town, not in Israel. I was bone-tired of running, of hiding from people and from myself. How many more Sams and Doughies and Axs lurked out there, ready to pounce on a woman who dared carve a life for herself? Or Peters to stir my hunger for love and leave me empty-handed? What was the point in continuing with life, fearing my own shadow, paranoid about my own safety? It would be easier to surrender to whatever fate they had decided for me – the Johnsons and Richard Mallen.

Suddenly the door opened and Rita entered with a tray. She saw me sitting on the bed and smiled one of her warm, friendly smiles.

'A very good morning to you, Miss Benson. I can't tell you how happy I am to see you awake. Doctor was getting worried about you,' she chatted, and put the tray on a small table in front of the window.

'Morning, Rita. How long have I been here?'

She turned to me, surprised. 'Why, since lunch time yesterday. The doctor said you were very tired and had to rest.'

'I see.'

'I hope you like this room. It's the warmest in the house, 'cept for the morning-room, that is. Gets the sun all day long. It used to be the doctor's room until his father died six years ago. He grew up in this room, building model aeroplanes and Spanish freighters. During school holidays he polished sea-shells for sale in the gift shop in town. So good he was with his hands,' she sighed. 'I knew God gave him those hands for a purpose. Today he's healing the sick with them.'

'Who brought my things here, Rita?'

'Why, Mrs Johnson had them delivered. Supervised it herself, she did. Oh, I could tell she's very fond of you. Wanted to take you to that monstrosity of a house out on the Bluff, but Doctor wouldn't hear of it. Said he was personally going to tend you right here. Never seen him like this before, you know,' she smiled secretively.

'Like what, Rita?'

'In love, of course.' She smiled again. 'Even arranged a few days off from that hospital of his, for the first time in sixteen years, I tell you. I've been despairing that he'd ever find the right woman, but then I've always been pessimistic by nature. It's a good man you're getting, Miss Benson. They don't come finer than Doctor Richard.'

I stared at her, trying to grasp the implications of her words. Then I realized the poor woman wasn't in his confidence, didn't know I was a prisoner here and not a guest. She poured coffee into a delicate cup.

'Cream?'

I nodded.

'Sugar?'

I nodded again. She held the cup towards me. 'I'll serve breakfast in the morning-room in half an hour. Doctor wants you to join him there.'

I shook my head. 'I'm not hungry, Rita.'

'And I say you are. Not a drop you had since the Lord knows when, and thin as a rake you are. I make the most delicious

210

croissants, got the recipe from the late Mrs Mallen herself. Just wait till you taste them.'

I didn't have the energy to argue.

The carpeted corridor upstairs was hung with family portraits. Rita pointed to a stern-looking man with severe eyebrows and a drooping moustache.

'That was Dr Ernst Mallen, Dr Richard's father. Had the meanest eyes you ever saw on a man, but a heart worth gold. He was the most adored man in this town, may his soul rest in peace. And here . . . right next to him is Mrs Marjorie Mallen. Now wasn't she just the loveliest lady? And so kind-hearted too. Gave free piano lessons to the poor kids round here, she did, and loved every minute of it. Never raised her voice to no one in her life. Her piano is still downstairs in the morning-room. Sometimes Doctor Richard plays it, but he's nowhere near as talented as his mother.'

I recognized Richard's eyes in hers – dark and gentle, the promise of a smile in their depths. Except for yesterday, when he had plunged the needle into my arm.

'This here is little David, the first-born. He was sadly afflicted but a gentle boy all the same. Dr Richard often took him to school for a day, but those cruel little buggers took the mickey out of him and upset his brother. So he never got no learning, not that it would've done him any good. He died young.'

I recognized the slanted eyes and lack of expression characteristic of Down's Syndrome victims.

'And look at Doctor Richard. He was eighteen when this one was done, just finished high school.'

I gazed at the portrait of a young man with a frank, honest gaze.

'But enough of all this chatter. When you're feeling better I'll show you the others in the library. They were a proud family, the Mallens. Liked to keep their images preserved.'

I followed her down the carpeted staircase. She stopped in front of a closed door. 'Here is the morning-room. Go right in and make yourself at home,' she said before hurrying down the passage.

I turned the door handle, went in and paused just inside the room. Richard was standing in front of a large bay window, his broad back to me. When he heard me he turned round.

'Good morning, Carla,' he greeted. The aroma of his pipe smoke hung in the sunny, spacious room.

'Good morning, Richard.' I returned his greeting the way one greeted total strangers.

'I'm glad you decided to join me. Will you sit over here?'

The table had been designed for a large family, with eight chairs around it. He pulled a chair out for me and waited until I was seated before seating himself at the head of the table. He poured two small glasses of orange juice from a jug and put one in front of me.

'May I presume you slept well?' he asked, his eyes on me.

'Did I have a choice?'

'No, I guess not,' he smiled. 'But I don't see how else I could've persuaded you to come home with me.'

'Why was I supposed to go anywhere when I have a home of my own?'

'Because that isolated cottage is an unhealthy place for you right now. You needed to get away from it, for a while at least. I think you know that, Carla, but you're very stubborn about your independence. Admirable, but harmful under the present circumstances.'

'What are the present circumstances?'

His eyes met mine. 'You haven't come to terms with your ordeal and the longer you're alone the worse it'll get. I want to help you, Carla.'

'And if I decide to go back there right now?'

'If you want to know if you're a prisoner here, the answer is no. But I think you'd prefer being here to being at Pelham's Bluff. Meryl was determined to take you there and I know just how overpowering she can be. She always was an intense girl, intent on having her own way. She collects people the way connoisseurs collect works of art. She's totally sincere but at the same time she exploits her role as Mother Superior in Oliver Bay. Not everyone is as indulgent towards her as Cyril.'

'Are you also convinced that I'm insane?' I asked bluntly.

'I'm not convinced of anything. Insanity is a word we use when we don't understand another person's state of mind. I think I understand yours.'

212

Rita entered with the breakfast trolley, positioned it next to the table and left again. Suddenly I realized I was famished. I couldn't remember when last I had eaten something. Unashamedly I helped myself to the ample fare, while Richard watched me with an amused expression. We ate silently.

He confused me. Yesterday I had been convinced he meant me harm, that he was a willing participant in the Johnsons' plot, now I doubted it. He didn't behave like a jailor at all and I sensed no danger from him. What amazed me most was that I had made my terrible confession and still had my freedom. There was no cold, pitiless prison waiting for me, no flashing cameras, no shocked outcries over my crimes. Meryl Johnson had decided that I – no we – had been justified in doing what we had done and no one in this town dared oppose her.

'Do you play tennis?' he asked conversationally.

'I haven't played for years.'

'I'm only an amateur myself. Would you play a game with me later this morning? There's a court just behind the hospital.'

I pushed my plate aside, the hunger suddenly gone. 'I killed those men, Richard,' I blurted out.

'Carla, Carla,' he said, reaching for my hand across the table. 'Stop believing something so downright absurd. You could no more kill another human being than I could.'

'Oh yes. I killed two of them at the factory. I shot them first, then loaded their bodies onto the conveyor belt. It carried them to the mincer where they were chewed up in a matter of seconds. I don't regret doing it. They didn't deserve to live after what they did to me and Peter. And Ax . . . Ax was waiting for me when I got home from the party. He attacked me with a knife and threatened to kill me, but I strangled him with fishing line. There was an awful lot of blood in my bedroom, but someone cleaned it up and even replaced the carpet.'

'Carla, don't you realize what you're saying is totally illogical? How could a frail woman like yourself overpower a man of Ax's stature? Especially a man with a knife?'

'He held the knife against my throat . . . here,' I said, raising my chin so he could see the cut.

He reached out and touched my neck gently with his fingertips. 'It looks like a nasty scratch. Carla . . . Ax's torso washed up just north of Jutter's Point last night. He fell overboard from a harbour tug early yesterday morning. It seems he got entangled in the tug's propeller. It decapitated him . . . crudely. They're still looking for the head. Whatever happened to Ax wasn't strangulation. I examined the body myself. And two men were with him at the time he fell overboard. Up to that point he was very much alive.'

'Who were the two men?'

'Why should that matter?'

'It matters a great deal. Who were they?'

'You won't know them. One is Rick Bedford, the other Mark Woods.'

So Meryl had more people in her pay than I had anticipated. She was a very enterprising lady.

'When you do the autopsy you'll know he died long before they say he fell overboard,' I said stubbornly.

'There's no need for an autopsy. I've already released the body to the undertakers.'

I couldn't believe to what lengths Meryl had gone to cover our crime. I doubted the head would ever be found, for surely the terror of Ax's dying moments would be etched on those grotesque features. And Richard . . . he was protecting me too. He was a doctor and had to know that Ax hadn't died in a tug accident. I stared at the remains of my meal, suddenly nauseous. I could go somewhere else and relate my gruesome story, but without evidence to substantiate it, who would believe me? They were more likely to institutionalize me and throw away the key.

'Carla, I want to tell you an extraordinary story. But first, let's sit over there by the window. You're shivering and the sun will warm you.'

I allowed him to lead me to the large bay window where we sat down on easy chairs overlooking the murky blue of the Atlantic beyond. Richard poured our coffee and handed me mine, then he lit his pipe while I lit a cigarette.

'Carla, the mind is a very powerful thing. It can make us believe whatever we want to believe, to whatever degree we want to. If you really believe you killed those men, I guess you did in every sense of the word. The story I'm about to tell concerns a man, let's call him Bob, who worked for a meat wholesaler. They transported frozen carcasses in refrigerated trucks over a three-hundred mile radius, working in teams of three. One day, just

214

after completing their last delivery, Bob accidentally got locked in the refrigerated hold. The others, unable to find him, set off on their three-hundred mile journey back to base, unaware of the tragedy taking place in the hold.'

He sucked on the pipe and blew the smoke upwards. I waited for him to continue.

'Bob hammered frantically with his fists on the walls of the truck, trying to attract attention, to no avail. He realized he would never survive the journey in that sub-zero temperature. I'm going to die in here, he thought, panic-stricken. At first he made a brave attempt to keep warm and mobile. He jogged in the confined space, did push-ups, pretended he had a skipping rope. Eventually he was so exhausted he just slumped into a corner. It's no use, he thought, I'm going to die. He took out his notebook and decided to record his sensation until the last moment, so that people would know what he had suffered. "My muscles are aching," he wrote. "The cold is affecting my bones, numbing my senses. I can't feel my skin anymore, I have difficulty breathing, my lungs hurt very badly. Now I can only move with the greatest of effort. My thoughts are confused. Now I'm beginning to feel incoherent. Soon I will be dead."'

He paused to drink his coffee. I looked at his hands, noticed the artistically long fingers with the immaculate, square-shaped nails. They were gentle, healing hands that had soothed my aching body in its blackest hour. They had examined every inch of me, assessing the damage caused by other callous hands.

'And did he die?'

'Yes. When they reached their destination, the other two opened the back of the truck and found him sitting erect in a corner – dead. He had all the symptoms of having frozen to death, except for one thing. The truck's refrigeration unit had broken down after the last delivery and the temperature inside was only slightly below normal. There was no reason for Bob to have died other than that he had convinced himself he was going to die. Just as you have convinced yourself you killed those men and need to be punished.'

I held his gaze, suddenly lacking the desire to convince him. Perhaps, just perhaps, he was right and the last six months of my life had merely been a frightful nightmare, or worse still, a figment of my over-active imagination.

'The ramifications of a trauma such as the one you experienced are manifold. We all want to believe we're in charge of our bodies and our destinies. We believe we have the right to create our own environment, that we're entitled to function within that environment. Which is correct, of course. So, when our self-created world is violated, we're stripped of the basic sense of security that is vital for our survival. Suddenly our entire existence is threatened, our foundations laid on a shaky sea of mud. We're no longer in charge of ourselves, but vulnerable to the evil whims of strangers. The resultant anger is a natural reaction and the mind creates its own relief to cope with the shock . . . in your case, the killing of those who had dared violate your world.

'There is no punishment fit for the crime such as that perpetrated on you, Carla. It will take a great deal of time before your faith in your world is restored, but it will be restored. I'm going to help you to see it objectively, to analyse your reactions, to come to terms with it. And while we're at it, I want you to stay here. I want you removed from the environment that caused you so much pain, and only when you're ready will I accompany you back there.'

'I can't . . .'

'Yes, you can. You owe it to yourself. This is a big house and Rita is very lonely here. I spend most of my time at the hospital and she'd love to have a companion, someone to take care of. You'll have all the privacy you need, for whatever you need to do. Please, Carla . . . I want to help you. My motives are purely unselfish.'

I looked at him. Nobody's motives were purely unselfish. Everyone wanted something from somebody. Time would tell me what Richard wanted from me, but I already had my suspicions.

In the weeks that followed I discovered the many facets to Richard's personality, and discovered some of my own too. He was infinitely patient, protective and caring, yet firm and sometimes downright bullying. While the winter snow fell outside, we sat in front of the fireplace in the sitting-room, sipping wine and talking, while the fire crackled and spread its warm glow throughout the room. I spoke of my childhood almost absently, as though it

216

had happened to someone else, and even managed to discuss Arthur Benson without a measure of anger. Some evenings, when I withdrew into my shell and feared the exposure, he would question me mercilessly, and more than once I fled from the room, hating him and his pat answers for everything. I often spoke of the murders, but he continued to treat them as hallucinations of an outraged mind and I started believing they were. It was safer that way.

Gradually Richard too started sharing his world with me. He spoke of the hospital and his patients, of his childhood in Oliver Bay, of his family and friends. I liked to listen to his deep voice, to imagine him as a boy, as a cherished son, as a compassionate doctor. Often, when he stayed away until late at night, I would stand by my bedroom window, waiting and watching the driveway until his car pulled in. I missed him on the days when he returned too late from the hospital and I had to wait until the next to see him.

Rita not only became the loving mother I never had, but a valued friend too. Soon I was helping her to prepare meals, to polish the silverware, to remove the books from the library shelves and dust and replace them with care. She told me all about her years in service with the Mallens, bringing the family to life for me. She taught me to crochet and to knit, simple skills that delighted me. We spent many hours in the morning-room, drinking tea and talking. She often mentioned her grandchildren in Milwaukee, and expressed a wish to visit them before she got very much older, in the same breath emphasizing that she could never leave Richard alone. She loved him like a son and wanted to see him settled first.

Meryl phoned almost every day, inviting me to Pelham's Bluff. I declined politely, but that didn't deter her from phoning again the next day. I wasn't ready to see Meryl and be reminded of that night she had been in my cottage, her eyes glinting with excitement. I preferred to believe that Richard was right in presuming the murders had never taken place except in my mind.

The most amazing aspect of my life as a guest in Richard's home was the return of my lost inspiration. One morning I sat down idly at my desk, put a blank sheet of paper into the typewriter, and without warning the words just flowed. My fingers couldn't move fast enough to keep up with the torrent that poured from my mind. I came alive in front of that typewriter, felt my heart pumping new life into my veins. Day after day I wrote and wrote until the sun set and I was drained.

One day my false sense of security was rudely shattered, reminding me that there was no room for complacency in my life. Meryl telephoned while I was doing revision in the morning-room. I took the call on the extension.

'Carla? Something hysterical has happened and I thought you'd like to know about it,' she said, her voice low with suppressed excitement.

I didn't want to know but refrained from saying so.

'Cyril's public relations department brought a letter to his notice this morning. It was sent by an old lady down in Little Rock. She lives alone with her two cats and has been buying Johnson's Pet Food for ten years. She claims it's of the highest standard and her cats simply love it.'

My hand on the receiver started trembling, my stomach contracted painfully.

'Are you still there?'

'Yes.'

'Well, her cats just smelled the last can she opened and walked away. While scraping it into the garbage can she noticed a peculiar oblong object in it, rinsed it under the tap, and . . . you guessed it! It was a bullet! She was very indignant and demanded that Johnson's Fish Factory take more care with their products. Cyril instructed the department to send her a case of Johnson's Pet Food – free of charge,' she concluded, and laughed with obvious glee.

The call hadn't been made in malice. Meryl was genuinely tickled by the incident. It was her way of thriving on challenge and defying fate. But instead of glee I suffered a horrible vision of a cat licking at a plate of human brains. I replaced the receiver, trembling with a cold fever. It hadn't been a nightmare after all. The murders had been real and I was a killer.

I got dressed and drove into town with the intention of ordering more paper from Uncle Billy. This was going to be the first time I would see him since Ax's death and I was somewhat apprehensive. I really liked Uncle Billy. There was a simplicity about him that was very appealing, and a tenacity that was admirable. If I had known a grandfather I would've wanted him to be like Uncle Billy. To my surprise there was no hostility in his manner. He even seemed pleased to see me, smiling his toothless smile.

'Been orderin' your paper same's usual,' he announced proudly, indicating the large stocks on a nearby shelf. 'Thought you'd be back soon, I did. Never told you I had a sister used to write short stories when she was young. Used anythin' she could lay her hands on, even the inside cover of the Bible. "'Tis like a force inside me, Billy, drivin' me on," she once told me. "It never gives me peace."'

I thanked him and bought the entire stock.

'Five children she had in as many years and died with that hunger for writin' in her eyes. Don't you ever let nobody stop you, you hear?'

'I won't, Uncle Billy.'

Just before I left, he said something that made me freeze in my tracks.

'Lost the last of the fam'ly I had. Now it's only me left. Imagine old Billy Reevers outlivin' everyone else,' he said, shaking his head in wonder. 'I'll be closin' this here store soon, ain't no point in carryin' on. Not with Ax gone too.'

I examined his face but there were no signs of accusation. 'I'm sorry, Uncle Billy. I wish it could've been different . . . for both of us.'

'It ain't you but the Man Above decides what's best for us, Carla, and who are we to argue? They never did find the head, you know. I woulda liked to bury all of him, not leave some of him to the sea.'

Instead of returning to my temporary home, I just kept driving after starting the car. For two weeks now I had surrendered to Richard's diagnosis that the mind created its own relief for trauma in the form of realistic illusions, but I had been a fool for believing the past could be erased. It was inside me like a living organ.

The country road was muddy and slippery after the recent snowfall, but I continued the hazardous journey until I reached Wreckers Strand. I left the car beside the road and walked towards the massive coral reef that fringed the coast, the low-flying sea-gulls my only companions. I climbed a rock and sat on its peak, impervious to the bitterly cold wind, and allowed my

219

thoughts to stray to that young man named Peter Dreifuss-Jones, a descendant of the breakfast cereal Dreifusses. I tried to recall his face but couldn't. Instead it was Richard's, with its gentle eyes and mellow features, that filled my vision. I also tried in vain to recall the woman who had arrived in Oliver Bay, a seemingly perfect future carved out for herself. Both Peter and the woman had died that foggy night in June, but whereas I was being given a new lease of life, Peter was not. I had avenged him but there was no solace in the fact. The path of revenge was strewn with corpses and a lonely old man who didn't have the will to continue.

Darkness came early. It crept across the ocean like a physical presence and settled all round me. I stumbled over shrubs towards the car and drove back to Oliver Bay. I could no longer postpone the inevitable – making a decision about my future. I knew for a fact that I could never return to Eve's Nook and pretend to myself that nothing had happened. Besides, there were more summers ahead and more men who would view my isolation as an open invitation to abuse. Since Christmas was only twelve days away, I decided to go to Israel and spend the festive season with Theresa and Gavin before making a final decision about my future.

Richard was waiting at the gate when I arrived back, his face a mask of anxiety. I experienced a deep sense of guilt when I saw the naked relief there. I should never have allowed him to get this close to me. When I got out of the car, he embraced me unexpectedly.

'Carla, Carla . . . I've been so worried about you,' he muttered in my hair. I sensed the tension in his body but hardened myself against the desire to respond to his embrace.

Rita met us at the front door and shooed me inside like a wayward child. My teeth were clattering from the cold, and she led me directly to the fireplace.

'Sit yourself down here, girl. I'll bring you some warm soup,' she said in her motherly way. The sense of belonging here with them threatened to overwhelm me. Ideals die hard, granted, but they had to die if I wanted to continue living.

Richard offered me a tot of brandy and I accepted gratefully. He poured it from the wall cabinet, handed it to me, then poked the fire in the grate.

'Did you go back to the cottage?' he asked, his back to me.

'No. I drove out to Wreckers Strand. I've almost forgotten how desolate it is out there,' I replied, sipping the drink.

He replaced the poker and turned round. 'What happened today, Carla?'

I looked at him, recognized the question in his eyes.

'Uncle Billy said they never found Ax's head,' I said tonelessly, lowering my gaze.

He knelt in front of me and took both my cold hands in his. 'Stop doing this to yourself, Carla. Haven't you suffered enough? Has it ever occurred to you that Ax Reevers and his mates were the lowest form of life? That however he died it was probably too good for him? I saw you after the attack, remember? What they did to you was inhuman. They damn near killed you and walked away without a backward glance. And what's worse . . . the law allowed them to go free.'

'I know.'

'Then forget the crazy notions that you killed them. Can you do that? Or at least, try?'

I nodded, wondering how I was going to tell him that I had to leave. That I couldn't stay in Oliver Bay and be constantly reminded of the horrid past. That I woke sometimes in the middle of the night and felt blood dripping from my hands. How was it possible with that light in his eyes?

22

I arranged for the only realtor in Oliver Bay to put my cottage on the market and use Fran Westcott in New York as a forwarding address. I booked my flight to Israel, then sent a telegram to Theresa advising her of my arrival. I had two days left in which to say my farewells to Richard, Rita and all that was Oliver Bay. I would not be returning here. Instead I would take my unfinished novel to Israel and complete it there, with the beautiful bay of Haifa to inspire me and anonymity to cloak me.

Time was running out fast, but I sadly lacked the courage to tell Richard of my decision. I postponed it from minute to minute, hour to hour. I knew my presence in his home made him happy and that he wanted more from me than I could give. It was in his eyes whenever they lingered on me at the dinner table, or in the glow of the fireplace, or when he arrived home late from the hospital to find me still awake to share a glass of hot chocolate.

As though sensing my impending departure, he arranged more time off from the hospital and tried in many ways to amuse and distract me, but I couldn't respond. I was quiet and remote, lacked an appetite and slept badly. On the morning before my departure I announced at breakfast that I was going for a stroll on the beach. When Richard asked if he could accompany me, I agreed, hoping that the opportunity would present itself for me to tell him.

We started our stroll at Jutters Point, away from the factory and the cloying smell. The air was bitterly cold, but invigorating too. It was low tide and the beach was strewn with seaweed and marine debris that had washed up during high tide. There were blue bottles and starfish and bits of red crab, and the sea-gulls were having a field day pecking at the juicy morsels. The winter sun shimmered on the gentle rippling ocean, two trawlers were passing on the horizon. Richard took my hand in his, and I allowed him to hold it. We spoke little, but whenever he looked at me there was a question in his eyes, until I avoided looking at him.

'Carla . . . do you remember the first time you came to my house for dinner . . . you asked me why I never married.'

'Yes.'

'The truth is . . . I've never met a woman with whom I wanted to share a hot chocolate in front of a crackling fire, or whose happiness was more important than my own . . . until I met you.'

'Richard, please . . .'

'No, please let me finish. I've been happier these past two weeks than I'd ever been . . . coming home and finding you there, seeing you smile one of those rare smiles, smelling your perfume in the house, hearing you in the library, or typing upstairs. It feels so right having you there, I don't want it to change . . . ever again.'

Suddenly tears were pouring down my cheeks and sobs were choking me. And his arms were round me and I smelled the caramel of his pipe smoke clinging to his clothes and to his skin. I

222

tasted it on his lips when he kissed me, and I cursed God and the devil, whoever was responsible for this bad timing.

Then I broke free and ran blindly across the sand, with the cold wind tearing at my face and burning my lungs. I ran past the car and along Oliver Bay's narrow winding streets until I reached his house. I ignored Rita's startled cry and raced up the stairs to the bedroom that had once been his, then mine for a while. I closed the door and leant against it, gasping for breath.

My bags were packed, my typewriter and unfinished novel in their own travel bag. I paced the room restlessly, checking a few times to see that I hadn't forgotten anything. Early tomorrow morning I would be gone, never to see Richard Mallen again, or be reminded of Oliver Bay and the ominous closeness of its community. I sat down on the edge of the bed, feeling empty. A cold breeze was blowing through the open window and rattling the wind chimes. There was a sad and lonely refrain in the sweet tinkle. And the hours passed and the light faded and night fell for the last time for me in Oliver Bay.

Shortly after dark Rita knocked on the door, announcing that dinner was ready to be served. I thought almost sadly of the grey that was turning her hair white and the grandchildren who were waiting for her in Milwaukee. After a while she went away and I was alone with the wind and the chimes again.

Richard came some time later. He entered the room after a short knock, carrying an armful of chopped wood. Without speaking he closed the window and proceeded to light a fire in the fireplace. He remained sitting there on his haunches, watching until the flames licked busily at the air and spread a warm glow through the room. Only then did he turn and look at me. Our eyes met in the red glow of the fire, and I recognized the naked plea in his. I sat motionless while he got up and approached me.

He sat next to me on the bed, reached out and cupped my face. When he kissed me his lips tasted incredibly sweet. Then, slowly, he unbuttoned my jacket, and I allowed him to, in spite of the fear that clutched at my heart. I owed Richard something for the kindness he had displayed when I most needed it, and if this was the only way to thank him then so be it.

He undressed me very slowly, his dark eyes never leaving mine, and I allowed myself to be drawn into the loving glow I saw

223

there. Once I was naked, he undressed himself, while our eyes remained locked. When the red glow of the fire danced on our naked flesh, he gently pushed me back until I lay flat on my back, then leant across and cupped my scarred breasts. Fear lay in the pit of my stomach when I recalled the last time a man had touched them in brutal lust, but his gentle, rotating fingers gradually eased the pain of memory and I felt myself relax. He kissed each scarred nipple before his lips travelled down, kissing my bare thighs, my legs, my feet, sending waves of pleasure through my body, then they travelled back slowly, until they met mine – open and waiting. His lips were teasing mine, softly at first, then with increasing passion until I strained myself against him.

His hands were expert, dispelling the lurking fear and rousing desire, until I wanted to beg him to take me, now! When he finally penetrated me, I wept softly, both with relief that there had been no pain and because this would be the only time for us. He moved with gentle, rhythmic strokes that had me arching my back in an effort to take more of him, deeper and deeper until we seemed to be one body.

'I love you, Carla. Dear God, how I love you!'

His lips were on my face, kissing away the tears. They claimed mine with the gentle passion of a man who had waited a lifetime for this moment. My orgasm exploded suddenly and in pulsing waves, and I clung to him until I felt his body shudder too.

We continued to hold each other, and his hands continued to caress my body, almost absently.

'Don't go, Carla.'

His voice was hardly above a whisper, his lips moving against my cheek.

'You . . . you know?' I whispered.

'Yes. It's been in your eyes these past few days. Ever since you returned from Wreckers Strand.'

'You knew and you didn't say anything?'

'I said it today. I love you, Carla. I want to marry you and keep you safe with me.'

I moved away from him and sat up. 'I killed those men, Richard.'

He reached out and touched my shoulder. 'I know that too, Carla,' he said quietly.

'You do?' I asked, stunned. He nodded. 'Then all that talk about the power of the mind . . .'

'Shhh,' he said, laying a finger on my lips. 'I killed them too. Many times. I injected them with air, I plunged scalpels into their hearts, I had them on the operating table and turned the oxygen off. Who is more guilty? You or I?'

'But why you?'

He sat up too and put an arm round my shoulder. 'I'll tell you why. Many years ago . . . when I was only fourteen years old, my father started discussing his medical cases with me. It was his way of preparing me for my predestined future and showing his respect for me. It made me feel sort of grown-up being treated with such regard, and I felt my interest grow. One night he told me he had seen the worst case of physical abuse in his career that day. Meryl Griffiths had been brought in early that morning. In addition to having been raped, she'd been stabbed repeatedly in her genitals and anus, her breasts were slashed. All the bones in her face were broken, her teeth too. She needed four pints of blood and one hundred and sixty stitches. My father said it was nothing short of a miracle that she was alive. He took me to the hospital, showed me her X-rays and allowed me to sit with her. I watched her agony for eight horrifying months, and I hated the animals who had done that to her. I didn't think such monsters deserved to live. The intensity of my reaction startled even me, and I discussed it with my father. I didn't think I should take the Hippocratic Oath when I felt that murderous. He explained that doctors are fallible beings too, susceptible to the same emotions as anyone else, and that I shouldn't be ashamed of it. But at the same time I shouldn't allow my emotions to cloud my reason. Doctors were there to heal, not to judge.'

We sat in silence while I absorbed his words, then he spoke again.

'During those eight months Meryl had nine operations to re-pair the damage to her body, and each time I saw her swathed in bandages and in pain I wanted to kill those bastards.'

'Richard . . . did you love Meryl?' I asked softly.

'If pity is a form of love . . . yes. She deserved all the pity she could get, there wasn't much of that going around here. This town chewed her up, swallowed her and spat her out. Very much like you. Yours was the second-worst case of physical abuse I've seen, and all that old anger resurfaced. For weeks I wanted to seek them out myself and wipe them from the face of the earth. I killed them over and over, Carla . . . in my mind.'

'I went a step further. I actually killed them and . . .'

'It doesn't matter! Don't you understand that?' he said heatedly. 'We won't ever, ever have to discuss this again. As of now you have no past.'

'I can't stay in Oliver Bay. I don't want to be reminded of the past,' I said, breaking away from him.

'Where do you want to go?'

'To Israel . . . for a while. After that . . . I don't know.'

'Is it only Oliver Bay that drives you away? If this was any other place, would you have stayed here with me?'

I looked at him, realized how important the answer was to him.

'I think so,' I said uncertainly.

He smiled and kissed my bare shoulder. 'Then how about a place like New Orleans? I hear the Gulf of Mexico is much friendlier than the Atlantic.'

'New Orleans? Why New Orleans?'

'Because an old friend of mine, Malcolm Bryers, realized a childhood dream we shared. He's building yachts for the superrich and making a handsome living out of it. He's been nagging me for years to join him in a partnership, but I've never been motivated enough to consider the proposal. Now I am.'

'Richard . . . I don't want you to do this. You're a doctor, not a yacht builder. I'm not worth the sacrifice,' I objected.

'Oh yes, you are. Don't for one moment believe otherwise. Besides, I became a doctor to please my father. I loved him far too much to disappoint him.'

'But your roots are here, your family home . . . everything.'

'I have no roots, Carla. I'm the last of the Mallens. The house . . . we could get something even nicer in New Orleans and have the furniture shipped there. Rita's been wanting to retire for years now, but she didn't want to leave me "uncared" for, as she puts it. I can't think of one good reason why I should stay in Oliver Bay. We'll go somewhere where no one knows us and make a fresh start.'

I leant against him, my face in the hollow of his neck. I felt the pulse of his jugular against my lips, tasted the salt of his skin, and

I ached to believe there was a new life waiting for us in New Orleans.

'Will you marry me?' he asked again.

'My past . . . it'll always be there . . . between us.'

'You have no past, Carla. All I know is that I love you and I have no future without you.'

'I have to leave in the morning, Richard. I need some time alone. Everything's happened with such startling speed these past few months. If you can wait . . .'

'How long?'

'A month, perhaps more.'

'Will you come back?'

I still hesitated, the answer seemed so final.

'I promise not to fart in bed, or break wind at the dinner table. And I'll shave over the weekends. And since you can't bear children any more, I can't ever blame you for ruining my life with those screaming brats,' he teased.

We looked at each other and burst out laughing. Soon we were rocking each other.

'In that case . . . how can I refuse?' I laughed.

23

New York was gripped in the clutches of a severe winter. The city stood sterile in its white cloak of snow, while shoppers thronged the pavements in a last-minute dash for Christmas gifts. There was a festive air in the busy streets and crowded shops, in spite of the cold outside.

I stayed overnight at a small, busy hotel on 67th Street. The pulsing life of Manhattan made me nervous, and already I was missing Richard and the serenity of his home. While I lay in bed that night, listening to the incessant din of the city, the sirens and hooters that pierced the night, I couldn't help but remember the silence of Oliver Bay, disturbed only by the roar of the ocean and the cries of sea-gulls. During the early hours of the morning I stood by the window and stared out onto the street below, noticed the debris of humanity still littering the pavements, and I wanted to be anywhere else but here.

I got up early and made my way downtown to Fran Westcott's office. Her secretary told me she was out of town for a week, but she had the contract with the television network ready for signature. Afterwards I enjoyed a generous breakfast at the Café des Artistes on Park Avenue, an ignoble but fascinating place I had frequented while living in New York. The clientele were struggling writers and painters and sculptors and actors and actresses, even this early in the morning. At Bloomingdale's I selected Christmas gifts for Theresa and Gavin – a hand-carved alligator waist belt for Gavin and an Italian leather handbag for Theresa. Finally, soon after noon, I took a taxi to J. F. Kennedy Airport.

I was early and strolled into a bookshop where I bought the latest issue of *Newsweek*. The departure lounge was crowded, but I found a fairly quiet corner where I drank the tasteless, tepid coffee I had bought at a kiosk. The snow had turned to sleet outside and I wondered if my flight was going to be delayed. Idly I paged through *Newsweek*. Now that 1986 had drawn to a close, the year was under review. It had been the year of the *Challenger* space shuttle explosion that had rocked the world and dented the invincibility of the American space programme. It had also been the year of the Chernobyl disaster in Russia, the final effects of which would not be known for years to come. It had been the year of increasing international terrorism and the brief baring of teeth between President Ronald Reagan and Colonel Mohammar Gaddafi, of large-scale riots in South Africa, of low oil prices and unpredictable gold prices.

It had been a strange and tempestuous year for me too. A year in which I had realized a life-long dream of owning a private little cottage by the sea, of sharing a need and raw passion with a young man, of being the victim of a cruel and sadistic rape, of becoming a killer. And finally, of being given another chance at happiness.

I came across the article towards the end of the magazine. It was one of those articles featuring the personal achievements of an outstanding citizen. His face stared at me from the page with that almost innocent, uncertain smile that had charmed me so. His blond hair was ruffled, his green eyes clear and almost trans-

228

lucent. There were an older man and woman standing on either side of him, hugging him proudly.

Stunned, I read the article that gradually turned my blood to ice. Peter Dreifuss-Jones, heir to the Dreifuss breakfast cereal empire, aged 23, had just completed a gruelling ten-thousand mile, cross-country cycling trip in an effort to raise funds for a Los Angeles charity. Touched by the plight of a private organization caring for abandoned children, he had acquired sponsorships for every mile of his arduous journey through deserted countryside, rugged mountains and overcrowded cities. Asked why it had been necessary to go to such extremes when the required sum wouldn't have dented the Dreifuss fortune, Peter explained that he had wanted to make a personal sacrifice, for only by doing so could he feel a personal involvement with the organization.

His proud parents explained that Peter had always been an achiever, striving for perfection in whatever he tackled. He thrived on challenges, explained his mother, Deborah Dreifuss-Jones. Even as a child she had found it almost impossible to keep the reins on his imagination. As a safety precaution they had hired a bodyguard to tail him, but suffered an anxious three weeks when he lost Peter. He only caught up with him again at a seaside resort called Mackerel Bay.

When asked what aspect of his journey was the most memorable or the most dangerous, Peter grinned before relating a hair-raising event in a small fishing village on the east coast. While spending a foggy night on the beach, he had suffered an un-provoked attack by three drunken fishermen, who were under the misguided impression that he had a fortune stashed away in his rucksack. After beating him into unconsciousness, they had dragged him to the pier, where they fastened a bag of stones to his legs, intending to throw him into the oily, stinking waters of the harbour. He had regained consciousness while they were lifting him, and screamed. A woman had come running along the pier, forcing the men to drop him and run off into the night. She had nursed him back to health at a plush seaside estate called Pelham's Bluff, made a generous contribution towards his cause, and sent him off with a new bicycle and rucksack. It concluded by saying his parents were delighted to have him home in time for Christmas.

'What about me, Peter? What about me?' I muttered, staring out the large windows towards the sleet-covered tarmac. 'What about all the lies?'

Only in New York can one weep in public and not attract attention. I wept softly – not for myself but for Richard and Rita. For suddenly I knew I wouldn't be meeting Richard in New Orleans in the new year, and Rita wouldn't be spending her last years with her grandchildren in Milwaukee. My task wasn't yet completed. Instead of going to Israel, I had to take the first plane to Los Angeles.

And kill Peter Dreifuss-Jones.